Theological Principles
of Egyptian Religion

American University Studies

Series VII
Theology and Religion
Vol. 59

PETER LANG
New York • Bern • Frankfurt am Main • Paris

Vincent Arieh Tobin

Theological Principles of Egyptian Religion

Foreword by
Roland G. Bonnel

PETER LANG
New York • Bern • Frankfurt am Main • Paris

Library of Congress Cataloging-in-Publication Data

Tobin, Vincent Arieh
 Theological principles of Egyptian religion / Vincent Arieh Tobin.
  p. cm. — (American university studies. Series VII, Theology and religion ; vol. 59)
 Bibliography: p.
 1. Egypt—Religion. I. Title. II. Series: American university studies. Series VII, Theology and religion ; v. 59.
 BL2441.2.T63   1989   299'.31—dc19   89-2539
 ISBN 0-8204-1082-9   CIP
 ISSN 0740-0446

CIP-Titelaufnahme der Deutschen Bibliothek

Tobin, Vincent Arieh:
Theological principles of Egyptian religion / Vincent Arieh Tobin. Foreword by Roland G. Bonnel. – New York; Bern; Frankfurt am Main; Paris: Lang, 1989.
 (American University Studies: Ser. 7, Theology and Religion; Vol. 59)
 ISBN 0-8204-1082-9

NE: American University Studies / 07

© Peter Lang Publishing, Inc., New York 1989

All rights reserved.
Reprint or reproduction, even partially, in all forms such as microfilm, xerography, microfiche, microcard, offset strictly prohibited.

Printed by Weihert-Druck GmbH, Darmstadt, West Germany

In memory of my mother
Lena McBain Moser Tobin

Table of Contents

Foreword	ix
Preface	xvii
List of Abbreviations	xxi
Introduction	1
I. The Nature of Egyptian Religion	5
II. Myth and Cult in Egypt	21
III. The Egyptian Gods	35
IV. Mytho-Theology of Creation	57
V. Ma'at	77
VI. The Egyptian Kingship	89
VII. Osiris	103
VIII. Immortality	125
IX. Universalism and Monotheism	153
X. Egyptian Morality	173
XI. The Egyptian Theological Synthesis	195
Select Bibliography	217

Foreword

Roland G. Bonnel

Ancient Egyptian religion provides material for an intriguing and fascinating study. Its gods were numerous, varied and colourful; its temples suggest the performance of mysterious and complex rituals; its texts appear to be full of rich mythology the details of which are frequently elusive. The remains of Egyptian religion appear to many to constitute a confused mass of symbols, beliefs and rituals, and attempts have been made to explain them by the assertion that Egyptian religion was an amalgamation of the different and frequently contradictory practices and beliefs of numerous traditions which had originally been separate and distinct. As a result of the unification of Egypt at the beginning of the First Dynasty (so this interpretation continues), the various symbols and beliefs of the earlier independent traditions were all accepted into a new religious synthesis. Hence, there appears to have emerged a religious tradition of many internal contradictions which no logical and rational mind could hope to comprehend in a coherent system. Hence, many have been able to see superficially some of the individual details of Egyptian religion, but have frequently seen no rationale of the total system.

A study of the individual gods of Egypt does not constitute a valid approach to Egyptian religion. An examination of Osiris as a deity of resurrection, for example, does have its value, for Osiris was indeed such. However, this aspect of Osiris cannot be divorced from the total picture of Egyptian religion, for an attempt to place Osiris and his function of resurrection in a category by themselves would produce a too highly compartmentalized understanding of the Egyptian tradition. So also an attempt to confine any of the other gods to some particular function and aspect would give some small understanding of their natures, but it would miss their real significance in the wider system of religious expression. The individual and specific details of any religion often present important points of interest, but such details are not necessarily the essence of the religion in question. Religions usually make wider statements about reality than can be comprehended in their isolated and individual symbols, for the main purpose of any religion is to enunciate some experience of the wider reality of life and the world. Any religion which does not do this has little chance for survival. If we desire to comprehend fully the meaning of any religious tradition, it is imperative to view that tradition in its entirety and to attempt to understand the cosmic statement which it is trying to articulate. The longevity of Egyptian religion, more than three thousand years, constitutes sufficient proof that its vision extended far beyond the concepts of the individual gods. What it presented was a universal and cosmic vision which was able to satisfy the spiritual needs and hopes of its adherents. To understand Egyptian religion in anything of a complete manner implies the ability to arrive at some perception of the abstract statements which that religion desired to make. Such a purpose is the aim of this present book.

An understanding of the cosmic affirmations of the religion of ancient Egypt is not an easy matter. The modern religious traditions with which the western world is familiar, namely Judaism, Christianity and Islam, have developed expressions which may be readily comprehended by the modern mentality. There has been no break with the original foundations of these faiths, and the individual development of each has been such as to keep alive the possibility of applying them to the contemporary world. The symbols and expressions of these religions are not foreign to us, and we may easily grasp the basic outlook of each of these religions. This is not the situation with the religion of ancient Egypt. The birth and evolution of its gods are lost in antiquity, its symbols had grown out of experiences which are not so relevant to the modern world, and its means of expressions were very different from modern methods of articulation. The modern mind is able to think in abstract concepts, and, due to the influence of philosophical reasoning, experiences no great difficulty in expressing reality in abstract terms. The Egyptian civilization did not have the benefit of abstract thought, and was thus forced to express cosmic ideals and concepts by means of symbols and myth. In order to arrive at some comprehension of what the religion of Egypt was actually saying we must start with the symbolic nature of its mythology.

In the past too much emphasis has been placed on the idea that Egyptian religion had its main centre in the cult, myth and belief playing a much more secondary role. This idea does contain some truth, for the Egyptians were not required to give assent to strict statements of belief and doctrine. It is also true that the performance of the state cults was of great importance, for these had the purpose of actualizing and realizing the cosmic principles for which they stood. However, it is necessary to be cautious in any attempt to see the cult as both content and expression of Egyptian religion. The cult, in both its ritual actions and its verbal expressions, was no more than an articulation of the religious ideals and values of ancient Egypt. It was not the actual *content* of religion. If such had been the case, then religion would have been little more than sympathetic magic. In such a situation we would be faced with a cultic and ritualistic system which had no concrete and specific content to give it lasting validity. Such cults would have had to develop and change constantly in order to meet the needs of the individual situations with which they were dealing. The scope of mere cultic performance and ritual would not have been able to provide material of a sufficiently substantial nature to give permanent value to the religion. We would then be forced to recognize the existence of different cultic rituals at different times and places, most of such cultic systems having very little relationship with one another. There can be no doubt that the Egyptian cult did undergo certain changes and developments in the course of its history. Such changes, however, were not simple acts of substituting the new for the old. They were rather newer and more complex expressions of the true content of the religion. Cult, as an expression of the religion, was also an expression which was efficacious of certain ends and goals, but the content of the religion was enshrined in the mythic symbols and narratives which formed the basis of the cult and which gave meaning to its rituals.

The myths of ancient Egypt appear to have had very little substance, there being few developed mythic narratives, and most of the myths being very brief and lacking in details. Hence, it can be an easy conclusion to state that Egyptian mythology was poorly developed and that it could not have played a major role in the religious system. One must, however, realize that the nature of true myth is not connected with a developed and detailed saga. Such may be the case if the myths are taken as the actual content of the religion, the traditions of the gods being seen as an account of the past 'history' of the universe. Myths in such a case would constitute the actual content of the religion, and would be dogmatic statements rather than true myths. Applying this approach to Egyptian religion, we would be able to state that the Egyptians believed certain facts about the various gods who inhabited the world of the divine, but the ultimate effect would be to make out of the Egyptian gods deities who were limited and restricted in their natures and their functions. The smallest amount of doubt or scepticism would have easily called such gods into question and caused the serious inquirer to realize that they were only figments of the human imagination. Such an impression may very easily be taken of the gods of Classical Greece as they are portrayed in the Homeric epics. The gods in these latter works appear as well developed and three dimensional figures who take active parts in the fictional narrative. They do not, however, appear as the type of deities who could be taken seriously by the mind which was seeking for the knowledge of a deity who would be valuable and meaningful in the spiritual life. They could not even be taken as serious personifications of nature or of the psychological constitution of man himself. The extended narrative which had developed out of the original MInoan-Mycenaean mythic elements had succeeded in turning the gods into beings who were obviously unreal and non-existent. The stories in which they appeared might be delightful and entertaining, but the true religious, spiritual and cosmic values of such gods were little more than non-existent. It is ironic, but true, that the highly developed myth, unless it has been developed with great theological skill, may eventually mythologize the mythic deities out of existence.

The heart of genuine myth does not lie in extended stories about the gods, for true myth does not attempt to lay down specific beliefs. It does not dictate comprehensible religious doctrines. The function of the myth is rather to symbolize, to point to the existence of a reality which cannot be understood or articulated in terms of logic. Hence, myth becomes the means of articulation which is used in the absence of rational thought. In such a means of expression the important element lies in the existence of the symbol itself. It does not lie in an extended narrative of what the symbol did or does. In the system of Egyptian mythology, Osiris, for example, was important for what he symbolized, and the latter had originally been portrayed by a number of symbols which had become conjoined to the mythic figure. Each of these mythic symbols had in itself a certain signification, and could have to a certain extent stood apart from the full body of the myth. One may even question whether or not there ever did exist a fully developed myth of Osiris. Despite the evidence of Plutarch, such was probably not the case. The central fact in the figure of Osiris was what he *was*, not what he *did*, his mythic actions being only the expression of his nature. In true myth it is sufficient for the mythic figure simply to be; his actions are only secondary. One might even question the fact that mythic figures really had to act at all. It is perhaps safer to state that the 'actions' of mythic figures are in reality their being and nature expressed in a manner which may be apprehended by the human consciousness. What cannot be conceived in a rational manner can, in the symbolism of mythic action, be portrayed graphically for the purpose of articulating the unchanging meaning and nature of the mythic deity.

If we apply this mythic principle to the figure of the creator god Atum-Ra of Heliopolis, we may interpret it in the same manner. The mythic action of Atum-Ra states that in the beginning he had arisen out of the primaeval waters of Nun and had taken his seat on the primaeval mound. However, the past tense of Atum-Ra's action was not important. More significant was the fact that Atum-Ra was continually and repeatedly rising out of the primaeval waters, and that this rising was expressed in a number of natural and historical events as a constant and continual process. However, one must proceed even further than this and state that the repetition of Atum-Ra's original appearance was a dramatic and graphic expression of the nature of that deity and the principle for which he stood or which was personified in him. Atum-Ra, mythically speaking, acted simply because he existed, and his action was the expression of what he was, the undefined essence which could not be comprehended intellectually but which was an unchanging factor of the physical universe.

It was this type of mythic expression which the Egyptian cult was designed to celebrate. Beyond the celebration, however, the cult was further designed to bring this mythic expression into reality, to make it present and active in the world of human experience. Without the myth to give it substance, the cult would have had very little value. It would not have been a valid religious experience or action, and it would hardly have been the spiritual mainstay of Egypt for more than three millenia. An investigation of Egyptian religion must, therefore, take the myth as its starting point. Such an investigation will not completely ignore the cult, for it will recognize that the cult was the expression of the mythic symbols. Nevertheless, it will be the mythic symbols which will be seen as the true heart of the Egyptian religious experience. Such an investigation, moreover, will not concern itself with the details of the mythic narratives, nor will it try to reconstruct complex characters for the various deities. Such a reconstruction could result in the creation of deities who were in reality unknown to the Egyptians. The myth must be stripped down to its bare essentials in order that it may reveal the abstract signification which lay behind it, and in order that this signification may not be obscured by a proliferation of unessential detail, much of which may have been no more than graphic dramatization.

All of this assumes that behind the concrete expressions of Egyptian myth and cult there lay an abstract concept of reality. Some may question whether or not this was a fact or if it is nothing but the attempt of a modern mind to impose on the Egyptian mind a way of thought which was foreign to it. Such an objection may have some validity, and it is necessary to admit that the Egyptians did not think in abstract terms, that they had not created a theological and philosophical synthesis in order to give meaning to the physical universe. They had not the ability to do so, for they did not have at their disposal the tools of abstract thought and speculation. The author of the present work would probably be the first to recognize such a fact. Nevertheless, the fact that the Egyptians did not think in abstract terms does not imply that they were unable to sense the abstract reality of universal being. The ability to do so appears to be an innate talent of the human spirit, even when this spirit is still unskilled in the methods of abstract speculation and articulation. If such were not the case, none of the great religious and philosophical systems would have emerged either in antiquity or in the modern world. What the Egyptians apprehended by those powers of perception which are deeper than the intellect they expressed through the concrete mythic symbols which they devised. The proof of this lies in the fact that the Egyptian mythic symbols readily lend themselves to a more abstract interpretation. It is also interesting to note that such an interpretation may be derived without twisting the mythic symbols and forcing them into a mould for which they were never designed. What the Egyptian mind was unable to do the modern mind can accomplish because of its familiarity with the realm of abstract thought.

The Egyptian mythic synthesis was, like the temples where the myth was dramatized, huge, far-reaching and all-encompassing. It attempted to take into itself every aspect of human life and experience. All things were seen by the Egyptians as parts of the universal and unchanging order of a cosmic Ma'at, a principle and force which arose from the divine creative force and which continually assured that the creative force was an effective reality throughout the universe. It was this order which the Egyptians attempted to express through their mythic formulations. The Egyptian mind, however, was not strictly theological in the specific sense of that term. As has already been stated, the Egyptians did not have the capacity for such abstract thought. Hence there arose the necessity of myth. However, in order that the term myth may not be misunderstood as being no more than a quaint invention of a simplistic ancient mind, the author of this book has preferred the term 'mytho-theology', that is, theology expressed in terms of myth, or myth which has a theological signification. Such appears to be a highly suitable designation for the Egyptian mythic system, for its intent was indeed the articulation of a theological order for the universe in an atmosphere and environment when theological speculation was not possible.

The attempt to discover the theological principles which lay behind the Egyptian mythic system is a legitimate one, for it is necessary to prevent that system from being seen as no more than a collection of ancient deities and symbols which could not be taken seriously and which have only an antiquarian curiosity for the modern mind. The achievements of ancient Egypt have often been overlooked due to a lack of understanding of the culture. Because of such a lack of understanding, modern scholars have often stated that Egypt contributed little to world civilization. Such an assertion is patently false once we realize the intellectual achievement which lay behind the Egyptian mythic system. In order to understand this system, however, it is necessary to translate it into terms which the modern mind can comprehend and accept as valid. Te average modern man is unable to read the Egyptian hieroglyphic texts in their original language, and so it is necessary to provide him with a translation of these texts in his own language. So it is with the Egyptian religious system. The modern mind does not think mythologically, preferring the abstract methods of philosophy and theology, and often not realizing that these too are no more than forms of expression. In order to make accessible to the modern mind the significance and meaning of the thought systems of ancient Egypt, these must be translated into modern terms. Such a translation does not create a new system of thought and then attempt to superimpose it upon the ancient Egyptians. In fact it does no more than reveal in somewhat different terminology the truths which were expressed in the Egyptian mythic systems, hopefully making these systems more intelligible to the modern mind and providing a wider and more open appreciation of the achievements of Pharaonic Egypt. It was that civilization which first gave humanity a cosmic sense of perception. Thus in the present work, myth has been interpreted as mytho-theology, and from this mytho-theology there has been extracted the meaning and principles of Egyptian theology.

The Egyptians, as one can see in the writings which they left behind, were highly conscious of the joys and the goodness of life. They sanctified and consecrated the force of life through their mytho-theology, recognizing the universal power of a creative force which gave meaning to everything and which assured the eternal and indestructible character of life. Through their mytho-theology they were able to perceive and apprehend the unity of the universe and the cosmic dimensions of the existence in which every individual shared. This book is an attempt to elucidate and interpret that principle, to reproduce the Egyptian achievement in a manner in which the modern reader will be better able to comprehend and appreciate it.

Roland G. Bonnel
Dalhousie University

Preface

The present work is concerned with a subject which many might be inclined to say never existed. Strictly speaking, the ancient Egyptians never knew the science of theology, at least not theology in the sense of an abstract and philosophical method of speculative thought. The principles of the religion of ancient Egypt were rather expressed by means of mythical statements and figures, symbols which attempted to give articulation to those ideals and values which later ages and cultures would be able to express by more rational and abstract methods. Theology as the modern world knows it was totally foreign to the Egyptian mind, a mind which was inclined to view the realities of the universe as concrete and tangible entities. About such entities one cannot really speculate, especially at a time when the human intellect had not yet evolved to that stage where abstractions may be seen as realities. Hence, the classical periods of the culture of ancient Egypt never evolved strict theological systems to express their spiritual ideals and values.

At the same time we would be gravely mistaken if we were to think that ancient Egypt expressed its religion through childish myths and fables, or that its gods were nothing more than the strange and fantastic beings portrayed in Egyptian art. True myth is never childish, and it is far from being mere fables. Behind all real mythological symbols there is hidden a concept of reality, a statement about the make-up and structure of the universe in which man lives. Such a concept is not necessarily a rational one or one which can be defined and analysed in abstract terms. Myths and mythic symbols do not constitute a system of figures which have a kind of allegorical value and which can be readily translated into terms which are more rational and more in keeping with modern mentality. Any attempt to treat mythology in such a fashion is both childish and futile, for it reduces myth to a level on which it may be seen as the quaint and even silly product of a somewhat juvenile ancient mind, one to be viewed with amusement and condescension, but not one to be taken in any way seriously. It is unfortunate that many are inclined to view myth in such a way, for they thus miss the true meaning of the content of the original mythic statements and fail to comprehend the very real wisdom and knowledge which was the achievement of the ancient mind. Of all ancient peoples the Egyptians least of all deserve such an evaluation of their mentality.

It is, furthermore, a mistake to view the Egyptian gods simply as they were portrayed in the temples and tombs of ancient Egypt. Statements which assert that Hathor was the goddess of sexuality and love, that Thoth was the god of writing, or that Amun-Ra was king of the gods, are in essence childish and superficial, totally missing the signification which these deities had in the Egyptian system of thought and method of articulation. We cannot, of course, deny that to many individual men and women of ancient Egypt such gods must have appeared as the anthropomorphic and theriomorphic beings who were portrayed in Egyptian religious art. Such, however, happens in every culture when the symbols of religion are accepted as dogmatic statements and concepts. Such a misinterpretation, however, does not in any way diminish the true value and theological significance of such figures. The full understanding of the Egyptian religious symbols may have been the property of only a few, but what is important is the fact that such an understanding did exist and that through it the Egyptians were able to express their essential understanding and comprehension of reality. The one factor which prevented Egyptian religion from moving into a more theological expression was the lack of an abstract and philosophical mentality. Such a lack, however, was not a totally insurmountable obstacle, for what they could not express in abstract terms the Egyptians expressed by means of their mythic symbols. Those mythic symbols contained an understanding of the essential structure and nature of the universe which was as profound and as valid as those of the most highly developed philosophical and theological methods.

It is for this reason that I prefer to speak in this book of the Egyptian *mytho-theological* system, a term which I feel expresses the reality of what Egyptian religious mythology was. Out of the myth of ancient Egypt one may quite legitimately abstract and construct a theological system which will provide some hints at the insights of the Egyptian mind into eternal realities. Such an undertaking is not only legitimate and valid; it is even necessary if the modern world is to have any true appreciation of the Egyptian intellectual genius. We shall, hopefully, thus be able better to understand the contribution which ancient Egypt made to the development of human civilization.

Insofar as this book is concerned not with Egyptian religion but with the theological principles of that religion, the reader will not find herein any complete account of the individual Egyptian gods or of the Egyptian myths. Such an account is not necessary for the purpose of this work and is, moreover, readily available in the many works already written about Egyptian religion. Nor have I attempted to deal in a historical fashion with the evolution of Egyptian religious expressions and practices. My main purpose has been to set forth what I comprehend to be the general principles of Egyptian theology, principles which did not change over the centuries or even over the millenia. It is my sincere hope that this work will enable the modern reader to obtain a more accurate concept of the spiritual values which made ancient Egypt the vital and living civilization which it was.

For the benefit of those readers who are familiar with the language of ancient Egypt, I have included a transliteration of most of the Egyptian texts quoted. To have included the actual hieroglyphic texts as well would have made the work somewhat cumbersome. Moreover, such texts will normally be readily available to most Egyptologists.

As in the writing of any book, thanks are due to various people. I would like here to mention especially Prof. Sarah Israelit Groll of the Hebrew University of Jerusalem who some years ago provided me with the opportunity of realizing a life-long desire to engage in the study of the ancient Egyptian language. It was also she who was gracious enough to act as director of my doctoral dissertation at the Hebrew University. Thanks are due also to Dr. Roland Bonnel, a true friend and colleague, who so carefully read the original typescript of this work and who also accepted to write the Foreword. I would be remiss if I did not also express my sincere thanks to Henri and Jeanne Bonnel of La Ferté-sous-Jouarre, France, whose home and warm hospitality provided me with the leisure and opportunity to write this book.

The cost of publication of this book was partially covered by a generous grant from the Senate Research Commmittee of Saint Mary's University, Halifax, Canada.

Vincent A. Tobin
Saint Mary's University

List of Abbreviations

ASAE	*Annales du Service des Antiquités de l'Egypte.*
BD	*The Book of the Dead.*
BIA	*Bulletin of the Institute of Archeology.*
BIFAO	*Bulletin de l'Institut Français d'Archéologie Orientale.*
CT	A. de Buck, *The Egyptian Coffin Texts.*
Davies, *Amarna*	N. de G. Davies, *The Rock Tombs of El-Amarna,* 6 volumes, London, 1903-1908.
GM	*Göttinger Miszellen.*
JAOS	*Journal of the American Oriental Society.*
JARCE	*Journal of the American Research Center in Egypt.*
JEA	*Journal of Egyptian Archeology.*
JNES	*Journal of Near Eastern Studies.*
JSOR	*Journal of the Society of Oriental Research*
LÄ	W. Helck, E. Otto, W. Westendorf, *Lexikon der Ägyptologie,* Wiesbaden, 1972-1983.
MÄS	*Münchner Ägyptologische Studien.*
MDAIK	*Mitteilungen des deutschen archäologischen Instituts Kairo.*
Pap. of Ani	E.A.W. Budge, *The Book of the Dead: The Papyrus of Ani,* New York: Dover Publications, 1967 (reprint of the 1895 edition).
PT	K. Sethe, *Die Altägyptischen Pyramidentexte.*
RSR	*Recherches de Science Religieuse.*
Sinuhe	*The Story of Sinuhe.*
Th.T.S.	*Theban Tomb Series.*
Urk. I	K. Sethe, *Urkunden des alten Reichs.*
Urk. IV	*Id.*, continued by W. Helck, *Urkunden der 18. Dynastie.*
Wb	A. Erman & H. Grapow, *Wörterbuch der ägyptischen Sprache.*
ZÄS	*Zeitschrift für ägyptische Sprache und Altertumskunde.*

INTRODUCTION

The Greek historian Herodotus, writing in the Fifth Century B.C.E., says of the Egyptians of his own time that they "are excessively god-fearing (θεοσεβέες) more than all people."[1] This impression on the part of Herodotus must have derived from the multiplicity of gods evident among the Egyptians rather than from any deeper or more serious comprehension of the nature of Egyptian religion. Herodotus claims to have knowledge of the mysteries of the passion of Osiris,[2] although he does not in this context use the actual name of the deity, and also of the mysteries of Isis whom he identifies with the Greek Demeter and whose rites he equates with the Greek Thesmophoria.[3] He himself admits, however, that he purposely prefers to avoid any deep discussion on matters of religion.[4]

Herodotus' tendency of making an identification between the Egyptian gods and those of the Greeks, a tendency which was not peculiar to him among the Greeks, serves as a prime example of a cardinal error frequently made by students of religion, that of seeing the religion of an exterior culture through the categories and expressions of one's own religious tradition. The identification of Isis with Demeter and the identification of Zeus with Amun-Ra both superimpose upon the Egyptian gods a character and nature which was not necessarily theirs. Although in the Egyptian tradition Amun-Ra was 'King of the Gods',[5] such a title is not necessarily elucidated by equating it with the expression 'King of the Gods'[6] as it was applied to the Greek Zeus. Such an identification can only result in an erroneous, or at best superficial, comprehension of the nature of the deities in the religious tradition under consideration. So also, a propensity to view the mythic traditions of ancient Egypt with the same attitude in which Greek mythology is often regarded can result in a total misconception of the significance of the Egyptian corpus of myth.[7]

At the same time one should not attempt to analyse the Egyptian religious experience in accordance with the character of the Judaeo-Christian tradition. There can, of course, be little doubt that certain affinities did exist between the religion of ancient Israel and that of Egypt, and it appears to be an inescapable conclusion that the Hebrew tradition owed a great deal to the earlier Egyptian systems. Hebrew religion, however, at an early stage developed a peculiar approach to its deity, seeing his manifestations and actions in the realm of historical events and in the realm of specific revelation to certain individuals. The Yahweh of the Hebrew cult was best seen in the very historical phenomena which moulded the destiny of the Hebrew people and in the words of the prophetic leaders of the nation who could preface their words with a phrase such as "The word of Yahweh came to me." Although the oracular did have its role in the Egyptian cult, the prominent means of divine revelation was its manifestation in the obvious phenomena of nature and in the on-going process of life itself. Cosmic events such as the daily return of the sun, the constant cycle of the seasons, and the yearly cycle of the rising and falling of the Nile all provided an assurance of the divine force which upheld and sustained the universe. The conquest of darkness by the light of the rising sun revealed to the Egyptian the power of the divine life manifest by and inherent in the sun god Ra. The rising of the Nile and the growth of the vegetation both pointed to the life force of Osiris which constantly and continually overcame the negative power of death.

The manifestation of a divine cosmic order inherent within the natural phenomena meant that for the Egyptian mind there was no need of a series of sacred writings which could contain and codify specific records of divine revelation. One cannot, of course, deny the important place played by such sacred writings as the Pyramid Texts, the Coffin Texts or the Book of the Dead. The function of these, however, was first and foremost practical, cultic and personal, designed to achieve for the individual certain ends and goals in the afterlife. It is important to stress the fact that they were not intended as dogmatic statements or doctrinal treatises which had to be accepted and to which men were required to give assent. Although certain statements from such texts may at times be used to aid our understanding of Egyptian theological principles, even this must be done with considerable caution lest we create out of symbolic and mythic statements a fixed dogmatic system which would have been foreign to the Egyptian religious experience. Nor do the texts of instructional literature have the sanctioned force of scriptural authority. Such outstanding texts as those of Ptahhotep, Any or Amenemope may well have been regarded as valuable for their moral philosophy, but such value depended solely upon the merits of the individual text, and none were regarded as a final moral authority. Such authority could be found only in the decrees of the Pharaoh whose words were regarded as the manifestations of Ma'at, the principle of cosmic order and righteousness.

Finally, in considering Egyptian religion one must beware of isolating particular areas or activities of life and labeling them as the specific phenomena identifiable as Egyptian religion. Strictly speaking, the Egyptians themselves saw no area of life which could be thus isolated. No division existed between 'church and state'; no aspects of life and conduct were outside the interest or domain of divine power; no separation existed between the sacred and the secular. Every human activity was regarded as being totally within the order and system upheld and sanctioned by divine power. If one were to attempt to offer a tentative definition of Egyptian religion, it might be said that religion consisted of life itself. To be 'religious' meant no more or no less than to live and exist, for by his existence the individual was automatically part of the universal divine order. Religion was not a mere aspect of human life, a set series of observances which could be performed and then forgotten, one's duties to the gods having been thus accomplished. Nor was religion a mere hobby or passing interest for the Egyptian. Religious experience was to be found not only in certain aspects of life, but in the full experience of the totality of one's existence, for it was throughout the whole of this experience that the divine power and interest was manifest and active. The gods, the natural order, the state, the king, the individual and even the dead were all integral parts of the one unified cosmic order. This order was sanctified insofar as it was the visible and tangible expression of the unchanging principle of Ma'at, the reality of which was given graphic expression through its personification as the deity who bore the same name, the goddess Ma'at.

Notes

[1] Herodotus, *Histories*, II, 37, 1.
[2] τὰ δείκηλα τῶν παθέων, II, 171, 1-2.
[3] *loc. cit.*
[4] τὰ ἐγὼ φεύγω μάλιστα ἀπηγέεσθαι, II ,65, 2.
[5] *niswt ntrw*

[6]Βασιλεὺς τῶν θεῶν.

[7]Although the basic roots of Greek mythology do without doubt lie in authentic mythic sources, much of its true mythic value had disappeared even by the time of Homer, and had become obscured and obliterated due to a heavy overlay of legend, saga and folklore. While many of the Greek myths as we know them in their Homeric and later forms do have a definite value of their own, it is often difficult to detect clearly the original significance of the genuine mythic element, a significance which had perhaps been lost even to the ancient Greeks themselves. The result is that the Greek myths are often taken at their face value by modern interpreters, or else are considered in their forms as fully developed narrative legends. The Egyptian myths, when viewed in this manner, may by comparison appear very simplistic and undeveloped. Thus there arises a false conception of the Egyptian mythic symbols. Such a concept of Egyptian myth serves only to conceal the actual depth of the true mythic signification and to mislead the modern mind with regard to concepts which were in all likelihood quite clear to the Egyptian mind. Egyptian myth should not be misconstrued due to any misunderstanding of its nature which may arise out of the Greek and Hellenistic traditions, traditions which have, unfortunately, been permitted to exert too strong an influence on the development of western thought.

I. The Nature of Egyptian Religion

What was the content of belief in ancient Egyptian religion? Such a question might appear as a natural query at the outset of a discussion of any religious tradition. This question, however, cannot properly be asked with regard to the Egyptian religious experience, or, if it is asked, it must be stated from the very beginning that no satisfactory answer can be given to it. The idea of 'belief' in the sense of the acceptance of certain defined tenets of faith is one which was foreign to the very nature of Egyptian religion, and hence one cannot expect to find any fixed and simple credal formulae by which that religion can be defined or described. One may with a fair degree of safety maintain that in such a sense of 'belief' the Egyptians believed nothing.[1] First and foremost, Egyptian religion appears as a system or systems of cult and ritual constituting a mythic and mystical experience which constantly re-affirmed and positively affected the power and indestructibility of the life of the individual, the state, the world of nature and the cosmos. Such a description implies a highly positive force in the religion of ancient Egypt, but it must be remembered that this description is of the religious experience, not of the content of belief.

A general perusal of Egyptian religion may lead one to the conclusion that it can be characterized by a total lack of philosophical and theological content, that it consisted of a totally "confused mass of material"[2] and that it was made up of a number of local unrelated cults. Within this mass of material and these various cults there is evident a large number of deities who often cannot even be seen as organized into a definite pantheon. This characteristic of confusion seems to be even more underscored by the absence of any central dogma, sacred scripture or one basic truth. The rationale of such confusion, however, has been well defined by Henri Frankfort who saw that the strength of Egyptian religion lay in its "multiplicity of approaches,"[3] that is, in its ability and willingness to admit the possibility of more than one legitimate and orthodox way. The concept of strict orthodoxy, so often a characteristic of the modern religious mind, did not hamper the freedom of ancient Egyptian thought, at least not until the time of the 'heretic' Pharaoh Akhenaten towards the end of the Eighteenth Dynasty. (Even here one may ask whether the objections to

Akhenaten's system were religious or political in nature.) The complex mythological system of ancient Egypt has been described by R. Anthes as being "completely free of those logics which eliminate one of two contradictory concepts and press religious ideas into a system of dogmas."[4] This freedom of Egyptian mythology to admit internal contradictions and to see them as compatible was the real strength of Egyptian religion. One may in fact maintain that such internal contradictions were not in reality contradictory but rather complementary, there being no strict dogmatic principles to define either orthodoxy or heterodoxy.

From the above it should be clear that the basic nature of Egyptian religion was totally different from the nature of religion as it is generally known in the modern western world, for the religion of ancient Egypt was unmarked by creed, dogma or belief. Nor were the Egyptians familiar with abstract philosophical and theological speculation. The main duty of the scribes of the House of Life was not a speculative or theological one; rather it was to ensure that the cultic rituals were duly and properly performed.[5] In the opinions of C.J. Bleeker[6] and of Drioton and Vandier[7] even myth had a relatively small importance, the main stress being placed on the performance of the cultic rituals. Hence, to place any emphasis on dogma or doctrine would be to distort the real significance of Egyptian religion. This opinion, however, must be tempered by a realization that cult is in itself an expression of myth and not simply a performance of empty or meaningless ritual. If we are to understand Egyptian religion as having its main basis in the cult, we must at the same time take into consideration the mythic symbols of which that cult was the expression. It is in these mythic symbols that the basic spiritual and theological values of Egyptian religion are to be found. The fact that the Egyptian language had no words to indicate 'religion' or 'belief' further serves to underscore the idea that such notions were not an integral part of the Egyptian religious consciousness.

In the past there have been those who have expressed the opinion that "there were deep mysteries beneath the surface of Egyptian religion."[8] Such an opinion seems to stem from a desire on the part of various early scholars of Egyptology to posit the idea that a deep esoteric knowledge existed in ancient Egypt. It is natural that such an interpretation should have arisen from the mysterious nature of the hieroglyphic script and from the awesome feelings so easily evoked by the Egyptian temples. The modern mind may (and justly so) be inclined to view such opinions with tongue in cheek. At the same time, it is necessary to stress the fact that one must beware of giving to the myth and religion of ancient Egypt any superficial interpretation. To be certain, we would be mistaken if we were to search for deep philosophical methods or arcane systems of knowledge in the Egyptian religious synthesis. We would, however, be equally mistaken if we were to view the Egyptian myths as simple and naive stories designed and invented to satisfy the questions of somewhat childish ancient minds. The gods, myths and rituals must rather be seen in the same light in which the Egyptian religious genius devised them, that is, as mythic symbols which were designed to express what could not be articulated, the myth itself being "an enunciation of a reality and not an explanation of this reality."[9]

The mythic and cultic aspects of Egyptian religion appear to have constituted a system of symbols contrived to express in graphic and perceptible form the mysteries of life and the universe. Such symbols did not make up a system of theology in the modern sense of the word, but were rather used to express theological concepts which could not as yet be articulated in abstract terminology. That is to say, behind the symbolic system of myth there did indeed lay a structured theological system,[10] not comprehended or expressed intellectually, but certainly apprehended in the experience of the cultic myth.

The cults in which the myths were expressed were basically community and state cults, having little if any interest in personal religious aspirations. In fact it appears that there was virtually no 'personal religion' whatsoever in the earlier periods of Egypt's history. (Personal piety became important only in the period following Akhenaten.) The communal nature of the Egyptian cults was totally in keeping with their mythic nature, myth being to the collective community what mystic is to the individual.[11] The primary purpose of the cult and the myth was the expression and maintenance of the cosmic order expressed therein. This does not imply, however, that the individual was able to find there no personal support, for in the Egyptian way of thinking the individual was contained within the cosmic order as an integral part of that order. Hence, by satisfying the religious needs of the state and community, the cult and its myth would have automatically met the conscious needs of the individual who was able to find his own stability within the wider order. This expression and affirmation of cosmic order may therefore be seen as one of the primary goals and principles of Egyptian religion.

If the Egyptian gave any type of intellectual assent to a dogmatic principle, it was to this concept of cosmic order, expressed through the figure of Ma'at, both goddess and abstract principle, the personification and symbol of such order. For the Egyptian mind, the cosmos, the order of Ma'at, was static and unchanging,[12] perfect even as it had come into being at the time of the creation. Because of this static perfection of the order of Ma'at, the Egyptian mind, unlike the Hebrew mind, had no need to apprehend history as a divinely guided process. Because the cosmos was already perfect, there was no need to posit a final goal to human history, nor was there any need of an eschatology or teleology.[13] This perfection of the cosmos, already realized from the very beginning, had only to be renewed and revitalized in the cultic rituals, rituals which both affirmed and effected such perfection. One may well wonder if any religion could ever express a more positive and more satisfactory ideal of cosmic existence.

Thus far it should be obvious that Egyptian religion was not designed to satisfy intellectual curiosity or to provide speculation regarding the origin of man and the universe. Its main function, that of expressing and renewing cosmic order, appears to have been highly pragmatic. The myth and its cultic expression literally held the universe together. Beyond this, however, religion also played a much more immediate role in that it was the basis of national stability. The state, already part of the wider cosmic order, was further strengthened in that it was the property of a ruler, the Pharaoh, who was himself a deity.[14] As a god incarnate and sprung from the gods, the Pharaoh was part of the mythic system and provided tangible and visible proof of the divinely supported nature of the state. In this connection one may note the personification of the royal throne in the goddess Isis, even the writing of her name[15] giving some evidence that such may have been one of her earliest functions and her actual origin. Through this deification of the source of royal power and authority as a personalized goddess, Egyptian religion mythologized the position of the ruler, placing him, although mortal flesh and blood, in a realm outside the course of normal human experience. Herein one can see a practical political importance in the mythic symbolism of Egyptian religion. Such symbolism stated that Pharaonic power derived its authority from the fact that the throne was the personal mythic deity Isis who imparted a divine nature to the ruler himself. This derivation of the royal power was expressed by the maternal relationship of Isis to Horus, the Pharaoh himself being considered as the incarnate Horus. A relief from Abydos, for example, portrays Seti I seated on the lap of Isis who bears on her head the horns of a cow as a symbol of motherhood. Even in the First Dynasty a king had called himself the "son of Isis,"[16] and in Spell 148 of the Coffin Texts Horus makes as his final claim to his rightful authority the statement, "I am Horus, son of Isis" (*ink Ḥr sꜣ ꜣst*).[17] This position of the Egyptian Pharaoh within the mythic system is mentioned here insofar as it was a central feature within that system and not simply a peripheral detail of it. The sanctification of the political order of the nation thus functioned as a central principle within the wider order of the system.

The cosmic nature of the religion of ancient Egypt is evident even in the origins of that religion. One should not, however, be too strict and dogmatic about the origins of Egypt's mythic system and leeway must always be left for other interpretations. Anthes, for example, has seen much of early religion, especially with regard to Horus, Osiris, Isis and Nephthys, as originating with the establishment of the monarchy in the First Dynasty.[18] To reject such a suggestion totally and to seek the origins of Egyptian religion solely in natural phenomena would be unwise, for it is reasonable that more than a single source must lie behind the complexities of Egyptian religious thought. Moreover, the Wars of Unification in the Predynastic Period obviously exerted a great influence on Egypt in the establishment of the monarchy. It is a plausible corollary, moreover that the establishment of this monarchy must also have been reflected in the development of religious myth, and hence one is probably justified in seeing the Osiris/Isis/Horus triad as having been greatly affected by the political events of the period. (Nevertheless, I am personally inclined to see earlier natural origins for the figures of at least Osiris and Horus.)

The order of nature and the cosmos was the primary source of revelation in ancient Egypt. Even a more sophisticated religious expression such as that of Akhenaten took its primary inspiration from the natural phenomena. In nature and the cosmos the Egyptian was able to perceive divine order and harmony, order such as was not readily evident in historical events as it was, for example, to the mentality of the Old Testament. For the Egyptian, the divine and the holy were revealed and made manifest in nature above all. The visible world was perceived and expressed, if not explained, in religious terminology, the earliest 'gods' being the controlling forces of nature. These primitive gods were usually local deities, there being no wider organized pantheon or spiritual realm.

With the emergence of wider conceptions of statehood, however, the purely local deities underwent a gradual process of assimilation, syncretism and organization, resulting eventually in a number of organized systems. Eventually it was the major powers and phenomena of nature which took central places as symbols of religious expression: the sun, the Nile, the fertile earth. The Nile, for example, was always constant, bringing yearly its new life and fertility. At times the inundation was not sufficient and the result would be famine, but the early inhabitants of the Nile Valley knew that eventually the river would rise again and life would be enabled to continue along its normal patterns. Men saw the yearly flood and the subsequent rebirth of vegetation, and, as a result, gradually came to experience the reality of revitalization. They soon realized that the new life brought by the Nile was the gift of a deity, and hence the association of the Nile with the efflux of Osiris was probably a simple matter when the latter deity established himself in Egypt.

The sun with its daily rising and setting displayed a regularity even greater than that of the Nile, and hence it was only natural that it too should become a symbol of the eternity of the life revealed in nature. Hence, in Akhenaten's Hymn to the Aten (if he was indeed its author) we find the following expression of the dependence of all life upon the life of the deity:

> Your rising is their life,
> Your setting is their death.[19]

As a result of such observations, the sun god at an early stage in Egypt's history became the main deity, or perhaps it would be more correct to say that the sun disc became the main symbol of the creative life and power which was perceived as inherent within the gods.

The life-giving powers of nature were not the only natural phenomena evident to the Egyptian. There was also the desert; there was also death and the realm of death. The desert was the very opposite of the fertile and life-giving black land of the Nile Valley, and hence it was an obvious development for the desert to become associated with the opposite of life and order. The Nile and the fertile land had the power to bring life and sustenance to mankind, but it must have been evident to the earliest inhabitants of Egypt that the fertility of the land could only be gained by the conquest of the desolate forces of the desert. The renewal of life was not, therefore, automatic. It was the result of a struggle in which the negative forces had to be defeated, just as Seth had eventually been defeated in the struggle with both Osiris and Horus. Hence, out of the natural cycle of nature and the seasons there emerged a mythologized account of the tension and polarity which existed between life and death, an account which was not only narrated in the spoken myth, but which was also experienced when this myth was ritually recounted in the cultic setting. The goal of this myth was that man might apprehend and perceive the divine order of the cosmos, the order of Ma'at, and that he might act and live in accordance with it so that all things might thereby be well and in order for the individual, the community, the state and the universe. This was the primary purpose and end of Egyptian religion. All else was secondary. The ultimate creation of the Egyptian mythopoeic mind, therefore, was a synthesis which included within itself the concepts of creation, fertility, life and its continuity, the political order of the state, and eventually the reality of individual resurrection in the afterlife. All of these were but various aspects of the one cosmic power of Ma'at.

One must be aware that the principles of Egyptian religion did not suddenly emerge in a fully developed form, but were rather the result of a process of evolution. In general the evolution of Egyptian religion may be seen in two areas: the individual deities and the overall perspective of life. With regard to the latter, its seems quite safe to maintain that a cosmic perspective had developed well before the end of the Fifth Dynasty when the first version of the Pyramid Texts made its appearance in the pyramid of King Unis at Saqqara not far from modern day Cairo. In these texts, and in the slightly later versions of the Sixth Dynasty, one can note the co-existence of two sets of symbols: a celestial symbolism centred around solar and stellar cults, and a system of symbolism centred around Osiris. It is important to note that the two systems of symbols were able to exist side by side without any attempt being made to create a rational syncretism of the two. Insofar as the Pyramid Texts contain a distinct "multiplicity of deities,"[20] they must be regarded as definitely polytheistic in nature, at least as far as concerns their mode of symbolic expression. To be sure, one cannot speak of any 'monotheistic' concept at this period of Egyptian history, even though so eminent a scholar as J.H. Breasted has suggested the emergence of a "non-national universal faith" in the Old Kingdom and has given to this faith the title of monotheism.[21] It is perhaps best to avoid at this stage the terms 'monotheism' and 'polytheism', both terms being essentially irrelevant to the Egyptian religious mind of the period. What was important for the Egyptian religious consciousness was the actual fact of the existence of the divine. In the Pyramid Texts the expression of this is neither polytheistic nor monotheistic, but rather symbolic. The term 'polytheistic' may in fact be applied here, but only to the actual system of symbols, not to the divine force itself which lay hidden behind these symbols. One must realize, however, that in the totally non-philosophical milieu of the Old Kingdom terms such as 'monotheism' and 'polytheism' would have been totally meaningless and were not even found in the vocabulary of the Egyptian language. What was important was the recognition of the divine, and whether the divine was singular or plural would have been a totally meaningless question to the Egyptian mind of the period.

The individual gods of Egypt gradually emerged at different times and in different places. Any attempt to trace the history of each one would be outside of the purpose of the present work. Hence, it must suffice to say that a number of individual deities were already known at the time of the Unification of Egypt at the beginning of the First Dynasty, having undergone a certain development in the Predynastic Period. Prominent by the time of Narmer were Neith, Hathor and Horus, the latter having possibly come into prominence as a result of the Unification of Upper and Lower Egypt. It is also possible that this was the time of the formulation of the myth of the conflict of Horus and Seth as a mythologization of the historical struggle between Upper and Lower Egypt. Hathor's prominence is illustrated by her place on the Narmer palette[22] where she appears in bovine form in her aspect of a mother goddess, the two portraits of her head flanking the name of Narmer. The symbolism here obviously reflects a concept of Hathor as the mother of the king or, as her name $Ḥt$-$Ḥr$ [23] ("mansion of Horus") implies, as a personification of the royal house.[24] Following the principle of mythologization, the figure of Hathor thus appears as a symbolic way of expressing the origin of the royal authority and divinity. Thus, even in the age of Narmer one may see an attempt to site the ruler within a wider cosmic setting. It appears, therefore, that the Unification of Egypt under Narmer (or Menes) did affect the development and evolution of Egyptian theology by the creation of a concept of the divine kingship. Such may well be understood as the natural outgrowth of the security and order which resulted after the period of the Wars of Unification. At the same time the formulation of a mythic symbolism around the person of the king would have given a stronger basis to the newly achieved unity of Upper and Lower Egypt. It is obvious, therefore, that at least to a certain degree early political events did contribute to the formulation of Egypt's religious principles. (At the same time this interpretation must be balanced by recalling the undeniable influence which the natural world had on the development of religion in Egypt.)

It may also at this point be asked to what extent the concept of a primitive mother goddess was prominent in early Egypt and how far such a concept affected the development of theology. Evidence for a type of mother goddess is already apparent in the figure of Hathor, in the figure of Mut (whose very name, *Mwt*, means 'mother'), and to a certain extent in Isis, although the actual origin of the latter was probably somewhat different, Isis being associated more with the royal throne although having a certain maternal aspect. The maternal aspect of Hathor is evident in the Late Egyptian story of Horus and Seth[25] where, at least at one point, she appears in more of a maternal role in relationship to Horus than does Isis. This maternal role of Hathor is also connected with her role as a goddess of love and sexuality, a role illustrated in a somewhat crude manner in the same story of Horus and Seth.[26] The primitive Delta goddess, Neith, also appears to have been an early mother goddess, a role illustrated by her title of 'Neith the Great, Mother of the Gods'. It has further been suggested that at a very early period an important religious role may have been played by a mother goddess who was associated with the sky.[27] There can be little doubt that some such concept must have been known in Egypt at an early period, and certainly its remains in the later periods are far from scanty. One should, however, be careful not to place too much of an emphasis on such a figure. While it is impossible to deny the maternal aspects in Egyptian religious symbolism, it must also be remembered that these are but one aspect of a wider system of myth. Certainly the Egyptians never knew an earth mother of the nature of the Greek Demeter despite the attempt of Herodotus to identify the Greek goddess with Isis. In the Egyptian mythic system the earth tends to be male rather than female. For example, in the Heliopolitan tradition the earth god is Geb, and in the tradition of Memphis it is Ptah, particularly in his role as Ptah-Tatenen,[28] who functions as an earth god. While the mythic traditions of Egypt did give due recognition to the maternal aspects of the divine, it did not place a preponderance of stress on it. In the Egyptian mythic system male and female deities appear to be well-balanced, the generative force and power of each being given its proper recognition.

The striving of local cults and various traditions for prominence must also have affected at least the content of the accepted mythic corpus. There was, for example, at an early period (pre-Pyramid Texts) a struggle between the sky religion centred around Ra of Heliopolis (On) and the religion of Osiris. Even though the two traditions had become sufficiently reconciled by the time of the Fifth Dynasty that both could be admitted to the Pyramid Texts, nevertheless the hostile attitude towards Osiris, noticeable at times in both Pyramid Texts and Coffin Texts, gives evidence that at an earlier point in history the Osiris tradition was regarded with abhorrence by certain segments of Egyptian society. Furthermore in the Fifth Dynasty, one sees an attempt on the part of the Heliopolitan priesthood of Ra to promote their own position by exerting an influence on the royal throne.[29] Such an event, although constituting a type of religious evolution, was an attempt not so much to change the content of religious experience as it was to promote the political power and influence of a specific religious group. The final result was that the position of Ra in Egyptian myth was greatly enhanced, as was the power of his priesthood. One cannot help here but note the influence of the political aspirations of the religious foundations of ancient Egypt, aspirations which were to play no small role in the subsequent centuries of Egypt's history.

The phenomena noted above are far from being the only events of their kind in ancient Egypt, nor are they necessarily the most important. The growth of Amun of Thebes during and after the Twelfth Dynasty was perhaps an even more dramatic example of religious evolution and change. Due to the political event of the deposition of the older Mentuhotep family by Amenemhet I of the Twelfth Dynasty, Amun rose from being a relatively minor deity to become eventually Amun-Ra King of the Gods, a virtually universal deity, by the time of the Nineteenth Dynasty. Here again it is necessary to note that the rise of Amun to prominence had little to do with religious needs and aspirations, but was the result of certain political events in Egypt's history. Obviously there can be little doubt that politics did affect the content of religious myth. One should note here in passing the abortive attempt made by Akhenaten in the Eighteenth Dynasty to oust the older deities of Egypt and to replace them with the Aten. There has already been much debate on the actual nature of Akhenaten's movement and much more is possible. For the present purposes, however, it is sufficient to say that the movement of Akhenaten, the so-called Amarna movement, represented an attempt to re-establish the political power of the royal throne on the basis of a religious organization and system alterior to the officially accepted cult of Amun-Ra of Thebes. As is well known, however, Akhenaten's attempt was doomed to failure for a variety of reasons, not the least of which was that by its very nature it was totally foreign to the Egyptian religious mind, having attempted to substitute a system of dogma and doctrine for the myth which had formed the basis of Egypt's religion for almost two millenia. Ironically enough, the major result of Akhenaten's movement was a further strengthening of the power of Amun-Ra, the deity whom Akhenaten had been most intent on supplanting.

Syncretistic tendencies in Egypt also made their contributions to the development of theological expression, if they did not in effect bring about actual changes in the mythic content of the religion. One may note, for example, the total identification of Ptah with the old Memphite earth deity Tatenen, resulting in the total disappearance of Tatenen into the new compound deity Ptah-Tatenen. So too, Min, the ancient fertility god of Coptos, was not infrequently identified with Amun, Horus or Osiris. Most common, however, was the tendency to syncretize the sun god Ra of Heliopolis with other deities. As a result there were produced such combinations as Ra-Horakhtey, Amun-Ra, Amun-Ra-Horakhtey, Sobek-Ra, Khnum-Ra, etc.[30] Most striking is the merging of Osiris and Ra in iconography in the tomb of Nefertari. Here the compound deity is portrayed as a mummy with the head of a ram topped by a sun disc and supported by Isis and Nephthys,[31] the latter two deities still performing the role which they so often have in association with Osiris. A further instance of identification between Osiris and Ra is found in a prayer in the Papyrus of Any.[32] One may, however, have strong doubts as to whether these last two instances were attempts actually to syncretize the two deities into one. More likely is the interpretation that such represent not the syncretization of two deities, but rather the conjunction of two sets of symbols, the two gods themselves still remaining as separate and distinct entities. The portrait which resulted in the iconography just mentioned was not so much a compound *deity* as it was a compound *symbol*.

With regard to the phenomenon of syncretism, one may well question whether true syncretism was all that prominent in ancient Egypt. There can be, of course, no doubt that over the course of history some syncretism did take place and that many of the gods must have owed their final forms to such a process. For example, Osiris gained much of his character through the absorption of other deities, namely Andjety of the Delta and

Khentiamentiu of Abydos. So also Ptah and Tatenen had been totally syncretized into one deity as already noted. Very frequently, however, what may superficially appear as syncretism is not such in reality. Amun and Ra, for example, merged into Amun-Ra, but this did not mean the disappearance of the two older deities and the creation of a new one. Neither Amun of Thebes nor Ra of Heliopolis ever lost their separate identities. What in effect emerged in such a combination was not a new god but a new mythic symbol, one in which both of the older deities were represented as conjoined into one expression of divinity while the separate existence of the two original hypostases was still recognized. Nor did the figure of Ra-Horakhtey imply that Horus and Ra were no longer worshipped as separate entities. The mythic figure of Ra-Horakhtey could be recognized as a symbol of divinity although the original Horus and Ra lost nothing of their character, nature or personality. Such a process cannot really be understood as syncretism, for true syncretism implies the absorption of one of the older gods into the other to create a new and indivisible hypostasis. Rather it is a sign of the peculiar ability of the Egyptian religious genius to express itself in symbolic terms, an indication of the Egyptian consciousness of the symbolic nature of the gods. Such expressions would not have been possible in a system which relied on the logic of philosophical theology, but it was possible (and even to an extent logical, or at least credible) in a system which made use of mythic expression to articulate its experience of deity.

The Egyptian religious mind was able to recognize both unity and diversity in the divine power. Divinity could be either one or many, and for the Egyptian mind it actually was both one and many. Such a statement, totally incompatible with rational thinking, is, nevertheless, fully acceptable when expressed in the symbolic terms of myth, for the actual purpose of mythic symbolism is to conjoin those elements which are totally inconsistent in terms of logical and philosophical thought. Such an understanding of the Egyptian approach explains the lack of any single orthodox religious synthesis in ancient Egypt. The one attempt to create such a synthesis, that of Akhenaten, failed for an obvious reason: the Egyptian mind was not yet restricted by a concept of orthodoxy of dogma which could give a basis for the denial of the validity of opposing concepts and expressions. The Egyptian mythic tradition knew and admitted a number of different religious syntheses, for example, the Osiris tradition, the Heliopolitan tradition, the Hermopolitan tradition, Amun-Ra of Thebes.

None of these, however, was incompatible with any other. Each one was able to make its own symbolic statements on the nature of the cosmos, and each one was correct insofar as it spoke in terms which were not dogmatic but mythic and symbolic. Symbolism, therefore, must be the key term in any attempt to understand the Egyptian theological mind.

Two further points should be briefly noted before ending this discussion of the nature of Egyptian religion. The first is the impact which the First Intermediate Period made on Egyptian religious thinking. The strong emphasis which the ancient Egyptians placed on the concept of life after death is well known, but during the Old Kingdom this immortality had been the prerogative of the king alone and of those of his nobles to whom he had been gracious enough to grant it. With the breakdown of royal central authority at the end of the Old Kingdom, the afterlife, no longer dependent upon the king, now became open to all who were able to provide for themselves the proper funeral rituals which would assure their survival after death. It was after this that the prominence of Osiris rose continually as he became the main deity who could afford continuity of life to all mankind. As a result, the hope of an afterlife became and would remain one of the main features and purposes of the Egyptian religious tradition.

The second point to be noted is the effect which the Egyptian Empire had on religious thinking, particularly during and after the Eighteenth Dynasty. Due to the foreign tribute won for Egypt by Thuthmose III, Amun-Ra of Thebes benefited greatly and hence his power and wealth steadily increased.[33] Gradually the stature of the gods of Egypt, especially that of Amun-Ra, grew to the point where they were seen as holding sway over all the foreign nations and not over Egypt alone. Such a concept is particularly evident in the Hymn to the Aten from the Amarna period. The logic of this is immediately obvious: if the Egyptian Pharaoh is universal ruler on earth, so also must the gods of Egypt be universal gods; and if Amun-Ra is the chief god of Egypt, so also must he be the main controlling force over all the world. Thus there entered the Egyptian religious mind the concept of a universal deity, a concept centred around Amun-Ra in his capacity as a sun god, or at least centred around his mythic symbolism as it was expressed in the sun disc.

To conclude this section of our study, let us state simply that the Egyptian mythic system of religious expression, a system which had taken its origins in the phenomena of nature and in the events of Egypt's political history, developed and evolved over a period of more than two millenia.

During the course of this evolution newer and wider concepts gradually made their way into the Egyptian system of thought. New mythic symbols were developed and older ones were discarded when the need for them was no longer felt. Hence, the variety and richness of the Egyptian mythic system grew into the complex and complicated synthesis with which we are now familiar. However, the basic themes and statements of Egyptian myth did not change. The main emphasis continued to be on the universal order of the cosmos and the abiding nature of Ma'at, the force which provided and symbolized that order. The Egyptian continued to recognize the never-changing foundation of the universe as the symbols and myths of his religion expressed it. The one major change which had taken place after the end of the Old Kingdom, one which must have appeared as a positive boon for all, was the fact that immortality beyond the grave was now a possibility for all people, nobles and commoners alike.

Notes

[1] In contrast to this assertion J.G. Griffiths suggests that the myths of ancient Egypt were traditions which the Egyptians actually did believe (J.G. Griffiths, *The Origins of Osiris and his Cult* [Leiden, 1980], 99). While it is possible that the content of the myths was actually accepted as factual and true by many of the commoners, such a literal acceptance is not demanded by the nature of authentic myth, and, if fact, contributes much to the destruction of the truly mythic nature of the material. The real value of myth lies in the fact that it is accepted and understood as symbolism, not as a dogmatic system.

[2] H. Frankfort, *Ancient Egyptian Religion* (New York, 1948), vi.

[3] *ibid.*, 4.

[4] R. Anthes, "Egyptian Theology in the Third Millenium B.C.," *JNES* XVIII (1959): 170

[5] H. Bonnet, *Reallexikon der ägyptischen Religionsgeschichte* (Berlin, 1952), 300.

[6] C.J. Bleeker, *Egyptian Festivals* (Leiden, 1967), 1-4.

[7] *L'Egypte*, 6th edition (Paris, 1984), 61.

[8] E. Hornung, *Conceptions of God in Ancient Egypt* (London, 1983), 12 (translated from the German *Der Eine und die Vielen*, 1971 by J. Baines).

[9] R. Bonnel & V. Tobin, "Christ and Osiris: A Comparative Study," *Pharaonic Egypt, the Bible and Christianity*, edited by S.I. Groll, (Jerusalem, 1985), 3.

[10] J.G. Griffiths (*op. cit.*, 18) states that a "consciously fashioned system of theology" may be detected in the Pyramid Texts, this theological system originating from Heliopolis.

[11] R. Bonnel & V. Tobin, *op. cit.*, 3.

[12] This aspect of Ma'at is not unlike the concept of λόγος in Greek philosophical thought.

[13] We cannot deny the fact that certain texts did indicate the idea of the end of the created order and a return to the original chaos, for example, Spell 1130 of the Coffin Texts and Chapter 175 of the Book of the Dead. Such texts, however, do not appear to be part of the official religious formulations used in the state cults. Moreover, such an 'eschaton' was not to be followed by a more perfect order as in Christian eschatological thought, but was to constitute a final end of creation and the re-establishment of the primaeval state of things. For a more detailed discussion, see E. Hornung, *op. cit.*, 162-165.

[14] J. Wilson, *The Culture of Ancient Egypt* (Chicago, 1951),72.

[15]

[16] W.M. Flinders Petrie, *The Royal Tombs of the First Dynasty* (London, 1901), II, Pl.II, Nos. 13,14.

[17] *CT* II, 226a.

[18] R. Anthes, *op. cit.*, 169ff.

[19] The original hieroglyphic text may be found in M. Sandman, *Texts from the Time of Akhenaten*, Bibliotheca Aegyptiaca VIII (Brussels, 1938), 95.17-18.

[20] E. Hornung, *op. cit.*, 24.

[21] J.H. Breasted, *Development of Religion and Thought in Ancient Egypt* (1912; reprint, New York, 1959), 6.

[22] Cairo Museum, JE 32169 (CG 14716).

[23]

[24] See R. Anthes in *JNES* XVIII, 193.

[25] Papyrus Chester Beatty I. For a translation of the text see M. Lichtheim, *Ancient Egyptian Literature*, II (Berkeley, 1976), 214-223.

[26] See M. Lichtheim, *op. cit.*, 216.

[27] R.T. Rundle Clark, *Myth and Symbol in Ancient Egypt* (London, 1959), 28.

[28] 'Ptah of the Risen Land', a reference to the primaeval mound.

[29] J. Wilson, *op. cit.*, 87.

[30] *ibid.*, 109.

[31] R.T. Rundle Clark (*op. cit.*, 158) suggests that in this context Ra and Osiris are "complementary forms of deity."

[32] *loc. cit.*

[33] J. Wilson, *op. cit.*, 184.

II. Myth and Cult in Egypt

One of the chief cultural characteristics of every ancient civilization was the fact that each had a mythology which was distinctly its own and which reflected its own level of culture and intellectual development.[1] If one analyzes, for example, the Canaanite mythic corpus, one finds therein at least two mythic traditions which had originally been quite distinct: the myths of the settled and urban Canaanite culture with their emphasis on the sophisticated deity El as head of the Canaanite pantheon, and the cruder myths of the more warlike Amorites who entered the area of Canaan late in the third millenium B.C.E. and gradually intermingled with the Canaanites, often by means of conquest.[2] Myths of the Amorite tradition place their emphasis on the god Ba'al whose nature was far less civilized and much more aggressive than the Canaanite El. In contrast to the Canaanite tradition, Hebrew mythology, although leaving numerous remnants in the Old Testament, has not survived in a detailed and organized form, and often has to be reconstructed and reconstituted. The reason for this is that most of the mythic elements were purged out of the texts in the process of editing by religious thinkers whose thought patterns were based on the historical rather than on the mythological.[3] Of all the ancient cultures, however, it is the Greek which has bequeathed to us the largest corpus of mythological material. Much of the Greek mythic tradition took its beginnings in the Minoan-Mycenaean world of the latter half of the second millenium B.C.E.,[4] after which it underwent a long process of expansion and development, the result being that much of this material can no longer be classified as true myth.[5] While this does not deny the authentic mythic basis of the Greek material, it does imply that the true mythic values may frequently be very highly concealed.

By comparison with the Greek mythological corpus, little is actually known about the myths and legends connected with the Egyptian gods, although considerably more information is available about them than is, for example, about the contents of Hebrew myth. The Egyptian texts contain numerous references to various mythical events and actions, but all too often these are no more than passing allusions, any full account of such events seemingly not having been recorded in permanent written form. It may well be that the reason for this was to prevent the various myths from taking any one definitive shape and form, and to allow for their fluidity and flexibility, *i.e.*, the possibility of change and development in content when such was necessitated by change and development in religious experience. It must further be remembered that the absence of a concept of sacred scripture would have rendered a permanent 'orthodox' version of any myth an impossibility. Finally, there appears to have been in ancient Egypt no large corpus of extended mythic narratives to be so recorded.

As for any extended narrative myth in ancient Egypt, the outstanding example of such is the cycle of the struggle of Seth with Osiris and Horus. If this tradition is taken as normative of Egyptian mythology, however, it should be only with a great deal of reservation. The Late Egyptian story of the conflict between Horus and Seth is quite obviously a literary work which contains a large amount of humour and cannot be taken as a serious mythic account. The only full account of the Osiris myth is that given in the writings of Plutarch, and one strongly suspects that this version of the story is one which has been constructed on Greek models of myth out of the individual component parts which the author may have known from Egyptian sources. The result is a Greek narrative which is based on Egyptian content but which does not necessarily contain an Egyptian understanding of the material involved. Egyptian sources contain numerous references to the Osiris myth, but no complete and unified account. Perhaps the Egyptian myths were already too well known to require any detailed recording, or perhaps, as has been suggested by Miriam Lichtheim, Seth's murder of Osiris was too terrible an event to be set out in writing.[6] On the other hand it may well be that the individual myths of the Egyptians were not developed in the fully detailed form with which we are familiar from the Greek tradition. Such an assertion may be seen as in keeping with the symbolic nature of the mythic traditions of Egypt, the theological and spiritual values of the myth being evident in the specific imagery and symbols rather than in any detailed elaboration of the narrative. The extended stories of Classical Greek mythology, when they are concerned with the gods, portray those gods as being little more than magnified human beings. Such 'myths' have in effect lost their true mythic and cultic features, and appear to be stories which exist only for the sake of their entertainment value. By way of contrast, the gods of the Egyptian mythic traditions do not appear as men, but as actual deities who possess an innate divine stature. More important is the fact that the Egyptian myths were more intimately connected with the cult,[7] and it is only within the cultic context that they became valid as symbols and efficacious in fulfilling their function.

Another extended Egyptian narrative may be mentioned here, namely the account of the destruction of mankind by the sun god Ra as contained in the *Book of the Cow of Heaven*. This text, recorded in five of the royal tombs dating from the Eighteenth to the Twentieth Dynasties, is written in the Middle Egyptian language and hence has been suggested to have originated during the Middle Kingdom.[8] The theme of the story is the account of Ra's destruction of men for their wickedness, a theme not unlike that known from Old Testament sources,[9] and one wonders if it may not have been influenced by the Semitic world. Nevertheless, the account reads more like a legend or a piece of fiction rather than a true myth, and perhaps it is in the class of fictional literature that it should be placed. In any event, it does not appear to belong to the normal mythic tradition of Egypt, for it does not reveal any true cosmic interpretation.

A proper understanding of the nature of Egyptian myth is an essential factor for the comprehension of its place within the religious synthesis. A mythic corpus is not simply a collection of stories from the past illustrating a type of heroic society or a golden age.[10] Nor is myth a simplistic and prescientific manner of explaining the origins of the universe and of man. For example, the account of the six days of creation in the first chapter of Genesis was never intended by the Hebrew theologians to be understood in a literal or fundamental fashion. The concept embodied in such a pericope may well be true and accepted as truth; but it is the *concept* which is to be accepted as such, not the symbol, which is only the articulation and expression of the concept. Thus, the Egyptian mythic figure which represents the sky as the goddess Nut (or as a cow or a vulture) was not intended to to taken by the Egyptians in a literal sense. Iconography of such a type was, to the Egyptian mind, a true and correct representation, but the truth of the representation lay in the signification of the symbol, not in its literal value. The sky was Nut (or a vulture or a cow) because it was part of the mystic and living divine order of nature. Its existence depended upon the divine creative force, a force which could only be represented symbolically and not literally. Hence, symbols which were totally different and even totally contradictory (contradictory, that is, to the logical and rational mind) could be used to express the same reality, and in such representations the Egyptian would have seen no dichotomy or conflict. The symbolic nature of the figures so used would have made conflict impossible. In like manner the sun god Ra could be portrayed as traversing the heavenly waters in his sacred barque, and to the mind of the Egyptian such would be a true description of the phenomenon of the course of the sun. At the same time, however, the truth of such an image would have been understood as implicit only because of the symbolic nature of the image, not in the symbol as a literal portrayal of the occurrence of the event.

The same principle may be applied to the iconography of the Egyptian gods. That Anubis had the head of a jackal, or Horus that of a falcon, or Thoth that of an ibis, was true in the sense of the mythic and symbolic. In such imagery the Egyptian was able to apprehend and perceive the mysterious life force of nature and the divine, but this apprehension was of a spiritual nature and could not be comprehended by the intellect. Hence, an iconographic expression of the divine could only be executed by the usage of symbols. Any non-symbolic expression of the divine would have been seen as totally incompatible with the nature of the gods and their realm. At the same time, no one symbol was able fully to express the totality of the spiritual concept thus described. Hence, the Egyptian religious mind and consciousness found it necessary to employ a multiplicity of symbols, for it was only this multiplicity of symbols which permitted the expression of "the infinite complexity of divine power."[11]

The complex system of mythic symbols formed for the Egyptian mind a synthesis, a mode of expression which the philosophical mind of a later age would be able to articulate in an abstract systematic theology. This capacity of the Egyptians to express the ineffable in symbolic and mythic terms perhaps demonstrates a greater reverence for the divine than do the most profound and abstract theological statements, for the latter statements far too often limit and define the divine by the creation of very narrow and stiff dogmatic assertions which are then accepted as 'correct' principles of faith and belief. It is surely axiomatic that no being or aspect of the realm of the sacred and holy can be comprehended by the intellectual powers of the human mind, and hence it is only through symbols that such may be expressed. The myth as a symbol, therefore, is neither a belief nor an intellectual assertion. It is rather an expression of an experience or the articulation of a reality which cannot be described in a literal manner. True myth, such as that which embodied the Egyptian principles of religious truth, far from being a naive expression of a simplistic belief, must be understood as a vital and creative intellectual force.

We may, therefore, define the Egyptian mythic synthesis as a series of symbols designed to express the inexpressible reality of the divine cosmos, the creation and sustenance of that cosmos, and the relationship of man and nature to the creative force. Since, however, myth is not a pre-scientific method of explaining these matters, one should not look for precise allegorical significance within the various elements of any one given myth. That is to say, one cannot expect easily and methodically to translate the mythic symbols into abstract philosophical thought, for true myth is far from being a simple allegorical narrative in which one expression or event stands for another. The Egyptian mythic narratives attempted to give expression to the idea that the creation and the cosmos had a meaning,[12] but that meaning was not easily to be discovered and rationally expressed through an allegorical interpretation of the details of the mythic narrative. In actual fact, the Egyptian myths contained very little of concrete substance which could be interpreted allegorically. "The [Egyptian] myth is hardly recognizable as a story."[13] While such a statement may not be applicable to all of the Egyptian myths, it is true for the majority of them. The myths themselves were usually very simple in their structure, but this simplicity did not prevent them from giving indication of an authentic and profound wisdom which was contained within their formulations. In fact, it was the very simplicity of the Egyptian myths which enabled them to do so, for their signification was not obscured by unnecessary details of narrative art. By way of contrast, the Greek myths are much more highly detailed and developed, but they have very little of spiritual or theological substance within them. Homer's 'myths', for example, appear to be designed more for entertainment than for edification. The Egyptian myth, however, was the exact opposite. Its purpose was not to entertain but to edify and, beyond mere edification, actually to effect the reality which its symbols expressed.

The reason and basis for the creation of a system of mythic symbols is the perception of the divine world as something which is numinous, wholly other, the *mysterium tremendum*,[14] that which is beyond the understanding and comprehension of the intellect and can be apprehended at only a much more basic and instinctive level, the level of the total personality. This numinous world of the divine had from the earliest periods of history been recognized by the inhabitants of the Nile Valley in the forces of nature. Insofar as the Egyptians did not, like the later Greeks, think in philosophical terms nor in terms of God as active in historical events as did the Hebrews, the development of a mythic system was necessary in order to express the apprehension of the divine world in a concrete and comprehensible manner. This nature, function and purpose of myth make it clear that a serious misunderstanding of mythology is at fault when a scholar can speak of the Egyptian tradition as "the vast accumulation of mythological rubbish inherited from the past."[15] The Egyptian mythic tradition did indeed constitute a 'vast accumulation', but 'mythological rubbish' it was not. On the contrary, the Egyptian mythic system demonstrated a deep theological acumen with but one mark to differentiate it from a philosophical system of abstract thought: its expression was not in the realm of the intellect, but in the realm of the symbolic, which is perhaps the better medium for an articulation of the unseen world of the wholly other.

 It is a commonly held belief that the time and place of mythological action is the past, a past so distant and removed in both time and nature from the contemporary world as to constitute an almost unreal realm. To a certain extent such an assertion is true, for the actual realm of mythic events has in effect no real relationship to historic time. Between the time of the mythic actions and the time which can be comprehended by historical memory there is no connection. Certainly the myths of the Greek tradition must be seen as having taken place at a time far removed from the later world in which they were recounted as legend and saga. So also it has been said that the Egyptians looked back to a mythic past when cosmic order had been established at the time of the creation.[16] To a certain extent this also is true, for, to the Egyptian mind, there was a time when the universe was brought into being, a time when the sun god ruled on the earth, a time before historical time. Such a golden age, however, is but one aspect of mythology, for mythology does not imply only looking back to a past so far removed as to be legendary. It implies also, and perhaps more importantly from a pragmatic point of view, a realization of that past in the present moment. True myth, when expressed ritually within the cultic setting, is in effect a dramatic realization, a bringing into reality in the present the ultimate truths articulated by the mythic system. Ritual cultic myth is in fact creation or re-creation of past mythic events with the intention that such events should become realities in the here and now.[17] Without such a realization of the myths, the cultic performance would be no more than a 'historical' commemoration having little if any effect on present reality. It is in this that the importance of the Egyptian cult may be found. The Egyptian concept of time was far different from the linear concept of time known in the modern world. The Egyptian mentality did not make a sharp distinction between past, present and future, and what had happened in the mythic past could well be seen as occurring in the present through its mythic re-enactment and recitation. This ambiguity concerning the specific time of mythic events is reflected in the structure of the Classical Egyptian language where verbal forms stress the perfective (completed) or imperfective (on-going and continuous) aspects of action rather than situating the action at a specific time in the past, present or future. Hence, a mythic event belonged to no specific time and could be experienced as a present occurrence, the Egyptian mentality being prone to experience time as a type of eternal now.

Cultic and ritual observances in ancient Egypt were many and varied, each temple having virtually its own peculiar rituals connected with the specific mythic associations of the shrine. Inscriptions and portrayals of the cultic rites on the walls of the temples have enabled scholars to reconstruct with a good deal of certainty the general principles and practices of such rituals. Like the general principles and myths of Egyptian religion, the cultic practices also underwent a long process of development and evolution,[18] but a description of this process is not the purpose of the present work. Nor is it our purpose to describe again the specific practices of Egyptian worship rituals. A few brief remarks, however, will not be out of place at this point.

Very little is known about the earliest Egyptian cultic practices, and thus it is impossible to make any secure attempt to trace the historical evolution of religious rituals. However, one may be quite certain that cultic practices originated from a dual source: rituals surrounding the person of the king and rituals connected with the orderly recurring of the various phenomena of nature. The latter type of rituals must be considered to be of a cosmic nature, intended to celebrate and even to effect the natural phenomena with which they were associated. It would be totally un-Egyptian to expect the rising of the Nile or the dawning of the sun to occur without the accompaniment of the appropriate rites. The question as to whether or not these phenomena would have taken place in the absence of the cultic ritual is not really relevant. The important point to be made is that the cultic rituals were the means whereby the actual *meaning* of the natural phenomena could be perceived and articulated. What the senses perceived in the natural world was given its signification by the performance of the rite which both imitated the natural phenomena and even caused them to be imbued with the religious meaning which they possessed. Without the cultic ritual the various phenomena of nature would have made no sense to the Egyptian mind, for the ritual organized these phenomena within the wider cosmic setting.

Rituals associated with the kingship were at an early stage also viewed in a cosmic light. The rites of the succession to the throne and the coronation of the new monarch, whereby the crown prince became the incarnate living Horus, were more than mere rituals of accession. It was through these rites that the new ruler was enabled to take his proper place in the divinely ordained system of nature and the political world, for these same rites functioned actually to create the divine nature of the monarch. Thus he was able to commence his rule as the official representative of the divine power on earth. Of such a nature also was the Sed festival, a topic too complex to be discussed here in detail, but one whose main purpose seems to have been the renewal of the royal powers or at least the proving and affirmation of the same. The cosmic nature of the royal religious ceremonies is evident in the fact that throughout Egyptian history it was the physical presence of the monarch which both provided the means and instrument of political and social order and also ensured the continuation of the blessings and benefits of the natural phenomena. More than a mere symbol of the assurance of such phenomena, the cultic figure of the ruler was even seen as their actual cause.[19]

At a relatively early stage in the religious development of Egypt, myth and ritual became inseparably interconnected with the result that the cult may be seen as the "actualization of the mythic pantheon."[20] Such was, of course, the result of a long process of evolution and development in the content of both myth and ritual. However, there can be little doubt that such a connection was inherent in Egyptian cultic practices from the very beginning. This fact must be underscored at this point in order to avoid the misconception that the cult alone was the central focus of Egyptian religion. While the main emphasis may have been placed on the correct performance of the cultic rites, it cannot be too strongly stressed that the cult was not more important than its mythic content. Without the myth the cult would have had virtually no real significance beyond a mere performance of a rite of sympathetic magic. The cult was important for no other reason than that it was the expression and dramatization of the myth, while the myth in turn was given relevance by its cultic expression. In other words, neither cult nor myth could have existed without the other. They were totally interdependent and in essence one and the same thing, the cult being a dramatic representation and the verbalized myth.

One of the chief characteristics of the performance of the Egyptian cult was its aspect of secrecy. The daily cult, as well as the major liturgical portions of the chief festivals, was performed secretly in the sanctuary of the temple by the priestly officiants. The actual event of the manifestation of the gods to the general populace took place only at certain great festivals, when the climax of the ritual appears to have been the public appearance of the statue of the god whose festival was being celebrated.[21] Two important theological points may be noted in this cultic practice. First, the aspect of secrecy is in keeping with the mysterious nature of the symbolic content of the myth. The actual deity himself is 'hidden', a characteristic expressed, for example, even in the very name of the Theban god Amun, whose name, *Imn*, means in the language of ancient Egypt "he who is concealed." Insofar as the essential nature of the gods was unknown to man, so was it fitting that also the rituals by which the gods were sustained be hidden and unknown. Because the mythic symbol functioned to conceal as well as to reveal the deity, it was also necessary that the performance of the cultic ritual should maintain a certain element of the secret and the unknown.[22]

Secondly, however, along with the aspect of secrecy there went also that of revelation. While the gods remained hidden and unknown, there was also the necessity of revealing the god to his followers. Hence, the public appearance of the deity at the climax of the ritual functioned to make this revelation a reality in the cultic[23] setting. What was actually revealed to the people was no more than an effigy of the deity, itself still a symbol, but such was sufficient to dramatize the important fact that the god had manifested his presence in the midst of his people. By such an epiphany the populace was assured that the divine power was in fact present with them, in the course of their history and in the continuation of the natural world, although still maintaining the hidden nature of its true personality and character. The 'hidden' and the 'revealed' were the two opposing and complementary marks of the Egyptian gods, and these two marks were symbolized in both the mythic tradition of Egypt and in the cultic expression of that tradition.

The texts which accompanied the cultic ritual consisted of three basic types: laudatory texts giving praise to the deity for those features of his nature and action which the cult was celebrating, intercessory statements requesting the favour or activity of the deity, and mythic statements expressing in the spoken word, and thereby proclaiming and revealing, the specific mythic action which was being commemorated and realized in the cult. The combination of mythic statement and ritual action was of prime importance, for it was first and foremost the power of the spoken word which gave its reality to the mythic concept and made the cultic action into an efficacious ritual. Thus, the revelatory aspect of the cult had its actualization in both the visual and aural aspects of the ritual. Hence, the religious festival became in effect "the ritual actualization of a mythical concept."[24] We must take strict note here of the concept of 'actualization'. The cult was not simply a commemoration of an event which had taken place at some point in the distant past; it was not simply an act of remembrance. Cultic commemoration rather implies that the mythic concept actually became real in the present moment, that the mythological action was in fact taking place in the ritual and that the reality of its occurrence was no less significant than the original event. In effect, the original mythic event and its cultic commemoration were one and the same thing. Thus the mythic event was seen as happening in the very presence and time of the devotees of the deity, and its practical effects were renewed for the purpose of accomplishing whatever benefit could be expected of them. In such a manner the Heliopolitan creation myth was ritually dramatized in the rites of Ra at On[25] and the creation event was thus actualized in the cult. So too the mythic traditions of Osiris were given their cultic realization at the festival of Osiris at Abydos in order to effect the continuity of life which was expressed in the Osiris myth. The ritual of the Pharaoh's succession to the throne must also be seen in the light of this mythic and cultic action. The latter action was both in effect and in reality a repetition of Ra's original action of the assumption of the kingship in the primaeval time of the creation.[26] Of importance also were the various rituals of *hieros gamos*, sacred marriages of the gods, designed to express and to effect the fertility of the principle of life itself. In this connection we may note the festival of Opet, the sacred marriage of Amun celebrated at Thebes, as well as the nuptials of Horus of Edfu with Hathor of Denderah, the latter two sites containing two of the most magnificent of the Ptolemaic temples.

It is impossible to overestimate the importance of the actualization of the myth in the cult. It must be noted, however, that the actual narrative details of the myth were not of any great significance. What was important was rather the symbolism of the various mythic figures and patterns. This latter fact may well explain the somewhat meagre nature of the Egyptian myths, there being no need to develop complex narrative patterns. The central point in the cultic dramatization of the myth was the underlying concept which that myth embodied.[27] As long as this concept was dramatized, the purpose of the cult was achieved, that purpose being nothing less than the renewal of the life of the world. Once that purpose was fulfilled, there was thereby guarantied the stability and well-being of the individual, the state, nature and the very order of the cosmos itself. According to such an interpretation, we may state that the cultic performance of the mythic ritual was in effect the establishment of the principle of Ma'at. In essence, therefore, myth could even be called a practical expression of, and means toward, Ma'at.

Egyptian mythology did not simply express legends of the distant past, nor was the cult performed for the purpose of receiving the favours of the gods. It was not, as Morenz has expressed it, a matter of *do ut des*, a situation in which man gives to the gods so that the gods may in turn give to man.[28] Rather it was a dramatization intended to realize the mystery of the divine presence within the created cosmos, to effect a re-creation of the universe, and to uphold Ma'at by ensuring the order and stability of the world. Such a purpose and function of myth and the cult, therefore, was a cosmic one; it was utilitarian and pragmatic, but in a highly positive, comprehensive and all-embracing manner. In short, the combination of myth and cult constituted a sacrament of the stability of the universe and of life itself.[29]

Notes

[1]This does not preclude the possibility of borrowing on the part of any one ancient culture from another.

[2]The latter is reflected mythologically in some of the accounts of conflict found in Canaanite mythology, On the myth of the conflict of Ba'al with El, see U. Oldenburg, *The Conflict Between El and Ba'al in Canaanite Religion* (Leiden, 1969).

[3]The result of this is that much of the mythic material of ancient Israel and Judah has been lost to the modern world. At the same time, however, some if its elements can be reconstructed, often through the interpretation of the Psalms, the cultic texts of the Jerusalem Temple.

[4]See, for example, M.P. Nilsson, *The Mycenaean Origin of Greek Mythology* (University of California Press, 1932).

[5]Unfortunately for the student of Greek mythology, much of the Greek material has been expanded by legend, folktale, saga and even by additions which in many cases may be defined as fiction, for example in the works of Homer and the classical dramatists. While this has had the result of providing the modern world with a rich literary heritage from the Greek world, it has also had the unfortunate result of colouring our conception of mythology. Hence, we often tend to look for myths to be well developed and detailed narrative accounts which set forth elaborate stories; we expect myths to be complex sagas, which usually in their inception they were not. It is, therefore, necessary to revise our expectations of mythology and to try to see it for what it originally was and for what it originally was intended to express.

[6]M. Lichtheim, *Ancient Egyptian Literature*, II (Berkeley, 1976), 81.

[7]R.T. Rundle Clark, *Myth and Symbol in Ancient Egypt*, 12.

[8]M. Lichtheim, *op. cit.*, II, 198.

[9]Genesis 6:5 - 7:24.

[10]Hence, the legends of the Trojan war as recorded by Homer can hardly be said to fall into the category of myth. They may be taken as legend or folktale, but not as true myth.

[11]H. Frankfort, *Ancient Egyptian Religion*, 19.

[12]C.J. Bleeker, *Egyptian Festivals* (Leiden, 1967), 11.

[13]*loc. cit.*

[14]An excellent discussion of the concepts of the 'Holy' and the 'Other' may be found in the now classic work of Rudolf Otto, *The Idea of the Holy*, 2nd edition (1923; reprint, New York: Oxford University Press, 1958), (translated from the German *Das Heilige* by J.W. Harvey).

[15]A.H. Gardiner, *Egypt of the Pharaohs* (Oxford, 1961), 227.

[16]C.J. Bleeker, "The Religion of Ancient Egypt," *Historia Religionum*, edited by C.J. Bleeker & G. Widengren (Leiden, 1969), I, 48.

[17]With regard to the time of myth, R. Anthes has remarked (*JNES* XVIII, 205): "The performance of a mythological procedure is closely related with the assumption that it mirrors an event which took place in the past." Such an observation cannot be contradicted, but it must be remembered that in the cultic performance of myth it is not the past time and the past tense of the action which is important. The important emphasis on time is in the present moment in which the myth is culticly performed, for the whole purpose of the cultic performance is to make the past real in the present. It is because the myth originally took place in the past that it must be culticly performed. Otherwise the past would have no relationship with the present, nor would the recounted myth have any importance or effect.

[18]While rituals and the content of the myths did develop and evolve, there was remarkably little change in the basic concepts of Egyptian religion, the basic structure and purpose of those concepts remaining essentially the same throughout all of Egypt's history. It is, therefore, possible to speak of general theological principles in Egyptian

religion without making reference to specific time periods and without attempting to trace a development in such principles.

[19] Also associated with the royal religious rites was a complex series of offerings made to the dead monarch and evidenced in the Pyramid Texts. Frequently the precise nature of these offerings is unclear, but the offering system seen in the Pyramid Texts was obviously connected with the worship, veneration and sustenance of the deceased monarch. This, however, goes somewhat beyond the simple practice of making offerings for the benefit of the dead. It was rather a further recognition of the cosmic nature of the monarch even after his death when he had become united with the greater divine powers. The cosmic nature of the Egyptian kingship was thus seen as encompassing both the present world and the next.

[20] S. Morenz, *La religion égyptienne*, translated from the original German by L. Jospin, (Paris, 1977), 119.

[21] *ibid.*, 129.

[22] It is quite possible that such secrecy may also have been intended to exert a certain psychological influence on the worshipper, and perhaps even to have a 'political' purpose as well. The element of secrecy, by which certain rites were viewed by the priestly class alone, must have done much to increase the prestige and position of that class and to strengthen its influence over the common people.

[23] I stress the term 'cultic' here, because a revelation within the confines of the cult does not violate the unknown and sacred nature of the gods, the cultic revelation remaining symbolic rather than actual. The gods were thus enabled to maintain their two important and complementary aspects of being both hidden and revealed.

[24] C.J. Bleeker, *Egyptian Festivals*, 39.

[25] *loc. cit.*

[26] *ibid.*, 40.

[27] *ibid.*, 6.

[28] S. Morenz, *op. cit.*, 134.

[29] I have purposely omitted any discussion of the nature and significance of the Egyptian temple architecture here, not because it is unimportant, but because it is not an integral part of the Egyptian theological synthesis. The temple was important for its symbolic value as an architectural representation of the primaeval mound of the creation and of the cosmos itself, being built, according to tradition, on the actual site of the original primaeval hill, the place of the creation. It was thus a visible expression of the act of creation and of the universe. That such was held true for every temple even further underscores the symbolic nature of the temple structure and of the myth which was dramatized therein, since obviously every single temple could not have been regarded as the actual historic place of the creation. Although this symbolic nature of the temple was highly important, the real importance of the structure itself was that it furnished a fitting and suitable setting for the performance of the myth, and functioned also as a dwelling place for the cult state of the deity. Detailed descriptions of the Egyptian temple may be found in the numerous works on Egyptian art and architecture, but for an elaborate interpretation of the meaning of the temple, I would refer the reader to E.A.E. Reymond, *The Mythical Origin of the Egyptian Temple* (Manchester, 1969). Although this study is

based primarily on the Ptolemaic temple of Horus at Edfu, it contains a great deal of interesting material.

III. The Egyptian Gods

The Egyptian term for 'god', *ntr*, (Coptic *noute*), provides no real indication of the basic meaning of the Egyptian concept of deity. Even the exact nature of the hieroglyph[1] with which the word is written is uncertain. Gardiner described it as a "cloth wound on a pole, an emblem of divinity,"[2] and Bleeker has suggested that it represents a pole with a flag,[3] a sacred object used to indicate the presence of a divine power. Hornung's opinion is that the sign grew out of a fetish, an inanimate object venerated at an early period.[4] Hence, the sign itself cannot be expected to shed any specific light on the subject which it signified. Any further discussion of the nature of the hieroglyph appears to be pointless, and one will probably be safest in adopting the fetish interpretation of the sign and viewing it as an abstract representation of the idea of divinity, the object depicted having no actual bearing on the concept expressed by it. Nor do the other two hieroglyphs commonly used as determinatives for the names of the gods[5] elucidate the nature of the concept of deity, the first sign being obviously connected with the ancient falcon god Horus and the second simply portraying a god in anthropomorphic form. A number of specific deities were also indicated by a series of various hieroglyphic signs:

𓀭𓀮𓀯𓀰𓀱𓀲𓀳𓀴𓀵𓀶𓀷𓀸𓀹𓀺[6]

Such signs, however, insofar as they were used for particular gods, did not say anything about the actual nature of those gods and their divinity, but functioned only as anthropomorphic and/or theriomorphic symbols of them, the anthropomorphic forms being somewhat later than the others.[7] What is important here is the obviously symbolic nature of the figures used for such representations; the various deities were thereby *portrayed* but not *depicted*. This avoidance of depicting a deity in the hieroglyphic system of writing is in accordance with the concept of the hidden and concealed nature of the gods as it was expressed in the mythic symbols of Egypt.

Moreover, the specific root meaning of the term *ntr* also appears to be quite uncertain. W. von Bissing has noted[8] the term *ntr* meaning 'natron', a substance used in purification, the verb *ntr* having the meaning of 'to be pure'.⁹ Following this pattern of thought, one might argue that the term *ntr*, when used of a deity, designated his or her purity, singleness or perfection.¹⁰ Such an interpretation of the term *ntr*, however, must remain no more than speculation, and the safest conclusion seems to be that it is an obscure word, one which reveals nothing about the Egyptian concept of divinity. Language, in this case, like the myths themselves, conceals rather than reveals the true nature of the Egyptian gods.

Even the iconography tends to conceal nature of the gods. The portrayal of Anubis with a jackal's head or of Hathor in the form of a cow should not be taken as actual portraits of these deities.¹¹ Such portraits are icons in the mythic and mystic sense, symbols of the hidden natures of the deities in question. According to Spell 491 of the Coffin Texts only the dead can know the true form (*ḫprw*) of a god.¹² This, however, does not imply that the living had no perception or experience of the gods. Mortal humans were able to experience the gods in the mythic liturgies of the cults. Furthermore, even before this cultic experience, there was a more basic and natural experience of the gods in the world of nature. Man's experience of the gods through the natural world must have taught him that the gods were 'good', *nfr* in Egyptian. This term had the connotation of a pragmatic goodness which could be perceived in the beneficial effects which the gods had on men and the world. Hence it was that the Pharaoh was frequently called 'the good god' (*ntr nfr*) in virtue of the fact that he was the one who mediated the blessings of the gods to the world of men. The gods of the Egyptians acted for the benefit of mankind, and particularly for the benefit of Egypt, their 'beloved land' (*t3 mry*). Unlike the Mesopotamian gods, the Egyptian gods did not represent a constant threat and a hostile force to humanity. The gods of Egypt had the constant intent to bestow their benefits and blessings on the world, a natural concept in a land where the regularity of the seasons and of the Nile was most dependable. The gods could thus be nothing else but a source of goodness for mankind. This does not, however, imply that the Egyptians were unable to recognize evil in the world. They did indeed recognize natural, political and moral evils, but they also recognized the fact that it would be the work of the gods through their goodness (*nfrw*) which would eventually set such evils aright. To the Egyptian mind and experience, life and the world were good, and hence any mythic expression of the gods also was bound to portray them as good.¹³

The gods, however, were not only good; they were also powerful, righteous, merciful and, perhaps above all in their nature and being, holy.

The Egyptian term for this latter attribute, ḏsr, may be translated as 'holy', 'sacred', 'splendid' (*prächtig*), 'beautiful' (*schön*), 'secret' (*geheim*).[14] The root ḏsr, moreover, has the significance of separating.[15] Hence, the concept of the holiness (ḏsrw) of the gods implied also that the gods were different from other categories of being. Thus, holiness in Egyptian thought appears, at least in the sense of the term ḏsr, to have had something of the same connotation as the Hebrew קדוש. That is to say, the gods were holy because they were totally different, separated and set apart from normal experience. The being and nature of the gods, and hence of the divine which they symbolized, was the classic *mysterium tremendum*, and not simply the *sacer* or ἅγιος. This holiness (ḏsrw) of the gods, however, was not necessarily the source of their important moral function in upholding the order of Ma'at, the term ḏsr seemingly not having acquired the moral connotations which the Hebrew קדוש did at the latest stage of the development of the latter term.[16] The Egyptian gods were righteous and upheld the order of Ma'at simply because they were part of that order and had therefore to support it. The holiness of the gods was not the first cause of their righteousness, but they were able to be totally righteous because of the fact that they were holy. The holiness and the righteousness of the gods and the divine realm were two separate and distinct characteristics which were related only accidentally.

The individual deities of Egypt appear to have been, like the mythic expressions in which they were embodied, more symbolic of the divine powers than indicative of specific divine hypostases. The symbolism of the divine which was embodied in the mythic gods was to an extent clarified by the very names of the deities themselves. One may note, for example, Amun 'the hidden one', Sekhmet 'the powerful one', Nun 'the primaeval waters', Kuk 'darkness', Huh 'infinity', Atum 'the complete one', Horus 'the distant one', Hathor 'mansion of Horus', and Isis 'the throne'. Many of the names of the gods, however, are not clear, and no definite meaning can be assigned to such names as Osiris, Ptah, Seth, Ra or Min. This is to be expected of deities whose origins may be lost in antiquity, but one must assume that the names of such gods were based on linguistic roots which in some way indicated their actual nature and function. An exception to this may be possibly seen in Osiris whose origin and name could well be from non-Egyptian sources.

The fact that many of the divine names can be given definite semantic significance points to the origin of at least some of the gods not as personal deities but rather as embodiments of specific aspects of the powers of nature. The Egyptian gods must be seen first and foremost as symbols, their hypostasization in specific anthropomorphic or theriomorphic form being an attempt to enunciate these powers in a personal and comprehensible manner. In the case of a number of gods it is clear that their function of personifying natural forces was by far one of their most important roles. We see, for example, the earth in the deity Geb, the sky in Nut, the grain and the Nile water in Osiris, the air in Shu, the sun in Ra, the desert in Seth, and the moon in Khons whose very name means 'the traveller'. Thus the impact made upon the early Egyptians by the natural phenomena was given its due expression by a process of mythologization. Such was not simply a naive method of explanation or a primitive means of rationalization of what could not be comprehended in a scientific manner. This deification of the natural phenomena and forces constituted a recognition by the ancient Egyptian of the essentially mystical nature of his environment. Due to an absence of any philosophical mentality, this mystical aspect had to be expressed through the mythic symbols which a non-abstract mentality could comprehend. Such an expression did not constitute for the Egyptian an actual form of 'knowledge', nor did it serve as a substitute for a scientific system. What it did do, however, was enable the Egyptian mind to express an understanding of the rational and ordered nature of the cosmos. The positive affirmation which was embodied in this expression permitted him to see the inherent goodness of the universe in which he found himself. The mythic system of the gods thus provided the Egyptian with his *raison d'être*, giving him an assurance that his universe had a meaning and significance, even if he was unable to articulate that meaning and significance rationally.

That the gods of Egypt were mythical is a fact beyond doubt, if by the term 'mythical' we mean deities who were symbolic of deeper forces and powers. They were not mythical, however, in the sense that the Homeric gods were mythical. The Egyptian gods had few extended mythological legends connected with them. They were not deities whose deeds were recounted in lengthy narratives; no sagas and folktales had developed their characters into the three dimensional beings such as one finds in the Greek tradition. The 'myth' of the destruction of mankind, noted in the last chapter, was a relatively late story which may have enjoyed a limited use. The extended account of the struggle between Horus and Seth belongs more to the realm of fiction than to that of myth, even though it may have been based on certain elements which were truly mythic. The full legend of Osiris comes to us by way of Plutarch who in all likelihood created a Greek myth out of Egyptian elements. Nor do we have any elaborate mythic legends concerning Geb, Nut, Hathor, Shu, Neith, Ma'at, Sekhmet, Ptah, Sobek or even Amun of Thebes.[17] The Egyptians appear to have developed no sense of epic literature with regard to their gods, and even their literary *genre* of the short story was seldom concerned with the gods. Even a quick reading of the story of the conflict of Horus and Seth makes it evident that its purpose was far from mythological in any true sense of the word. Even Herodotus went into no detail about the myths of Egypt, a fact which may lead one to suspect that such were unknown to him despite his claim to have been initiated into the Egyptian religious life.

As an exception to this non-developed nature of the Egyptian myths, one may be tempted to cite the example of the famous mysteries of Osiris at Abydos, and these may be even further extended by the numerous references to the battles of Osiris in the Book of the Dead. However, two points may here be raised in objection. The first is that we have little concrete knowledge of the Abydos mysteries and no specific text which may have served as the basis of the Osirian liturgy. Hence, it is impossible to state for certain that even these rites constituted a unified and extended dramatization of the Osiris legend. It is quite likely that such rites were centred on only a few basic incidents, those incidents which could be said in actuality to constitute the core of the Osiris tradition. Secondly, the varied references from the Book of the Dead do not necessarily imply any unified and extended account. It may well be that in such examples we are faced with no more than disconnected mythic statements based on a general tradition of the struggle of Osiris with Seth and the eventual vindication of the former. It may, on the other hand, be the case that the Osiris tradition had developed into a generally well detailed myth and that, due to the importance attained by that god in popular veneration, he had become an exception to the general pattern of the Egyptian gods. The fact, however, that no extended Egyptian source relating the Osiris tradition is extant seems to present a certain degree of evidence against such a supposition. It is unlikely that the Osiris tradition was anything like the extended account given by Plutarch. If even a shorter version of the myth existed, it would certainly have to be considered as an exception to the general rule.

All of this, however, does not decrease the mythic value of the Egyptian gods. If anything, it enhances such value. When a myth develops into a detailed epic-like account, such as, for example, the Greek tradition of Theseus, it runs a serious risk of losing its original signification and of being narrated more for its legendary and fictional value. The fact that the Egyptian gods seem not to have developed in such a manner would have made it possible for them to retain the symbolic nature of the mythic events and actions attributed to them. We may here adopt the attitude that the Egyptians developed no extended myths for the very reason that symbols cannot evolve into fictional accounts and still retain their full essence as symbols. Because the Egyptian gods were such symbols, they did not evolve as figures of an epic mythological tradition. Thus they were able to keep their symbolic aspects right up until the time when they were supplanted by Christianity, the latter tradition having a mythic system closely enough allied to that of Egypt to make it readily acceptable to the descendants of Pharaonic civilization. Thus, by their failure to develop a complex mythology, the Egyptians gods were able to retain their full mythic value until the end of their history as a viable religious force.

The purpose of the present work does not permit any kind of complete discussion of the individual gods of Egypt, nor is such a discussion necessary here. Nevertheless, a few remarks on some of the individual deities may help to illustrate the nature of the gods as a whole. Perhaps the richest mytho-theological[18] symbol among the Egyptian deities is the old creator god of the Heliopolitan system, the deity Atum who was at an early stage of Egyptian history equated with the sun god Ra to form the composite deity Atum-Ra. It has been suggested[19] that Atum and Ra were originally simply two "different aspects of a single god manifest in the sun." That Atum was, or at least eventually became, a sun god, is no doubt correct, but, as Anthes has suggested,[20] this solar aspect of Atum was not his most genuine characteristic. In the theological system represented by the mythic symbol of Atum, the latter deity had a significance which is much more basic and fundamental than that of a sun god, as important as that figure may be in Egyptian thought.

The name of Atum may be construed as a participle of the verb *tm* which may mean either 'to be complete' or 'to become non-existent'.[21] It is obviously the former meaning of the verb which is significant for the name of Atum, and the deity himself, therefore, was indicative of fullness and completion, *i.e.*, Atum contained within himself the totality of all creation. He was in fact the potential and source of all existent things and thus served as a symbol of the totality and unity of the created universe even before the latter had become a reality. From a theological view point we may state that in the system centred around Atum, the Heliopolitan system, that deity represented the unity which existed in the diversity of the creation. According to the Heliopolitan myth, Atum had risen out of the primaeval waters of Nun, and sitting on the primaeval mound (the first land to appear out of the waters[22] and the place of the first revelation of the sun god), performed the creative act by himself, this act being one of masturbation. This act of masturbation, which in logical thought should represent the very opposite of creativity, pointed in the Heliopolitan mytho-theological system to the fullness of creative power. Atum, as a symbol, was neither male nor female, nor should he be understood as an androgynous deity. He rather represented the fullness and completeness in which the masculine and feminine principles were combined into one unity in order to express the singleness and wholeness of the creative force. Such a mythic symbol embodies no dichotomy between the masculine and the feminine, but rather portrays them as two complementary aspects of the single generative force. Hence, in order to express the unity and singleness of the original action of creation, the Heliopolitan theologians used a symbol which was not dual or even androgynous. On the contrary, it represented a single principle which contained both sexual elements,[23] with the result that Atum was able to function in the Heliopolitan mythic system as an affirmative statement of the totality of the creation and the divine creative force. He was an Egyptian symbol of the fullness and oneness of both the created universe which had emerged from the divine life force and of that life force itself.

Further discussion of Atum in his aspect as a creator god will be found in the following chapter where the Egyptian myths of creation will be discussed. One further point concerning Atum, however, should be made at this point, namely the mythic connection between Atum as creator and the Pharaoh. Atum's rising out of the primaeval waters was represented in Egyptian by the verb $ḫ^ci$, 'to rise', normally written with the hieroglyph ⌒ which represents the rays of the sun rising over the primaeval mound. Herein is another symbol of creative activity, the symbol of the defeat of darkness by light. The same verb, $ḫ^ci$,, was also used of the ascent of a new Pharaoh to the throne, indicating that the succession of a new ruler was in effect a repetition or renewal of the original creative act whereby Atum had assumed his kingship over the world. The accession ritual thus became at the same time a creation liturgy signifying that the new ruler both established and guaranteed the stability of the created order. The primaeval kingship of Atum and the earthly kingship of the Pharaoh were mythically one and the same, and each accession to the throne by a new ruler was at the same time a renewal of the order of creation through the cultic repetition of the action of the verb ḫʿi,. A related symbol may also be seen in the Old Kingdom pyramids as the burial places of the kings, the pyramid being symbolic of the primaeval mound, and the king being buried therein so that he might repeat his participation in the divine life of the deity as a vital creative force.

Atum was thus a mythic symbol of the force of creation and stability, a symbol which, when dramatized in the cult, renewed and effected that force. Atum was not, however, the only symbol of such a concept. In the Memphite system there was found the ancient deity Tatenen, whose Egyptian name, *Tʒ-ṯnn*, has the meaning of 'the risen land', thus pointing to his significance as a personification of the primaeval mound of creation. Tatenen, however, was at a very early period connected with the god Ptah, a deity who, like Osiris, represented the fertility of the soil. By combining the two symbols, Ptah and Tatenen, into the one god, the Memphite theologians expressed symbolically the same reality as did the Heliopolitan system, using imagery of a similar nature and giving to it the name of Ptah-Tatenen instead of Amun-Ra. It was out of this Memphite tradition that there eventually came the famous document known as the *Memphite Theology*.[24] According to the teaching of the *Memphite Theology*, creation was first a divine thought, then a divine word, and finally a material reality which sprang directly from the action of the speaking of the word. The theme of the instrumentality of the divine word in creation is strikingly similar to the creative activity of Genesis 1, but whether or not a connection should be seen between the two traditions is another question. The importance of the *Memphite Theology* lies in the fact that, like other creations myths, it represents an attempt to find a 'First Principle', an attempt to elucidate the intelligent force which underlies and supports the whole universe.[25] The *Memphite Theology*, moreover, like the Heliopolitan system which had been centred around Atum, was an attempt to express the perfect unity of the divine world. The system of the *Memphite Theology*, however, shows a more far-reaching outlook than does the mythic system of Heliopolis, for it (the *Memphite Theology*) also created an ethical order and made it an integral part of its theological system. Also indicative of a more astute theological outlook is the attempt in the *Memphite Theology* to combine Ptah and Horus. Horus is shown as being a manifestation of Tatenen, King of Upper and Lower Egypt.[26] Finally, being self-begotten and creator of the other gods, the Memphite creator is similar in function and nature to

Atum in the Heliopolitan system. One should also note here in passing that the *Memphite Theology* attempts to a greater extent than the other traditions to formulate a complete synthesis of the major deities.[27]

In connection with Ptah and the Memphite tradition mention should also be made of Nefertem, who in the Memphite mytho-theological system was the offspring of Ptah and his consort Sekhmet. Sekhmet, whose name in Egyptian (*Sḫmt*) means 'the powerful one', appears as a very early goddess in the Egyptian tradition, one who was only later associated with Ptah. Not well defined as a deity, Sekhmet may possibly have been representative of a type of primitive and non-personalized *numen*. From Ptah and Sekhmet there emerged the god Nefertem, symbolized by the lotus flower. Anthes has suggested[28] that the element 'Nefer' in the name Nefertem may mean something like 'the new one', 'the youthful one', 'the regenerate one'. My own suggestion, however, is that the term *nfr* as it is used in the name of Nefertem may be taken in its normal meaning of 'good' or 'beautiful', the name Nefertem then signifying something like 'the good one is complete'. In such an interpretation, Nefertem, as the offspring of Ptah, would essentially signify the goodness of the fullness of creation. Thus the Memphite tradition of Nefertem would be basically the equivalent of the Heliopolitan mythic symbol of Atum. However one interprets the name of Nefertem, his significance is obvious: he was a symbolic statement of the reality of a divine creation which was good, complete and perfect. Nefertem was nothing less than the regenerative force of natural life personified and deified in the mythic symbol of the deity.

In the mythic system of Hermopolis it was the god Djehuty, commonly known under his Hellenized name as Thoth, who was the father of the gods, the Hermopolitan Ogdoad, the eight primaeval deities, and hence it was Thoth who was the basic source of creation. For the present purposes little more need be said of Thoth. It will be sufficient to state simply that in such a role Thoth also functioned as a symbol of the divine life force in creation, specifically as the source of the other deities. The role of Thoth as the scribe of the gods had very little, if any, bearing on his role as father of the gods, his scribal role belonging to the setting of the wider pantheon. As far as concerns the Hermopolitan mythic system, the central aspect of Thoth's symbolism was his representation of the source of divine life.

The deification of natural life in a personalized god is further evident in the ancient figure of Min of Coptos who, normally portrayed with an erect phallus, was representative of creativity through fertility. Min was in effect not really a personal god, but rather the generative force of nature, like Sekhmet, a type of primitive *numen*. The mytho-theological signification of Min is quite obvious: he was a recognition of the mysterious power which permits the procreation and generation of life. It would not be untrue to say that in some ways Min was a recognition of the sacredness of the natural function of sexuality. Of a similar function, although somewhat more restricted than Min, was the crocodile god Sobek, symbolic of the fertilizing powers of the Nile. Although basically a local deity connected with a number of specific centres, Sobek did function in a somewhat more cosmic aspect as a Nile deity. Thus he too may be seen as having the same symbolic function as the more universal deities discussed above, his importance in the total mythic system, however, being somewhat less.

With the deities who belong to the system of creation, regeneration and life we must also place the god Sokar. There appears to have been no specific myths associated with Sokar, nor was he ever portrayed as accompanied by a divine female companion.[29] Strictly speaking, therefore, Sokar was not a god of regeneration; he was rather a god of death whose abode was in the underworld. At the same time, however, Sokar did have a mythic symbolism in that he represented the reality of the power of life which is latent in death. Although not a god of life or regeneration, he nevertheless represented the *potentiality* for life. One might suggest that Sokar represented an Osiris-like figure without the realization of resurrection. What was contained in the symbolism of Sokar was an admission of the reality of the power of death, a personification and even deification of the total absence of life.[30] The symbolic value of Sokar, however, went beyond this and served as an expression of the Egyptian desire to offset this purely negative aspect of death. Sokar made the symbolic statement that even in death there is the latent potentiality for life. The main purpose of the festival of Sokar appears to have been to assure the constant regeneration of life.[31] In the wider context of the Egyptian symbolic system, the figure of Sokar had its importance in the fact that it represented an Egyptian acknowledgement of the grim reality of death. Thus he offsets for us the erroneous idea that the fear of death was unknown to the ancient Egyptians, who, according to much modern popular belief, stressed only the fact of the revival of the dead in the next world. It has, however, been aptly demonstrated that to the Egyptian mind death was indeed a powerful negative force, one which was feared and dreaded.[32] Sokar was the prime symbol of this fearful reality of death. At the same time, however, due to the flexibility of mythic expression and its ability to reconcile even two opposing concepts, Sokar, with his potential for life from death, also served as a further affirmation of creative and generative power.

In connection with the deities of life and generation, mention should be made of Hathor. As discussed earlier, Hathor appears to have had her main function in the generation of the king. Symbolic of the 'Mansion of Horus', as is implied by her Egyptian name *Ḥt-Ḥr*, she was a personification of the divinity of the ruler and of the legitimization of this divinity as a mark of the right of the individual king to hold the throne. Even such, however, represents an important aspect of the generative power of life, for it was the divine character of the ruler which was generated by the goddess Hathor. Hence, Hathor was seen also under the aspect of the divine mother, an aspect which was given symbolic expression in the cow imagery which was associated with her. Furthermore, Hathor had an important role as a goddess of fertility and birth, as a tree-goddess, as a goddess of sexuality, and even as a goddess of the dead,[33] the latter being quite obviously in virtue of her life-giving powers. In this connection we may note that Hathor played an important role in the Coffin Texts where she appears frequently as a source of the revivification of the dead. Nor can the role of Isis as a life-giving deity be overlooked, such being very obvious in her role as the mother of Horus, a role very dramatically described in Spell 148 of the Coffin Texts.[34] Such a role for Isis, however, is probably a derived one, since, as we have seen earlier, her main origin was as a personification of the royal throne. It is probably from this latter function that her maternal role later developed. Even though this latter role was a derived one, Isis nevertheless functioned symbolically as an Egyptian affirmation of the principle of life.[35]

The divine nature of Horus does not appear as so basically connected with the concepts of life and regeneration. Evidence points to the fact that originally there was more than one god who bore the name Horus, which appears to have derived from the adjective *ḥr*, 'distant'. The name Horus, therefore, 'the distant one', may have originally been a title rather than a personal name. As a deity who is 'distant', such a title could well be applied to Horus as a falcon god, as a sun god, or as the god who was incarnate in the Pharaoh. To be certain, the Egyptian texts give the impression that at least three different (although eventually related) concepts of Horus were in existence among the Egyptians: Horus as the lord of heaven, Horus as the ruling monarch, and Horus as the son of Osiris. Horus in his aspect as the lord of heaven was quite obviously related to Horus as the reigning Pharaoh, the latter being an incarnation of the heavenly deity. Horus as the son of Osiris was also related to the earthly ruler, since it was in virtue of his being the son of Osiris (the dead king) that the crown prince assumed the throne legitimately. Due to the eventual acceptance of the Osiris tradition as a legitimate system of symbolism, Horus the son of Osiris and Horus the lord of heaven became syncretized into the one deity, and both aspects were seen as incarnate in the one hypostasis in the reigning monarch. The main purpose of this identification between the supernatural Horus and the Horus incarnate in the ruler was the legitimization of the royal succession.

An interesting question arises in this regard. Which was the earlier concept, Horus as a supernatural being, or Horus as the reigning monarch? Did the title of the ruler derive from the deity, or did the personification of Horus as a mythic deity take its existence from the Horus who sat on the throne of the Two Lands? Such a question cannot be given any final answer, but there seems to be little doubt that the unification of Egypt must have played an important role in the formation of the Horus mytho-theology, which was probably formulated by the time of the First Dynasty. The opinion of Anthes is that the concept of the heavenly Horus took its beginning as a theologization of the earthly ruler, the latter being projected onto a deity who was celestial in nature but who had not originated as a cosmic deity.[36] Such an origin for the mythic deity Horus would make of him not a god of the natural order of the universe, but rather a god of the political structure which had originated as a result of the historical process and had subsequently been sanctified and consecrated by the creation of a deity of a celestial nature who could symbolize its divine basis of authority. It is a possibility that the truth lies somewhere between the two opposite poles. We may reasonably conjecture the existence of an original deity, Horus, who was a sky god in origin, but whose nature was later expanded by the imposition of the royal mytho-theology for the express purpose of creating a more cosmic basis for the state, a basis which would be more valid and binding than a simple political ideology. The result was the creation of a new deity, Horus, who thus became a cosmic deity reflecting the political structure of the Egyptian state, that same political structure thereby taking upon itself cosmic dimensions. Such a politico-theological creation then became the justification for the Egyptian governmental structure. In this manner there was created a means whereby the peculiar kingship of Egypt was given its foundation in the eternal and unchanging world of the divine. As a result, we may define Horus as a true cosmic deity who had come into existence as a political expediency, and who in turn transmuted the political system into a revelation and even extension of the cosmic order, his origins thus being both natural and political.

The sun god Ra appears to have been one of the oldest deities of Egypt, some indication of his antiquity being given in the biliteral root $r\,^{\varsigma}$ which comprises his name. The importance of Ra, even at an early point in the Old Kingdom, is evident from the prominent place which the solar cult had attained by the time of the Pyramid Texts. By the Fifth Dynasty, the cult of Ra had become the major royal cult, and had virtually subordinated the kingship to its priesthood. This control of the kingship by the Heliopolitan priesthood is attested by the story of king Cheops and the magicians in the Westcar Papyrus, in which story there is 'foretold' the birth of three sons of Ra who would be destined to take over the throne. This story, when interpreted historically, is obviously a justification of the rise of a new dynasty, the Fifth, which was under the sponsorship and influence of Heliopolis. As a result of this, the title 'Son of Ra' ($s\,\jmath\,R\,^{\varsigma}$), although in use earlier, now became the official designation of the ruler. According to the interpretation of Anthes,[37] this transition of the monarch from being strictly Horus to his new role as the son of Ra was brought about in order to strengthen the royal power. According to Anthes' argument, the king in his position of Horus was too far removed from the reality of politics to be of any real effect within the political order. Hence, by adding the Horus concept to the Ra concept and making the ruler the son of Ra, *i.e.*, vice-regent of Ra on earth, the effective political power of the throne was strengthened.[38] Whatever political implications may have been involved, the historical fact remains that from the Fifth Dynasty onwards Ra was the chief deity of Egypt. Moreover, even before this, during the earlier part of the Old Kingdom, the sun god Ra had merged with the older creator deity Atum of Heliopolis (On) to produce the composite deity Atum-Ra.[39] The final result of this process was the emergence of the most important of the Egyptian arrangements of the gods, the system of the cosmic deities of On, the famous Heliopolitan Ennead. Herein we find an arrangement of the nine chief deities (hence the term 'Ennead') in a system based on procreation with divine authority being held by the natural right of inheritance. The Heliopolitan Ennead in its descent from Atum-Ra may be illustrated graphically as follows:

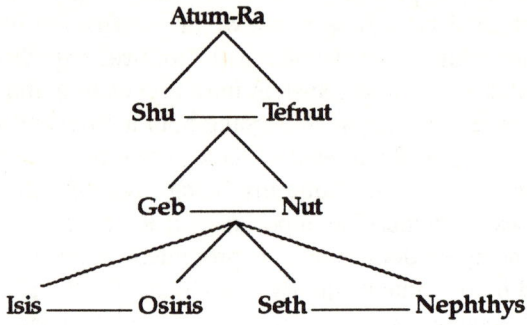

From Isis and Osiris was born Horus, eventually to become the heavenly counterpart of, and incarnate within, the earthly ruler. Horus was thus the fifth generation in the Heliopolitan system and in direct descent from the sun god in his form as Atum-Ra. Hence, in the politico-mythic system, the earthly ruler was both the incarnate Horus and the son of Ra by direct descent, the Osiris/Isis/Horus mythic system having merged with the solar system of Heliopolis. This mergence of the solar, Osirian and political systems was the main accomplishment of Heliopolitan mytho-theology, for it gave a tightly knit unity to the three systems, forming a synthesis of the three while still retaining the characteristic mythic symbols of each. Within this cosmological system, the place of the earthly ruler under the gods was clearly defined. The royal descent from both Osiris and Ra was still maintained, and the monarch became the direct representative of the Ennead. The worlds of politics and religion were thus combined into a total and complete unity, no distinction being evident between them.

During the Old Kingdom the sun god Ra had relatively few myths associated with him. However, due to his prominence, it was but natural that a fairly complex system of myth should develop around him. Hence, by the time of the New Kingdom, Ra had acquired numerous mythic symbols and traditions. The different variations within the mythic system associated with Ra are almost endless, and any attempt even briefly to outline them would be pointless. The important point about the Ra mythic system, however, was the actual cycle of the sun disc: its daily rising, its nightly journey through the underworld, and its rebirth on the following morning and the subsequent repetition of the cycle. The details within this general cycle present a very colourful and highly varied set of motifs, the interpretation of many of the specific details being highly ambiguous and doubtful. Any effort to give significance to each of these details could well be a futile undertaking and might only result in a total misunderstanding of the imagery involved. For example, during one stage of his nightly journey through the underworld, the boat of Ra was towed by a team of jackals. Such an image is probably not a true mythic symbol, but rather a graphic portrayal of the movement of the sun barque at a specific moment. Any attempt to impose a theological significance on such an image would be tantamount to treating the image as an allegory, and myth should not be taken in such a simplistic fashion. Hence, many of these varied portraits of the sun god should probably be understood as no more than attempts to express the various stages of the sun god's journey. In short, they are not true mythic symbols, but pictorial representations of the complexities of the actual journey and not intended to be interpreted in detail.

The important aspect of the mythic system of Ra, therefore, was the fact of the cycle itself, the birth of the god in the morning and his death at night, although the latter is never given specific expression. The one symbol on which strong emphasis was placed was the daily birth of the deity. The Book of the Dead, for example, speaks of the sun god as "the one who illumines the earth at his birth each day" ($\underline{hd}\ t\jmath\ r\ mst.f r\ ^c\ nb$).[40] In such an image we have a true mythic symbol intended to express the reappearance of the life-giving power of the sun, the reality of such power being so strong that it could only have been expressed through an image which itself was already one of life and generation. To the Egyptian mind, the daily sunrise was much more than a natural phenomenon; it was rather an event which caused the cosmic life of the universe. To express or to experience such a concept solely in terms of the natural movement of an inanimate object, *i.e.*, the physical sun disc, would have been incomprehensible to the Egyptian mentality, for it would have obscured the obviously meaningful structure of the cosmos. For the Egyptian mind, the sun was the source of life only because it was a living and personal embodiment and manifestation of divine life. The sun could not be an 'it'; it had to be a 'thou', and on account of it the cosmos was animated and filled with the positive force of life. Man could thus be assured that he was not at the mercy of inanimate natural forces, that his life was not dependent upon the mere chances and changes of natural phenomena. The life of the universe and of the individual was ordered and guided by a power which was both intelligent and beneficent, and therefore the world was positive and dependable. The Egyptian could thus be optimistic about his world, his life and his future, for these were assured and guarantied by the mythic symbol of Ra.

The situation of Amun of Thebes was of a somewhat different nature, his importance being due not so much to his mythic associations as to the political events which brought him to prominence. Amun was originally a relatively unimportant deity within the Egyptian system, being a member of the Hermopolitan Ogdoad, and coming to Thebes, whose chief deity had originally been the warrior god Mont, only during the First Intermediate Period.[41] It was due to the overthrow of the Mentuhotep family and the usurpation of the Theban throne by Amenemhet I that Amun gained his position. After the expulsion of the Hyksos and the reunification of Egypt at the end of the Second Intermediate Period, Amun of Thebes was combined with the older Ra of On (Heliopolis). This latter move was probably political in nature, an attempt to overcome any possible rivalry between the two deities and also to further strengthen the position of Amun within the Egyptian pantheon. As a final result, and also to a certain extent in opposition to the older systems, the Theban cosmogony was formulated. According to this newer Theban mythic system, Amun had begotten himself in secret, coming out of the egg on the primaeval mound, the site of which happened conveniently to be at Thebes. Everything else was then created by Amun, even Ma'at who was his daughter, just as in the Heliopolitan system she was the daughter of the creator god Atum-Ra. Amun himself became king of the gods, a possible reflection of the earthly Theban kingship. With him were associated his wife Mut and his son Khons, thus forming the Theban triad. Into this Theban mythic system the political system was grafted by interpreting the ruling monarch as the son of Amun-Ra, just as in the Heliopolitan system he had been the son of Ra, a title which was still retained in the official royal titulary. This position of Amun as the father of the monarch naturally meant that the power and prestige of his priesthood was greatly increased and magnified to the extent that, at least at certain periods of Egypt's history, the Theban priesthood was in virtual control of the throne. The political influence which Amun eventually attained is possibly best seen in the struggle between Ramses XI and Herihor at the end of the Twentieth Dynasty and the resulting virtual independence of Thebes with its line of priest-kings during Dynasty Twenty-One. So too, in the struggle between the religious organizations one sees the rivalry which emerged between the Heliopolitan priesthood and that of Thebes, a struggle which found a powerful expression in the Amarna movement when the heretic king Akhenaten brought against the power of Amun the older traditions of Heliopolis. That the Theban Amun and his clergy constituted a strong political force there can be no doubt.

One must, however be careful not to place too much stress on Amun as a political force. Although his influence in the realm of politics was immense, this did not prevent him from becoming a significant theological symbol. Around the figure of Amun, during the Eighteenth and Nineteenth Dynasties, there emerged the concept of universalism and a system of thought which gave rise to what some would consider a type of monotheistic system. The latter will be discussed at a later point. We may conclude these remarks on Amun by the statement that in the conjoining of Amun of Thebes with Ra of On the Egyptian mythopoeic mind was able to create a symbol which combined the two aspects of the hidden and the revealed in Egyptian religion. Amun, 'the hidden one', as his name implies in Egyptian, was at the same time Ra, the visible god who was manifest in the sun disc and perceptible to the eyes. Hidden and manifest, mysterious and revealed, Amun provided the ideal mytho-theological symbol of the mystery of the cosmos. At the same time he was the support and justification of Egypt's political system. Eventually he became also the support and justification of the Egyptian Empire. Thus, through certain accidents of history, through the ambitions of the temple, and through the mytho-theological talents of the Egyptian mind, Amun of Thebes evolved from relative unimportance to the position of being the virtual embodiment of the religious and political achievements of ancient Egypt. It is little wonder that he held the title of *niswt ntrw*, 'King of the Gods'.

Of the gods in general, it is significant that most Egyptian male deities had their female counterparts. We find, for example, Osiris and Isis, Amun and Mut, Ptah and Sekhmet, Horus and Hathor, Geb and Nut, Shu and Tefnut. Even the figure of the Aten (*itn*), the physical sun disc, was balanced by a female solar deity, the *itnt*,[42] although not in the theological system of the Amarna movement; Horus (*Ḥr*) and Ra (*Rˁ*) had their female equivalents in *Ḥrt* [43] and *Rˁt* [44] with reference to the queen. This balance of the male and female deities is evident in the Heliopolitan Ennead where all the gods, with the exception of Atum,[45] were balanced by a female counterpart. In the latter system even Seth had his consort in the goddess Nephthys, although in tradition Nephthys was more actively associated with Osiris than with Seth. The Hermopolitan Ogdoad also balanced its male and female principles in Nun and Naunet, Huh and Hauhet, Kuk and Kauket,

Amun and Amaunet. These deities of the Hermopolitan Ennead appear more as vague personifications of the force of life and generation than they do as active personal deities. Nevertheless, even in such impersonal deities the Egyptians saw fit to balance the male and female principles.

This pairing of the masculine and feminine was more than just a sense of balance on the part of the Egyptians as has been suggested.[46] It was rather a recognition of the complementary aspects of the male and female as concerns regeneration and the procreation of life. This is evident in the fact that from such divine pairs there frequently came an offspring indicative of the results of the procreative powers. The offspring of the various divine couples were then associated with the parents to form a number of divine triads which functioned as symbols of the continuity of life. In such a manner the mythic systems of Egypt deified the principle of regeneration, expressing in the divine triads the fulfilment and completion of procreation. At the same time this principle became an integral part of the cosmic order of the universe. We may note here in passing such well known triads as Ptah, Sekhmet and Nefertem; Osiris, Isis and Horus; Amun, Mut and Khons. An interesting triad of a somewhat different nature is found in Atum, Shu and Tefnut.[47] In this triad the duality of the parentage and the oneness of the offspring was reversed to produce a pattern wherein the single parent reproduced two offspring, one male and one female. The principle of reproduction was here maintained with the difference that it was in the offspring that the male and female principles were evident. The two offspring then became the source of the deities who were born in the next generation. At the risk of over-interpreting the mythic symbolism involved, it may be suggested that the apparent signification of this triad was the idea of the *single* creative principle manifesting its male and female *duality* in the act of procreation, the offspring themselves, being clear embodiments of the male and female, were then able to continue the reproductive pattern. Atum, however, remained as the symbol of the essential unity of the opposite sexual roles.

In summation, we may state of the gods of Egypt that they were symbolic of the active power of creation, life and regeneration. Due to them order and stability were assured within the created cosmos. Because of them the universe could even be viewed as a cosmos, an ordered pattern, rather than a series of unrelated phenomena. The gods were other than man and beyond human comprehension. Nevertheless, they were not beyond human perception. They could be apprehended in nature, in the cosmos and in life itself. They were of necessity many, for it was impossible for the Egyptian mentality to express the complexity of the cosmos by a single symbolic principle. Nevertheless, beyond the polytheistic symbolism which served as the vehicle of religious expression, one can sense that the Egyptian saw some unarticulated unity in the divine force which upheld the universe. This divine force was the vital and enervating power of life. This was the primary signification of the Egyptian gods: they were the essence of the cosmic life which expressed itself in the totality of all being.

Notes

[1]

[2] A.H. Gardiner, *Egyptian Grammar*, 3rd edition (Oxford: Griffith Institute, 1957), Sign List, R8.

[3] C.J. Bleeker, "The Religion of Ancient Egypt," 51.

[4] E. Hornung, *Conceptions of God in Ancient Egypt*, 38. From this fetish eventually derived the flags which were used in the official cult to function as symbols of the gods.

[5] and (A.H. Gardiner, *op. cit.*, Sign List, G7 and A40).

[6] *ibid.*, Sign List, Section C.

[7] E. Hornung, *op. cit.*, 40.

[8] See C.J. Bleeker, *op. cit.*, 52.

[9] *rein sein* (*Wb* II, 36).

[10] The Pyramid Texts give some indication of a connection between the term $n\underline{t}r$ ('natron', 'pure') and $n\underline{t}r$ ('god'):

> *Wsir Ppi m n.k n$\underline{t}$r.k n$\underline{t}$r.k.*
>
> O Osiris Pepi, take to yourself your natron
> so that you may become a god (*PT* 25a).

The text here seems to indicate that it is due to the natron ($n\underline{t}r$) that the dead king will be deified ($n\underline{t}r$), perhaps by the process of purification. This, however, appears as rather tenuous grounds on which to base a connection between the roots of the two terms, and it may in fact be no more than a word play. Hornung also points out that the derivation of the Egyptian term for 'god' from the term for 'natron' is unconvincing (E. Hornung, *op. cit.*, 41).

[11] E. Hornung, *op. cit.*, 117.

[12]*CT* VI, 69c, 72d.
   The idea that it is only the dead who can know the gods is tied very closely to the Egyptian concept of the dead as deified beings, beings who have become spiritualized and glorified (*sḫw*). In such a state the dead are beyond the boundaries and limitations of ordinary mortals, and hence their powers of perception and comprehension, now also spiritualized, are obviously able to perceive and understand things which normally lie beyond the human senses and the human intellect. Indeed, not only are the dead spiritualized to the extent that they are able to comprehend the gods, but they are in fact themselves deified and even identifiable with the gods. This is especially evident in the Coffin Texts where the deceased is identified most frequently with Osiris, but also with numerous other gods as well. Such an identification between the deceased and the various gods appears as an Egyptian symbolic way of stating that the life and being of the deceased becomes one with the life and being of the divine world, an idea not unlike the concept of θέωσις which is so common in many writers of the Greek patristic tradition, a term which expressed the identification of the individual soul with the divine essence and hence a process of actual deification. In the Egyptian mortuary texts we see that the dead man or woman can be identified with virtually any one of the gods, and not infrequently with more than one. The symbolic purpose of this is immediately evident. In Egyptian thinking the dead were deified and became part of the divine life force of the cosmos. Hence, it was natural that the dead should have the capacity to know the true nature of the gods, for the dead themselves had become one with the principle represented by the symbolism of the gods.

[13]In the texts from the Amarna period we see that Akhenaten's deity, the Aten, is praised above all else for his characteristic of goodness to mankind.

[14]*Wb* V, 610.

[15]A Pyramid Text (*PT* 1778b) speaks of "him who separates (*dsr*) the sky from the earth and the primaeval waters."

[16]In the Biblical Book of Leviticus it is the holiness (קדש) of Yahweh which demands moral action on the part of his people.

[17]On the god Amun see K. Sethe, "Amun und die acht Urgötten von Hermopolis," 1929.

[18]I wish to introduce into the text at this point the terms 'mytho-theology' and 'mytho-theological', to express the idea of myth which is used to express theological concepts or, *vice versa*, theology expressed by means of mythic symbolism.

[19]H. Frankfort, *Kingship and the Gods* (Chicago, 1948), Chapter XIII, n.1.

[20]*JNES* XVIII, 176, n.14.

[21]*ibid.*, 177.

[22]That the earth was symbolized by this primaeval mound is frequently brought out in the Pyramid Texts. (See, for example, *PT* 627, 640, 645, 648, 1587, 1652.

[23]A Coffin Text expresses this idea as follows:

> *ink Itm km's wrw* I am Atum who created the great ones;
> *ink ms Šw* I am he who begat Shu;
> *ink pn tn.* I am the He/She. (*CT* II, 160g-161a)

24The date of this document could still be questioned. J. Wilson (*The Culture of Ancient Egypt*, 58) had maintained that it was of a very early date, *i.e.*, the early Old Kingdom, a view once held also by Miriam Lichtheim (*Ancient Egyptian Literature*, I [1973], 51). However, a much later date has been suggested by F. Junge (MDAIK 29 [1973], 195-204) who would place the *Memphite Theology* in the Twenty-Fifth Dynasty. Since the contents of the work present a much more spiritualized concept of creation, *i.e.*, creation through the intellect and the spoken word rather than by means of birth and reproduction, it appears quite likely that the later date should be accepted.

25J. Wilson, *op. cit.*, 60.

26*Memphite Theology*, 13c.

27It has been assumed up to this point that the text known as the *Memphite Theology* was indeed intended as a theological treatise. In such a view, this document would illustrate the transition from a mythical system to one which was able to express itself in theological terms, even though those theological terms were still formulated in the traditional mythic symbols. One should note, however, that the suggestion has been made that the document was not intended as a theological text but that it was rather more in the nature of a hymn, a text intended for cultic usage (C.J. Bleeker, *Egyptian Festivals*, 17). If such was indeed the case, then the *Memphite Theology* would serve to underscore the cultic nature of Egypt's religion as opposed to the dogmatic and the theological. I would suggest, however, that, even if the text was intended for cultic purposes, it nevertheless shows the emergence of the theological as opposed to the strictly mythic and cultic.

28*JNES* XVIII, 177.

29C.J. Bleeker, *Egyptian Festivals*, 89.

30In contrast to Sokar, Osiris, who was also a god of the dead, embodied the power of life after the death of the mortal body. He was a revitalizing force. Sokar, however, lacked this revitalizing power, and was thus more like the Greek deity Hades.

31C.J. Bleeker, *op. cit.*, 86.

32See, for example, J. Zandee, *Death as an Enemy According to Ancient Egyptian Conceptions* (Leiden, 1960).

33C.J. Bleeker, *op. cit.*, 134.

34*CT* II, 209c-226a.

35In the context of the continuation of life, one quite obviously cannot overlook Osiris, the main deity connected with such a concept. His position was due to his growth as a god of rebirth in the next world, a natural extension of his character as a god of fertility in the earth and in the Nile. It is probably due to the personal hopes and aspirations of the general populace of Egypt that Osiris attained its prominent position as a god of resurrection. Due to the importance of Osiris in the Egyptian mytho-theological system, I prefer not to discuss him at this point, but rather to devote a separate chapter to him.

[36] *JNES* XVIII, 187.
[37] *ibid.*, 180.
[38] Although this is an interesting theory, Anthes himself admits that he has no real evidence for it.
[39] A.R. David, *The Ancient Egyptians: Religious Beliefs and Practices* (London, 1982), 46.
[40] *BD* XV, 13.
[41] A.R. David, *op. cit.*, 121f.
[42] *Th.T.S.*, I, 30.
[43] *Urk.* IV, 361,4.
[44] *Urk.* IV, 332, 11.
[45] In the case of Atum, male and female principles were seen as being inherent within his person. The reason for this may have been that the existence of a separate female hypostasis along with the original creator god would have detracted from the unity and completeness of the single creative principle.
[46] J. Wilson in *Before Philosophy*, edited by H. Frankfort, (Penguin Books, 1949), 50.
[47] In the Atum/Shu/Tefnut triad Jan Assmann has seen a possible source for an Amarna triad of the Aten, Akhenaten and Nefertiti (*Re und Amun*, Freiburg, 1983, 113f.; see also J. Assmann, "Palast oder Temple," *JNES* XXXI [1972]: 152-154.). In the Amarna system a number of other scholars have suggested different possible combinations to form a triad pattern. For example, we find such suggested triads as Ra, the Aten and Akhenaten (Davies, *Amarna* II, 15, n.2); Ra-Horakhtey, Shu and the Aten (S. Morenz, *La religion égyptienne*, 169f.); Ra, the Aten and Akhenaten (R.Anthes, "... in seinem Namen und im Sonnenlicht," *ZÄS* XC [1963]: 1-6). However, such triads do not seem to have symbolized the generative force of nature in the same graphic manner as did the traditional Egyptian triads, for in the Amarna system it appears that it was the Aten himself who was the sole and single source of all created life. One must, moreover, beware of attempting to formulate what may well be artificially created concepts of an Amarna triad. If any such triad did indeed exist in Amarna theology, it was probably of relatively little importance.

IV. Mytho-Theology of Creation

Every religious system which is mythologically based must also have its myths of creation. Such myths consist necessarily of two main component elements: a divine creative force which is the source of the universe, and a mythical process through which the creative force acts in order to accomplish the work of creation. Even such a highly theological account of creation as is recorded in the first chapter of Genesis uses the mythic symbolism of the speaking of the divine creative word ("And God said..."), followed by a graphic statement of the appearance of the various phenomena called into being by the speaking of the word. No serious theologian, however, would maintain that such a description was intended as a literal and historical account of the origins of the universe. What is contained in this account, an account which was very possibly a poetic liturgy, is the simple but profound theological statement that all things depend on the power of the divine creative force for their very existence. Any religious account of creation (be it mythological or theological) should not attempt to go beyond such a statement. That is to say, religious accounts of creation do not express either scientific or historical facts. They do provide an explanation of the universe, but this explanation is expressed in terms of a metaphysical basis and rationale of its existence. To a certain extent, theological accounts of creation provide a kind of articulation of the method by which all things came into existence and by which they are constantly maintained, but this articulation of the creative method does not, and was never intended to, answer the question "How?" in terms of the precise mechanics of creative activity. If we again refer to the account of creation in the opening chapter of Genesis, we see that the theologians who composed that account took care to avoid giving the impression that it was historical in nature. For this reason they used the very specific Hebrew verb ברא (*bara*) to denote the divine activity in creation, a verb which contained no overtones of normal human creative activity, and one which was totally free of any connotation of specific mechanical means or methods. Thus, any concrete imagery which might suggest a historical and scientific description was avoided in this specific account. Having established the exclusivity of the divine mode of creation, the Hebrew theologians were then free to utilize mythic imagery[1] for the rest of the narrative.

Any attempt to draw a comparison between this Hebrew account of creation and the Egyptian accounts would be somewhat tenuous for the very reason that their respective compositions were separated in time by more than two millenia. The Hebrew account was the product of a time when abstract theological speculation was starting to become a possibility, whereas the Egyptian accounts were the products of an age which was still tied to a mythic and symbolic way of thought and expression. Nevertheless, the Hebrew account serves to emphasize by way of contrast the more mythic nature of the Egyptian accounts. Insofar as the Egyptian accounts were more mythologically oriented in their expression than was the Hebrew account, one must be all the more careful not to interpret the Egyptian accounts in a fundamentalist manner. The Egyptian creation myths were not factual and historical accounts; rather they were symbolic ones, and the different symbols used in the various Egyptian creations myths must be seen as simply different ways of articulating the same reality. The Egyptians themselves, at least the priestly classes who were responsible for the formulation of the myths, were without doubt quite well aware of the non-historical nature of the myths, understanding them as symbols which gave expression to the structure of the universe.[2] We cannot, therefore, maintain that the Egyptians had several different theories or doctrines of creation. What may be stated is that the Egyptians used several different systems of mythic symbolism to express the reality of creation, systems which evolved at different religious centres. Since such systems were symbolic, it is obvious that the Egyptians themselves must have seen no contradiction among them, the symbols themselves being subordinate to the theological truth which they embodied. In such a way it is possible to speak of a single Egyptian concept of creation. We must stress, however, that this was a single *concept*, not a single articulation of the concept. The concept may remain basically the same, even though its expression and articulation may vary widely in the usage of the symbolic language.

The Egyptian and Hebrew accounts of the creation show a strong contrast in yet another area. In the Hebrew system the creator deity was always one and the same, the Yahweh of Biblical tradition, who, due to the historical process of ancient Israel, had become very much a henotheistic, and later monotheistic, deity. This necessitated the total exclusion of all other symbols of the divine from Hebrew theology. In Egypt, however, the historical process had not developed in such a manner as to cause the acceptance of one deity at the expense of all others. As a result Egyptian thought was able to express the person of the creator by a number of different deities with no inherent or apparent contradictions. It was only during the period of Akhenaten that official theology could recognize only one symbol of the creator. This exclusivity is strongly evident in the text which has been accepted as the classic expression of Amarna theology, the hymn on the west thickness of the tomb of Ay, the famous Hymn to the Aten. In this text creation is described as the activity of the Aten alone: "You have created the earth according to your own desire, you being alone."[3] In the earlier periods of Egypt's history, however, such exclusiveness was not found in religious thought or symbolism. Hence the Egyptians were able to give recognition to a number of creator gods and systems of creation mythology. At Heliopolis and Hermopolis the creator deity was seen in the sun; at Memphis it was Ptah who was responsible for the universe, especially by means of the spoken word, as we have already seen in the Memphite Theology; the Theban tradition gave Amun the credit for creation; at Elephantine it was the potter god Khnum who was taken as a symbol of the divine creative power. All of these gods, however, were not anthropomorphic creators who acted in a specific and defined fashion to bring the universe into being. They were rather symbols of the mysterious and undefinable force of life which was inherent in the very nature of the divine. No one symbol (except the Aten in the case of Amarna theology) usurped the place of any other or made any other obsolete and invalid. The absence of a concept of orthodoxy of dogma made such an event impossible.

For the Egyptian mytho-theological mind creation was of the ultimate importance, for all things had come into being at some specific point, and there was no concept of an eternally existent cosmos. The universe had to have a beginning, and before that beginning there had been nothing. A Pyramid Text speaks of the time before the creation as follows:

> The sky had not yet come into being;
> The earth had not yet come into being;
> Mankind had not yet come into being;
> The gods had not yet been born;
> Death had not yet come into being.[4]

One should not, however, state of this time before the creation that there had been nothing in existence, for the Egyptians seem to have had no philosophical notion of a *creatio ex nihilo*. In the beginning there had existed chaos, the primaeval waters of Nun, a single existent reality in which there was a primitive demiurge, a type of Prime Mover, if one may express it in terms of a later philosophical vocabulary. Such a philosophical expression, however, would have been totally non-Egyptian, nor would the Egyptian mind have seen the need for an abstract elaboration of the primary substance of the universe. For the Egyptian mythopoeic mind it was sufficient to state that before the creation there had been only the Nun. This Nun, however, was not so much a primary substance or form of matter, but rather a mythic symbol of the abstract reality of the full potential of being, a principle which contained within itself both the masculine and feminine forces which were necessary for generation and procreation.

This symbol of the primaeval waters appears to have been the basic principle of all the Egyptian systems of cosmogony, for it was common to all the myths of creation.[5] The logic of water as a primaeval symbol is evident immediately when one considers the yearly phenomenon of the rising of the Nile as the potential source of the life and rebirth of nature. Hence Nun, the primaeval water, must have presented itself as the most dramatic and graphic symbol to express the ultimate life source from which the creation had emerged. At the same time, despite the positive potential for life and order, the primaeval waters of Nun essentially represented a principle of chaos for the very reason that such a shapeless and formless mass implied an absence of the order and stability required in a created cosmos. The Hermopolitan tradition especially stressed this negative aspect of the primaeval waters. Nevertheless, the Egyptian mentality was able to recognize at least the *potential* for life and order with the primaeval waters, for, according to a Coffin Text, Atum created the eight Heh (Chaos) gods "... according to the word of Nun, in infinity, in the primaeval waters, in gloom and in darkness."[6] By another mythic symbol, however, the begetting of the Heh gods was attributed to Shu, who in the Heliopolitan tradition was, along with his sister Tefnut, the first offspring of Atum. Spell 76 of the Coffin Texts provides the following imagery:

> I am he who begot the Heh gods again,
> In infinity, in the primaeval waters,
> In gloom and in darkness.
> I am Shu, the one who begot the gods.[7]

Spell 78 of the Coffin Texts also attributes the birth of the Heh gods to Shu, elaborating the imagery as follows:

> O these eight Heh gods,
> Whom Shu conceived,
> Whom Shu begot,
> Whom Shu created,
> Whom Shu knit together.[8]

The Heh gods, therefore, symbolic of the chaotic nature of the primaeval waters of Nun, appear as the offspring of Atum in one tradition and of Shu in another. This double symbolism of the generation of these deities may thus appear contradictory, but the signification of the symbolism is not. What was important here was the actual generation of the Heh gods within the primaeval chaos, the beginning of the complex generative system from which the creation would eventually emerge. That the Egyptians could attribute the birth of these deities to two separate divine hypostases, hypostases which were themselves related by the imagery of generation, points to the complex nature of the generative activity of the divine life force. Shu begot the Heh gods, but Atum also begot the Heh gods, an apparent contradiction in terms of logic, but not in terms of mythic symbolism. Only in such a manner could the Egyptian mytho-theologians have expressed the inexpressible activity of the divine world. Only by means of a plurality of symbols could the mysterious have been articulated without losing its mystery in a futile attempt at logical articulation.

The Heh gods were enumerated and expressed in the Ogdoad of Hermopolis, the eight-fold grouping of these deities. Here we find the Heh gods expressed under the form of four divine couples: Nun and Naunet, Huh and Hauhet, Kuk and Kauket, Amun and Amaunet. In each of the four pairings of the deities, we see gods who were not representative of specific divine hypostases, not personal, mythic and anthropomorphic gods, but rather deities who were by their very names statements of the principal characteristics of the primaeval chaos out of which all things would eventually emerge. Nun was symbolic of the primaeval water itself, the undefined source from which all things were to come; Huh was indicative of boundlessness, infinity, chaos, the absence of shape and form in the time before the creation; Kuk was the negative force of darkness; Amun was the 'hidden one', the mystery of the divine force which in the chaotic state of pre-creation was not yet manifest or evident, 'hidden' also because of the unknown nature of the divine. No myths were attached to these deities because their nature was entirely and completely impersonal. They were, therefore, unable to act in any form of mythic symbolism. Their importance lay in the fact that, through the characteristics which they symbolized, they expressed the negative nature of the primaeval chaos. They were the actualization of the nothingness which existed in Nun, a nothingness which, due to the principle of completeness in Atum, would become the source of all that exists. Thus, nothingness and totality were balanced in the primaeval waters, two contradictory and opposing principles which encompassed all that would eventually exist. The Heh gods were the foundation principle of the Egyptian mytho-theology of creation, symbolizing the reality of chaos, but at the same time pointing to the creative potential within it.

The potential for generative activity was symbolized by the association of feminine deities with each male deity. Thus, in the Hermopolitan Ogdoad Nun was balanced by Naunet, Huh by Hauhet, Kuk by Kauket, and Amun by Amaunet. Such a balance of the masculine and feminine provided the totality of procreative power required for the production of life. The creative life force of Egyptian mythology was, therefore, neither masculine nor feminine. It was rather the equal balance of the male and female which made the emergence of the creation a reality. The Egyptian creation was thus a cosmic reflection of the normal reproductive processes of nature, such processes being deified by their reflection in the cosmogonic myths of the cult.

The same principle of balance between the masculine and feminine was evident also in the Heliopolitan Ennead. Here we see Shu paired with Tefnut, Geb with Nut, Osiris with Isis, and Seth with Nephthys. Even the first principle, Atum, appears to have had within himself both the male and female principles as noted above. When compared with the Hermopolitan Ogdoad, which had a basic simplicity in the four pairs of cosmic Heh gods, the Heliopolitan system presents a more complicated pattern of theological symbolism. The Heliopolitan Ennead may be divided as follows into three different levels of mythic existence:

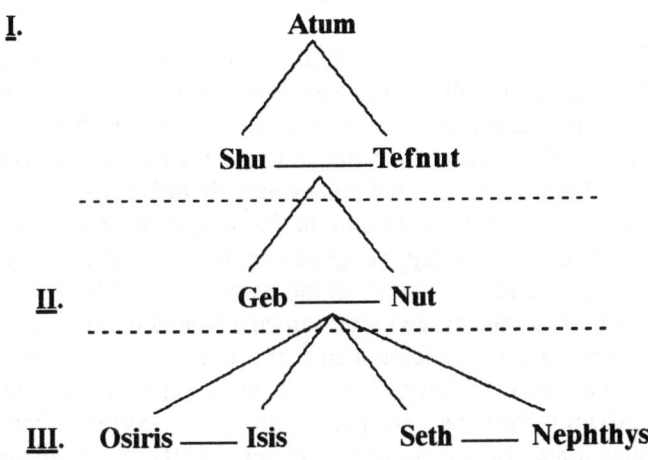

The first of the above levels, that on which are found Atum, Shu and Tefnut, may be said to represent the primary principle and action of the creation. The figure of Atum here is symbolic of the totality of the creative force, containing within himself both the male and female principles, and representative, therefore, of the fullness of generation and procreation. Shu and Tefnut who belong on the same level of symbolism, although chronologically posterior to Atum, are essentially the same principle as Atum himself. Shu and Tefnut, whatever other mythic symbolism may be seen in them, are in their essence the actualization of the male/female principle within Atum. Whereas in Atum this principle is combined in one hypostasis, in Shu and Tefnut it is divided into its two component and complementary elements, thus giving full hypostatic expression to male and female and signifying thereby a situation where the power of generation and procreation can be active in a natural manner.

The deities of the second level, Geb and Nut, although still signifying the fertile principle of the life force, also represent a stage of creation wherein the basic structural features of the universe, earth and sky, are articulated and laid out as separate entities. With the emergence of Geb and Nut the physical structure of the universe is completed and the creation has in fact taken place. Thus, in the first level of the Heliopolitan Ennead one may see a progression from pure potentiality in Atum to an effecting of that potentiality in Shu and Tefnut. This in turn leads to the second level of the

Ennead wherein the created universe evolves as an actualization of potentiality in Geb and Nut.

The mythic figures of the third level (Osiris, Isis, Seth and Nephthys) bring the mythic symbolism to a level which may be called, in a broad sense of the term, 'historical'. Herein we see the establishment of the earthly kingship in the person of Osiris and also the start of the conflict between Osiris and Seth. This conflict will eventually be brought to its completion in the Horus and Seth pericope and the establishment of the historical kingship of Upper and Lower Egypt, governed by the earthly king as the direct descendant and representative of the cosmic powers.[9] In such a manner the Heliopolitan mythic system represented a complete mytho-theologization of the cosmic order of creation and the temporal order of royal power[10] which was thus an integral part of the cosmic order. The Heliopolitan Ennead may thus be interpreted as a full mythic symbolism of the actualization and existence of the cosmos and the Egyptian state, combining them both into one unity and justifying the political role and position of the Egyptian monarch. Although the latter was not directly dependent on the male/female balance of the gods of the Ennead, it did nevertheless grow out of them by the generative process. Hence, the political order was not only seen as a created phenomenon, it was understood also as a *procreated* one.

The principle of the pairing of the masculine and feminine and the principle of androgyny were both important in Egyptian religion, for they expressed, as we have seen, the fullness and totality of procreative power. Jean Leclant has given numerous references to androgyny in the mythology of ancient Egypt,[11] indicative of the importance of such symbolism. Even in the Amarna theological system, which was relatively free from the traditional Egyptian mythic symbols, certain indications of an androgynous character may be seen in the deity. We find, for example, that the Aten is addressed: "You are the mother and father of everyone whom you create,"[12] and "You are the mother who bears everyone."[13] It appears that the mythic symbol of androgyny, or at least a tendency to combine the masculine and feminine principles in the gods, was so deeply ingrained in the Egyptian religious mind that even Akhenaten, despite his zeal for doing away with the old, was unable to avoid it in his own theological expressions. It must, however, be stressed that this expression of androgyny was used here as mythic and verbal symbolism and was not meant to be taken literally.

The importance of the male/female imagery in the Egyptian mythic systems is clearly seen in the birth imagery which was frequently used in the accounts of creation, an imagery frequently expressed by the use of the Egyptian verb *msi*, 'to beget' or 'to bear'. Here it should be noted that the usage of such imagery was for the Egyptian mind a totally natural one, for, in the consciousness of the Egyptian and in his very observation of nature, the cosmos was something which was alive.[14] Even the creator himself, the sun god, had been born and was reborn each day,[15] although the birth imagery in this case was represented as self-generation. A hymn to Ra in the tomb of Horemheb, for example, describes the sun god as "the one who begot himself and bore himself by himself."[16] Self-generation is, of course, an impossibility except within the context of a mythic image, and cannot be taken literally, but can refer only to the self-sufficiency of the creator deity with regard to every action and aspect, even with regard to his own birth. Even the praises of the Aten in the Amarna movement state "you beget yourself every day without ceasing," (*msy.k tw r ꜥ nb bn irt ḏbw*).[17]

Before proceeding, it may be useful at this point to make a few brief remarks on the Theban cosmogonic system. This system, which developed after the rise of Amun during the Middle Kingdom, was naturally centred on the god Amun, later expressed after the Hyksos period as Amun-Ra. Like the other creator gods, Amun was also self-sufficient, and also like them he was the father of the gods and the source of creation. However, little would be gained in the present context from concentrating on the Theban cosmogonic system as interesting as it may be in its own right. The Theban system had little of originality to add to the general Egyptian mythic systems, although we should note that it was from the worship of the Theban Amun-Ra that there eventually emerged the universalist tendencies found during the Eighteenth and Nineteenth Dynasties. To the credit of Amun-Ra, therefore, it must be admitted that it was his religious organization which was responsible for bringing Egyptian religion to one of its highest achievements. However, it should also be stressed that the growth of Amun was due mainly to the attempts of the Theban clergy to promote him to the position of chief deity of Egypt, and thereby to promote the Theban strength and supremacy throughout the country. The Theban system did not have the same antiquity as did the other creation myths, but was rather a later invention which had evolved, as we have seen, from political aspirations more than from religious and spiritual ideals. The basic principles of Egyptian creation mythology had taken shape long before the advent of Amun, and it was to them that Amun owed the true basis of the theological formulation of his own system.

We have dealt above to some extent with the interpretation and significance of the Heliopolitan mythic system. Due to the importance of this system, however, it is advisable at this point to look at some of the textual evidence concerning the emergence of the creator god Atum and the creation itself. According to the texts, Atum had come into existence within the primaeval waters of Nun, his generation having been from himself. *i.e.*, he was self-created as is stated in Utterance 587 of the Pyramid Texts:

> Hail to you Atum;
> Hail to you, Kheprer, the one who came into being by himself.
> You were exalted in this your name of Height (Ka);
> You have come into being in this your name of Kheprer.[18]

The names given to the newly emerged creator deity in this text are all symbolic of his nature. As Atum, he is the complete one; as Ka, he is the Height, the one risen as the sun disc upon the primaeval mound; as Kheprer, he is the one who is constantly in a state of becoming,[19] *i.e.*, the sun disc in the course of his daily journey. In the combination of Atum-Kheprer one detects the two elements of completeness and becoming in the deity who is thus conceived as both active and static. The same concept is expressed in Chapter LXXXV of the Book of the Dead: "I have come into being by myself with Nun in this my name of Khepri."[20] In the same context Atum is described as the sun god Ra: "I have come into being ... as Ra."[21]

The creator deity, Atum-Ra-Kheprer, thus emerged in the form of the sun disc, having been self-generated within the primaeval waters, and sat upon the primaeval mound establishing thereby his kingship over the creation which he was about to effect. The symbolism here is two-fold: the birth imagery, *i.e.*, the emergence of life from life, and the imagery of the risen sun which brings light against the darkness. This appearance or revelation of the sun god Atum-Ra was both an act of self-creation and an act which functioned as an emanating creative power, the creation of light by the action of the rising sun nullifying the negative force of darkness. Hence, the appearance of the deity and the effecting of creation are identical. We may note here the similarity in imagery with that of the creation myth in Genesis 1. In the latter version the first movement of creation takes place in three stages: the existence of the primaeval chaos, the action of speaking on the part of the creator deity, and finally the emergence of light. In the Heliopolitan tradition we see the same three basic stages: the primaeval chaos, the action of the deity in rising from the waters,[22] and finally the emergence of light as a result of the divine action. At this stage of creation, in both the Hebrew and Egyptian traditions, the creative force has attained a certain potentiality; it has produced the element of light which will then serve as the source of more tangible things, the light itself being essentially the symbolic expression of creative power.

The first creative action which follows the emergence of the light is Atum's production of Shu and Tefnut, both of whom may be interpreted at this point as air deities.[23] It is important to stress here that the male and female principles which had been united in the figure of Atum are now diversified in the figures of Shu and Tefnut, thus making possible the normal generative process. The birth of Shu and Tefnut is described in Utterance 600 of the Pyramid Texts:

> O Atum-Kheprer, you were exalted on the height;
> You shone on the *benben* in the temple of the *benu* in On.
> You spat out Shu, you spat out Tefnut.
> You placed your arms around them like the arms of a ka
> So that your ka might be in them.[24]

According to the tradition reflected here, Shu and Tefnut were born through Atum's action of spitting, the symbolism of life-giving moisture being quite evident. Such an interpretation of the action of spitting appears more likely than the suggestion that spitting implies creation by means of the spoken word, as has been suggested.[25] By a different piece of symbolism the birth of Shu and Tefnut was the result of Atum's masturbation, as may be seen in Utterance 527 of the Pyramid Texts:

> He is Atum, the one who came into being and who masturbated in On.
> He placed his penis in his fist
> So that he might have sexual pleasure thereby,
> So that the twins might be born, Shu and Tefnut.[26]

As symbolic expressions of the unusual birth of Shu and Tefnut the mythic traditions alternate between spitting and masturbation on the part of Atum. (Spell 76 of the Coffin Texts, for example, stresses the fact that their birth was due to spitting.[27]) In actual fact the specific symbol makes little difference. Both spitting and masturbation represent birth by an unusual manner and from a single parent. It has in fact been suggested that masturbation and spitting are one concept.[28] The main point to note here is that the Egyptian mind had no difficulty in accepting both symbols, realizing that they were only symbols, to express the birth of Shu and Tefnut, a birth which mythically had to take place by an unorthodox method insofar as Atum was the combination of the male and female principles. Through the birth of Shu and Tefnut the Heliopolitan mythic system represented the actual appearance of the diverse masculine and feminine principles. As a result of this, the creation was able to proceed by means of the normal patterns of procreation. The further details of the Heliopolitan tradition need not concern us at this point, for the central signification of the myth has been brought out in its symbolic representation of the emergence of creation and life from the first principle which was inherent within Atum, and, even before Atum, was inherent in Nun, the primaeval chaos, as a potential force which had only to be realized and actualized. The actualization of this force, therefore, became the pivot point of the whole mythic tradition.

One specific symbol within the creation traditions of all the various shrines of Egypt served as a focal point to conjoin the myth with the ritual actions of the cult. That symbol was the primaeval mound itself, the mound whereon the newly-born deity had sat in order to carry out the task of the creative process. There can be little doubt that the symbol of the primaeval mound evolved from the observation of the natural phenomenon of the hillocks of land emerging from the waters of the Nile when the inundation began to subside each year. In this the Egyptian was able to observe a graphic representation and portrayal of the original emergence of the land from the primaeval waters. Furthermore, since the emergence of the land after the flood was the start of planting and of natural reproduction from the soil, it was even more to be expected that the primaeval mound should become the symbol of life. In the cultic ritualization of the appearance of this primaeval mound, the sites of the major shrines were interpreted in each tradition as having been the original place of the primaeval mound, and the latter was the basic signification of each temple and shrine. This primaeval mound was situated at On, Memphis, Hermopolis, Thebes or wherever the specific cult centre happened to be located. The temple thus became in a cultic sense the centre of the world, for it was, ritually speaking, the site of creative activity and the source of creative power. Finally, the temple was seen also as the permanent dwelling of the cult deity, his presence being represented there by his cult statue around which the rituals were performed.

The basic signification of the cult at each shrine was the celebration, representation and actual repetition of the divine creative action in the present moment. The final result of the cult was the renewal of the created universe and the renewal of the order of that universe, *i.e.*, the order and structure of Ma'at. The temple was the setting in which the cult deity repeated and continued his defeat of the powers of chaos and non-being. It was the mystic structure where the mythic reality of creation was given a cultic expression and a tangible reality. In this we are brought back to the very pragmatic and practical purpose of the cult, for the ritual renewal of the creation was the assurance of the re-establishment of the universal order. Creation myth and creation cult (the official state cults of Egypt) thus gave man the assurance that the order of the cosmos would be maintained and that the universe, the state and the individual would continue their ordered existence in a positive and optimistic manner. Creation mythology, performed in the cult, was not simply a commemoration or a means of giving an answer to the "How?" of creation. It was in effect creation itself. Egyptian religion encompassed, therefore, no less than the totality of universal life. Creation was not a single action; it was repeated and realized each day in the rising and rebirth of the sun god and the subsequent re-establishment of universal Ma'at. It was realized also in every cultic festival, in the succession of a new Pharaoh to the throne, and even in the rebirth of the dead. Creation mytho-theology thus touched every aspect of life, both public and private, in ancient Egypt. It would be difficult, therefore to over-emphasize its importance.

Nor did the symbolism of creation play any less important role in the Amarna movement. It is true that, due to the nature of the movement, no specific graphic myths of creation were formulated. Furthermore, it seems that cultic worship did not centre on the actual ritualization of the creative action, but rather on the person of the deity himself, the Aten. This worship of the Aten, however, was none the less an acknowledgement of his creative aspect. At the very outset of the famous Hymn to the Aten, after the recognition of the beauty and goodness (*nfrw*) of the god's dawning, the deity is addressed as "the living Aten, the source of life" (*pʒ Itn ʿnḫ šʒʿ ʿnḫ*). The impression one takes from the text is that the rising of the sun was again an assurance of the life-giving force and power of the god.

The setting of the sun is described:

> Your setting is on the western horizon,
> While the earth is in darkness in the fashion of death.[29]

Here it is as if with the setting of the sun, the symbol and revelation of the Aten, the created universe has again returned to the darkness (Kuk) of the mythic primaeval chaos. With the rebirth and return of the sun disc the world is again aroused to normal activity, normal only because with the return of the Aten there has returned the natural order of the world:

> The earth brightens when you are risen on the horizon,
> When you shine in the Aten of the day-time,
> Expelling the darkness and sending your rays.
> The Two Lands are festive, wakeful and alert,
> For you have aroused them.[30]

In the Amarna system no other deity was afforded recognition; it was the Aten alone who was the giver of life and it was by his agency alone that men were able to live:

> To you yourself belongs length of life,
> And it is only through you than men live.[31]

That life and the power and right to bestow it belonged solely to the Aten was a natural tenet of Amarna theology, for in that theological system the Aten was the sole creator of all that existed:

> You are the one who made that which did not exist,
> The one who made them in their entirety,
> For they have proceeded from your mouth.[32]

The impact which the created universe had made on the Egyptian mind and consciousness was so strong that it pervaded every aspect of the religious life of the culture. Even the heretic Akhenaten could not escape giving as his main praise to his deity the acknowledgement that the greatness and power of that deity lay in his obvious manifestation in the world which he had created. No Egyptian religious tradition and myth could ever be divorced from its tie to the creative principle, for the creative force was the very foundation and centre of understanding and comprehension.

It is an interesting point that the major source of our knowledge of Egyptian creation myths, and the place wherein references to the creation are frequently made, is the mortuary literature of Egypt. The Pyramid Texts, the Coffin Texts and the Book of the Dead are more than abundant in their repetition of the creative motifs. The question arises as to why was the theme of creation and the birth of the creator deity so important in such texts. The answer to this question is a simple one, but it illustrates the profound impact of creation theology on the Egyptian mind. Mortuary rituals were of necessity founded on creation theology. The hope of the deceased was that he would by means of such texts and their accompanying rituals be enabled to identify with the creator god in his repeated and on-going creative activity and nature. In such a manner the deceased would himself be reborn within the living cycle of the cosmic creation. Creation, as we have already seen, was nothing less than the totality of life itself. In incorporating the mythic expressions of creation into the mortuary texts, the Egyptian was conscious that he was thereby infusing those texts with the one certain means of the continuation of his own personal life beyond the tomb. In the mythopoeic mentality of the ancient Egyptian there was the understanding that wherever and whenever creation took place there could be no power of death. Hence, the Egyptian hoped that in death he would be identified with Atum, with Ra, with Nun, for thus the continuation of his life would be guaranteed. It could not have been otherwise, for in such an identification he would have become no less than the very force and power of universal regeneration. Thus, in Chapter XVII of the Book of the Dead, the deceased is made to say:

> I am the great god who came into existence by himself,
> Nun, who created his own name as a god
> In the primaeval time of the gods.[33]

Thus, for the Egyptian, although death was still an object of fear, a terror which he had eventually to face, it was not an object of ultimate despair. He knew that in the face of the creative power of the universe death could have no lasting dominion over him, for that creative power was life itself, everlasting and enduring.

One final question remains to be asked about the Egyptian concept of creation: was there a purpose in the created universe? Had the creator god acted in order to bring about eventually some specific end and goal? Did the world have some final development towards which it was evolving? Would there be an eventual *telos* or *eschaton*? Unfortunately, such a question must remain unanswered, for no Egyptian text outlines any specific reason and purpose for the creation. The creator god, it appears, had simply performed the act which was inherent in him by his very nature, and the Egyptians do not seem to have asked why such an event took place. One may, of course, hazard a guess at an answer, but any answer thus provided will be no more than speculation. Perhaps the creator acted in order to produce the beauty and goodness (*nfrw*) of the perfect order of Ma'at. The creation may thus have existed as a work of divine art, an end in itself, having and needing no other justification. Perhaps the answer to the question may be found in the doctrines of Akhenaten: the god created because of his love (*mrwt*) and goodness (*nfrw*), and creation was thus an expression of his personality. The creation myths did not go so far as to try to explain the "Why?" of the creation any more than they had attempted to explain its "How?" What they did state, and very clearly through their use of mythic symbolism, was that the world existed as a manifestation of the divine; because the divine existed and was itself the force and power of life, creation had of necessity to have come into being. The manifestation of the divine which was afforded in the creation could be neither known nor articulated in an intellectual manner; it could only be apprehended and experienced in the mythic symbolism of the cult.

Inseparably connected with the concept of creation, in fact an integral part and even cause of the created order, was the principle and reality which was the continued support of the universe. That principle was the goddess Ma'at, to which we must now turn in order to give some measure of completion to our understanding of the Egyptian mytho-theology of creation.

Notes

[1] The mythic imagery in the account in question, however, was restricted to the image of the spoken word.

[2] R.T. Rundle Clark, *Myth and Symbol in Ancient Egypt*, 226.

[3] ḳmꜣ.k tꜣ n ib.k iw.k wꜥ.t (M. Sandman, *Texts from the Time of Akhenaten*, 94.17).

[4] *PT* 1466: *n ḫprt pt n ḫprt tꜣ*
       n ḫprt rmṯ n mst nṯrw
       n ḫprt mt.

[5] R.T. Rundle Clark, *op. cit.*, 35.

[6] *CT* II, 24a: *ḫft mdw Nnw m ḥḥw m nnw m tnmw m kkw.*

[7] *CT* II, 5e-6a: *ink wṯt ḥḥw wḥmw*
       m ḥḥw m nnw
       m tnm m kkw
       ink pw šw wṯt nṯrw.

[8] *CT* II, 19c-d: *i ḥḥ 8 ipw iwr.n šw*
       ms.n šw ḳmꜣn šw
       ṯsi.n šw.

[9] It is important to remember that Atum's first appearance and his creative act was also the establishment of the kingship, Atum himself becoming the first king of the universe. Not only is the creation of the kingship contemporary with the creation of the universe, but the two are essentially the same. In this system of mytho-theological thought cosmos and kingship are totally inseparable and interdependent.

[10] For a more extended treatment of the Osiris/Horus/Seth traditions, see R. Bonnel & V. Tobin, "Christ and Osiris: A Comparative Study" in *Pharaonic Egypt, the Bible and Christianity*, 1-29.

[11] *Syria* 37 (1960): 7f.

[12] *ntk mwt it n iri.k nb* (M. Sandman, *op. cit.*, 12.10).

[13] *ntk mwt mst bw nb* (*ibid.*, 84.6).

[14] H. Frankfort, *Ancient Egyptian Religion*, 17.

[15] E.A.E. Reymond (*The Mythical Origin of the Egyptian Temple*, 111f.) makes reference to a possible myth of the death of the sun god after his creation of the world, a suggestion based on the texts from the temple of Edfu. The death of the creator god, following this interpretation, would then have been the occasion for a new stage of the creation. Although there appears to be no other evidence of the mythic death of the sun god, such could be reflected in the symbolism of the sun god's sojourn in the underworld during the night. If this was actually interpreted as a 'death', then it would make the symbolism of rebirth each morning much more dramatic and graphic, underscoring the idea that the new day was also a new creation.

[16]*wtt sw ms sw ḏs.f* (*Hieroglyphic Texts from Egyptian Stelae &c., in the British Museum*, 8 parts [London, 1911-1938], 552 [VIII], pl.27).

[17]M. Sandman, *op. cit.*, 75.14-15.

[18]*PT* 1587: *ind̠ ḫr.k Itm*
ind̠ ḫr.k H̱prr ḫpr ḏs.f
ḳi.k m rn.k pw n ḳỉ
ḫpr.k m rn.k pw n H̱prr.

[19]Note the doubled 'r' in the name Kheprer, an Egyptian grammatical device to indicate repeated or on-going action.

[20]*ḫpr.n.i ḏs.i ḫn ˁ Nwn m rn.i pw n H̱pri.*

[21]*ḫpr.n.i ... m R ˁ*

[22]In the Hebrew myth the deity did not originate within the waters, but, due to the more sophisticated theological level of the period of its composition, was totally other than and outside of the creation. Hence, in the Hebrew myth the action of the deity was expressed as one of speaking, imposing his power upon the material of creation from the outside, and the absolute distinction between creator and creation was thus maintained. In the much earlier Heliopolitan system, however, there was not that same distinction between creator and creation. "Creator and creation merge in Egyptian religious thinking," (F. Friedman, "*šḫ* in the Amarna Period," JARCE XXIII [1986]: 101).

[23]I. Shirun-Grumach, "Remarks on the Goddess Maat," *Pharaonic Egypt, the Bible and Christianity*, pp.173f.

[24]*PT* 1652a-1653a: *Itm H̱ prr ḳỉ.n.k m ḳỉỉ*
wbn.n.k m bnbn m ḥwt bnw m Iwnw
i ššn.k m šw tfn.(n.)k m Tfnt
di.n.k ˁwy.k ḥỉ.sn m ˁ(wy) kỉ
wn kỉ.k im.sn.

[25]R.T. Rundle Clark, *op. cit.*, 44.

[26]*PT* 1248: *Itm pw ḫpr ms ỉw m Iwnw*
wd.n.f ḥnn.f m ḫf ˁf
iri.f nmmt im.f
ms s ỉty snnt šw ḫn ˁ Tfnt.

[27]*CT* II, 3g-4a.

[28]J. Zandee in *ZÄS* 100 (1973), 71f. What is more likely is that originally both spitting and masturbation were combined in the action of Atum, and what the god spit out as Shu and Tefnut was actually his own seed whereby he had impregnated himself.

[29]M. Sandman, *op. cit.*, 93.17.: *ḥtp.k m ỉḫt imntt*
tỉ m kkw m sḫr n mt.

[30]*ibid.*, 94.3-4: $ḫd\ t\ ꜣ\ wbn.ti\ m\ sḫt$
$psd.ṯ\ m\ itn\ m\ hrw$
$rwi.k\ kkw\ di.k\ stwt.k$
$tꜣwy\ m\ ḫb\ rs\ ꜥḥꜥ\ ḫr\ rdwy.$
$ṯsi.n.k\ sn$
[31]*ibid.*, 95.18.: $ntk\ ꜥḥꜥ\ r\ ḫꜥw.k$
$ꜥn\ ḥ.tw\ im.k$
[32]*ibid.*, 46.15.: $ntk\ ir\ n\ wnt$
$ir\ nn\ r\ ꜣw$
$pr.n.w\ m\ r.k.$
[33]$ink\ nṯr\ ꜥꜣ\ ḫpr\ ḏs.f$
$Nwn\ pw\ ḫm\ ꜣ\ rn.f$
$pꜣwt\ nṯrw\ m\ nṯr.$

V. Ma'at

The concept of Ma'at as part of the Egyptian theological synthesis may be defined in a number of ways: as a symbol, as an abstract principle, or as a personal goddess having a specific hypostatic existence in her own right, none of these definitions being necessarily exclusive of the others. To attempt, however, to select any one of these as an exclusive definition of Ma'at and thus to eliminate the other possibilities would be to distort seriously the concept for which Ma'at stood in the Egyptian mythic system. In some ways it may be easier to state what Ma'at was not than to define categorically what it was. Ma'at, although frequently used in a symbolic manner, was not a mere symbol. Ma'at may, of course, be seen under a symbolic aspect, but at the same time it went far beyond the nature of a symbol, being in fact the actual reality which it symbolized. Ma'at was at times seen by the Egyptians as a personal goddess, but to restrict it solely to such a role would be effectively to eliminate the central place which Ma'at held in the Egyptian systems of thought. More than symbol, more than principle, and more than goddess, Ma'at represented, perhaps even more than the creator deity himself, the true foundation stone of the stability of Egyptian religious thought. Ma'at was, if one may attempt to define it briefly and simply, the basis for the unity of all things, the basis of cosmic order, of political order, of morality, of life itself, of art and science, and even of good etiquette in normal everyday affairs.

No other culture of the ancient or modern world has evolved a single concept which is so totally all-inclusive as was the Egyptian concept of Ma'at. The Greek world developed the concept of δίκη (*diké*), frequently translated by terms such as 'justice', 'righteousness', 'custom', 'manner', 'order', 'punishment', but its signification varies from context to context, and it appears never to have gained the all-embracing role which Ma'at held in Egyptian thinking. Only in the Athenian dramatist Aeschylus, and particularly in his trilogy the *Oresteia*, did the concept of δίκη begin to approach the Egyptian Ma'at. Even here, however, despite the positive force which is implied in Aeschylus' usage of the Greek term, δίκη was not able to move beyond its position of an abstract principle, and it was able to remain an effective force only so long as it was recognized as such. Moreover, the negative traits which so often appeared in the Greek concept, overtones which were clearly fatalistic, punishment for human sin, human mortality, tended to detract from the positive force which it did hold. To the Greek mind, δίκη was as much of a threat as it was a blessing, for it served to place a restraining force on human thought and action, holding man in check and threatening him with dire results if its principles were in any way violated. Although this restraining force of δίκη did function in a positive manner to prevent wrong-doing, it also had a very negative impact through its threatening aspect of punitive action in the event of sin or crime. Creative action was, therefore, a very minor part of this particular Greek concept, and its positive value was limited.

In order to express anything of the fullness which was contained in the Egyptian Ma'at, the Greek language had to have recourse to terms such as θέμις ('right', 'order'), μοῖρα ('fate', 'portion',), σωφροσύνη ('discretion', 'self-restraint', 'moderation') and ἀρετή ('virtue', 'nobility'). This plurality of terms to express the various concepts which were all inherent within the Egyptian Ma'at only prevented the Greek mind from developing a more unified and inclusive principle of order. Hence, instead of a single concept which could bind the perception of reality together into a unity, the Greek mind had eventually to formulate complex philosophical systems in an attempt to integrate its understanding of the universe and human life, systems whose very complexity and abstract nature must have frequently made them incomprehensible to the ordinary mind.[1]

In contrast to the more restrictive δίκη of Greek thought, the Egyptian concept of Ma'at provided a positive and constructive single principle of order. Ma'at was eternal and unchanging, always strong, good and benevolent in its nature, never a threat to human happiness. Man was assured that in every event of life and human history Ma'at would always prevail. As a result, the Egyptian was able to view the universe in an optimistic and hopeful manner, for that universe was static, always secure, having no necessity of change or evolution towards a higher and better mode of existence. Because of the reality of Ma'at there could not possibly have been any better mode of existence, for the cosmos was already perfected. For such a reason, the Egyptian religious and moral mind was never forced to develop any concept of an eschatology or even a teleology. Such were simply not needed. Indeed the very possibility of an *eschaton* or a *telos* would have contradicted the perfection of Ma'at.[2] J. Wilson has described Ma'at as "the cosmic force of harmony, order, stability and security... the organizing quality of created phenomena... the just and proper relationship of cosmic phenomena."[3] Ma'at, according to Egyptian mythic symbolism, had been established at the time of the creation and was the principle which allowed the created universe to continue its existence in an ordered fashion. Without Ma'at there could have been no universe; there would have been, on the contrary, only created disorder, a state which would have been inconceivable and even self-contradictory to the Egyptian mind, for disorder would not have been creation. Nevertheless, the cosmic order of Ma'at was not totally unshakable, for it was possible that at times it could be disturbed. Such disturbances, however, were only temporary, for the order of Ma'at was seen by the Egyptian as something which was eternal and which could never be totally and finally destroyed.

The centrality of Ma'at in Egyptian thought is evident in the place which it held in the Heliopolitan creation myth. Here Ma'at was identified with Tefnut the daughter of Atum, and thus appears to have been at the very foundation of the whole created order. Without Ma'at, therefore, there would have been nothing in existence. This identification of Ma'at with Tefnut may be seen in Spell 80 of the Coffin Texts where Atum says:

> Tefnut is my living daughter;
> She shall be with her brother Shu.
> Life (Ankh) is his name;
> Ma'at is her name.[4]

The same text further stresses this relationship between Atum and Ma'at, giving her a specific active importance even within the life of Atum:

> Kiss your daughter Ma'at,
> Placing her at your nose.
> Your heart will live,
> For she is not far from you.
> Ma'at is your daughter
> With your son Shu whose name is Life.
> You will eat of your daughter Ma'at.[5]

Here Ma'at, begotten by Atum at the time of the creation as a type of active First Principle of creation, appears personified as a goddess. Such a personification, however, is definitely secondary to her role as a symbol of cosmic order. The above text also illustrates a further symbolic function of

Ma'at in the action of Atum's placing Ma'at to his nose and kissing her, and also the action of Atum's eating of Ma'at. The first of these symbols portrays the importance of Ma'at by showing her as the very breath of life to Atum, while the symbolism of Atum's eating of Ma'at further implies that it is by Ma'at which the god lives. Both of these symbols were quite clearly intended as imagery, imagery which portrayed the centrality of Ma'at even in relationship to the gods. Ma'at was in effect that principle by which the divine life was continually renewed. Without Ma'at even Atum himself, the actual source of created order, would not have been able to exist. Ma'at was thus more than only the principle of universal order; it was an integral part, an inseparable aspect, of the cosmos, without which that cosmos would not even have existed. Ma'at in effect was that which permitted the creation actually to be an ordered cosmos.

As a result of the concept of the eternally stable and unchanging nature of Ma'at, the Egyptians evolved a very optimistic outlook on the world; or the reverse may in fact be true, namely that the development of the concept of Ma'at was the result of the natural optimism which was already existent in Egyptian society. Which of these two suggestions actually represents the truth makes very little difference. The important point is that Ma'at was the embodiment of Egyptian optimism, an optimism which is particularly evident in the writings of the Old Kingdom. Consider, for example, the optimism of Ptahhotep who takes the attitude that, if a man lives by the principle of Ma'at, his life will prosper and all will be well with him. To the Egyptian mind, Ma'at was the most enduring natural principle known, powerful and everlasting, as the story of the Eloquent Peasant puts it:

> Speak Ma'at, do Ma'at,
> For it is mighty, it is great, it endures.[6]

> Do Ma'at for the sake of the Lord of Ma'at,
> The Ma'at of whose Ma'at endures.[7]

Like *The Eloquent Peasant*, the text of Ptahhotep also stresses the unchanging and unchallenged power of Ma'at, a power which has never been shaken since the 'age of Osiris', the golden age of civilization and culture. Throughout the texts of both the Peasant and Ptahhotep, Ma'at appears as a positive force for justice and right. In such texts, one is beginning to approach the moral aspects and demands of Ma'at, and these in turn are but a further indication of its power, for it is perceived as a force which pervades all human affairs. Not only was there a natural universal order within the cosmos, but, because of this natural order, human and state affairs had to be conducted with righteousness and justice. A righteous and ordered cosmos of necessity demanded a righteous and ordered life on the part of those who inhabited it. Anyone who did not conduct his life in such a fashion was of necessity seen as incongruous with the innate nature of the universe and of human society.

The demand of Ma'at for righteousness in human affairs points to the importance of the role of the Pharaoh, for his main duty was to maintain the cosmic order of Ma'at,[8] particularly as it pertained to the political realm and to human affairs. Because of this role, the ruler held the title of the 'good god' (*ntr nfr*). He was, however, considered 'good' not simply because he was beneficent and providential to mankind, but because he was the living instrument through which the eternal practical goodness and beauty of Ma'at were realized in the world and in human and political affairs. The goodness of the good god was in essence nothing else than the goodness and power of the creator god who had first fashioned the universe. The faith in the power and ability of the Pharaoh to right wrong, to drive away evil and to restore Ma'at in the land may be seen in the text known as *The Prophecies of Neferty*. Herein is described a situation where disorder and wrong have become prevalent throughout the land, with the result that the whole structure of society and life has collapsed. Nevertheless, the writer of the text expresses his own assurance that such will be set aright by the coming of a good king, who, in the historical context which gave rise to the document, was Amenemhet I, the first ruler of the Twelfth Dynasty. The result of the deeds of this good king will be that:

> Ma'at will return to her throne.
> For evil (*isft*) will have been driven away.[9]

The 'prophecy' of the coming of the good king Ameny (Amenemhet I) was, of course, written *post eventum* and thus it reflects a historical situation which had already taken place rather than one which was yet to come. This, however, is of no real importance. What is important here is that the text reflects the same faith in the certainty of Ma'at as does *The Eloquent Peasant*. In the latter, the faith in the power and certainty of Ma'at allows even a humble peasant to find the courage to plead for his rights against a member of the nobility. In order to do so, he dares to importune even the royal throne itself, but the basis of his daring rests upon the conviction that the justice of Ma'at cannot be challenged. One can hardly imagine that a Homeric Greek would find such courage in his world where δίκη held sway.[10]

Because of the power of Ma'at, there was in Egypt, even in times of social disruption, the belief that order and right would eventually be victorious. Such a re-establishment of order, when it did take place, would have been nothing other than the re-establishment of the order and principle of Ma'at within society.[11] If the Egyptian had found himself in a situation where he could have had no such hope in the final victory of Ma'at, then life for him would not have been worth living. Such is the situation depicted in the famous *Dispute of a Man with His Ba*.[12] Here one sees a picture of a man who actually contemplates committing suicide because of the breakdown of social order and morality within the land. The shock engendered by this situation was obviously felt as so terrible that suicide appeared the only possible solution to a life which, because of its lack of order, was meaningless and unbearable. Normally, however, it was the place and function of Ma'at to ensure that such situations did not arise, and, if they did arise, to see to it that order would be re-established and the state of the land again set right.

Because of the strength of Ma'at and its embodiment in the person of the Pharaoh, the Egyptians had no permanent law codes until the Persian and Greek periods.[13] Such, however, was no more than natural. Given the earthly presence of an individual who was himself a god incarnate and the embodiment of the force of order and righteousness, no law codes were necessary, nor could they have ever substituted for, or even augmented, the role of the monarch. On the contrary, an organized law code which was intended as a basis of order within the land would have appeared to the Egyptian mentality as a blasphemy. It would have constituted an attempt to place a lifeless and codified system of statutes in the place of a living and vital principle of right, a principle which was, furthermore, a manifestation of the divine. Ma'at was embodied in the Pharaoh; he was a living and effective law as opposed to a lifeless code of behaviour. No force could have been more powerful for the maintenance of righteousness and justice. In the person of the Pharaoh righteousness and justice virtually dwelt among men, a situation which in its positive overtones sounds almost like a

Biblical description of a Messianic age. In ancient Egypt the earthly presence of the Pharaoh did in fact transform the land into a type of Messianic kingdom on earth. Such at least was the official doctrine of the royal office, and whether or not such was actually realized makes little difference. The important point is that the ideal existed.

Although our main concern here is with Ma'at as a principle and as an effective force, we cannot overlook the fact that there also existed in ancient Egypt the concept of Ma'at as a personal goddess. The question here arises as to which of the two concepts of Ma'at was the original one, Ma'at as a principle or Ma'at as a goddess. With regard to the first concept, we do find the opinion that the importance of Ma'at depended "more on her mythological activity... than on a personified principle."[14] In the latter interpretation, Ma'at appears to have been basically a personalized air goddess closely connected with Shu and involved with him in the action of creation. C.J. Bleeker also presents a similar opinion.[15] It may possibly be that case that the mythological actions of Ma'at constituted an important aspect of her personality, but the fact still remains that with the personified goddess there was associated an abstract principle of which she was the specific symbol. To make even a tentative decision on this question would require a full investigation of the history of Ma'at, a task which is neither in the interest of the present study nor within its limits. Whatever the actual history of Ma'at may have been, the fact does still remain that it was the importance of Ma'at as a principle of order which contributed to its significance in the Egyptian theological system. My own inclination is to view the personification of Ma'at as a development from the abstract principle, at least from a rudimentary perception of the existence of an undefined but obvious order within the cosmos. As a mythological figure Ma'at seems to have been for the most part somewhat colourless and two-dimensional. Hence it is difficult to imagine the emergence of an important abstract principle out of the personalized goddess.

One must, on the other hand, seriously question whether or not the Egyptian mentality was sufficiently inclined to the philosophical as to be able to develop an abstract principle and then personify it at a later stage of development. It may indeed be safer to adopt the opinion that the figure of Ma'at had its development basically as an abstract principle which was at the same time expressed in the only manner in which the Egyptian mind could express such an abstraction, *i.e.*, by means of the concrete symbol. The latter would be to say that Ma'at was a true mythic symbol, as were many of the other deities. Atum, as we have seen, was both a creator god and at the same time a personification of the principle of creative power, no distinction having been made by the Egyptian mind between the god as a symbol and the god as an hypostatic deity. Atum had been thus personified simply because the principle of creative power was a reality, and as a reality it could have been portrayed only in terms of a figure which actually did exist. Such appears also to have been the case with Ma'at. In order to have any kind of 'real' existence, Ma'at had to be a tangible being. Hence, it was personified and expressed in a graphic manner as a personal deity. To the mythopoeic mind the existence of universal order would have naturally implied the existence of the personal goddess, and the denial of that goddess would have been tantamount to the denial of the principle of order. Order, however, was very real to the Egyptian perception; his experience of the world and of nature would have confirmed this. Hence, Ma'at as a goddess had to be real and existent; her reality was proven through normal human experience of the natural world around him.

Despite the opinions noted above, I would suggest that the real importance of Ma'at did not rest upon its position as a personalized and mythological deity, but rather on the cosmic order which was embodied in that deity. The goddess Ma'at thus became a sacramental symbol of the existence of the cosmic order which she embodied, so that no distinction existed between Ma'at as a principle and Ma'at as a goddess. In the figure of the goddess Ma'at, order in the cosmos was not simply an abstraction and an intellectual principle. It did not depend upon the ability or inability of man to comprehend and to understand it. Through the mythic figure of the personal deity Ma'at, the Egyptian expressed his own consciousness of this order and affirmed in his cultic rites that Ma'at was indeed a reality which was stable and enduring. The primary purpose of the Egyptian cult, as has already been discussed, was the realization, re-establishment and maintenance of the cosmic order. So that such could take place, that order had to be, at least to the mythopoeic mind, a real and integral part of the divine system. As an abstraction it could not have been so. Hence, Ma'at took its reality from the fact that within the cult it was expressed in terms of an hypostatic deity. Had it not been thus, then Ma'at as order would have had for the Egyptian mind very little, if any, meaning. Nor does the view of J. Assmann that Ma'at was a pneuma-like and life-giving substance[16] add anything to the mytho-theological nature of Ma'at. As a mythic symbol, Ma'at could hardly have been taken as a 'substance', and it was basically the mythic symbol of Ma'at which was important in the Egyptian theological expression. Above all else, therefore, Ma'at remained the mythic symbol of the divine principle of the order which existed in the universe, inherent within the universe from the very beginning of its existence and as an essential element of the fact of its creation. The personalized deity was but an expression of this order, although the mythic symbol was inseparable from the reality. Thus, the question as to which came first, goddess or principle, is relatively unimportant. They were one and the same entity, and any attempt to separate them would be totally in opposition to the function of myth and its symbolism.

Although it is not the purpose of the present work to deal in detail with the Amarna period, and although Akhenaten's movement does not appear to have made any significant contribution to the Egyptian concept of Ma'at, nevertheless a comment should be added here on Ma'at in the Amarna system. Opinions on Akhenaten's concept of Ma'at have varied from one extreme to another. J.H. Breasted, seeing in the Amarna period a movement of high moral consciousness, described Akhenaten's Ma'at as signifying righteousness and moral order.[17] At the opposite extreme R. Anthes has seen the Amarna concept of Ma'at as being no more than truth, the actual expression of the way things are in their reality.[18] Such an interpretation could give some significance to the expression of realism in Amarna art (although one need not necessarily feel inclined to give any particular philosophical justification for that specific artistic phenomenon). It is impossible within the context of a brief discussion either to refute or to defend totally the interpretation of either Breasted or Anthes, or indeed to deal with the full range of opinion on the subject. One may, however, at least offer a personal opinion.

The north thickness of the tomb of May at Amarna has an inscription wherein May describes Akhenaten as "the one who placed Ma'at in my body."[19] The result of this is that May is also able to state immediately, "My abominations are lies."[20] This contrast of the two Egyptian terms $m\jmath^{c}t$ and $grgw$ seems to suggest that an interpretation of Ma'at as 'truth' might be quite appropriate, at least in this context. Ay in his tomb was also able to state, "My mouth holds Ma'at" ($r.i$ $\underline{hr}$ $m\jmath^{c}t$).[21] Such an expression seems to indicate that the Amarna concept of Ma'at was that it was some type of an abstract principle of truth which enabled one to distinguish between right and wrong, between truth and falsehood. It may further be understood as the ability on the part of the Amarna nobles to accept the truth of

Akhenaten's doctrinal system. Such an interpretation of Ma'at at Amarna may, however, be somewhat broadened into a wider concept of its nature by adding to it the following description, that at Amarna "the understanding of Ma'at is the understanding of the essential nature of reality."[22] Thus the Amarna concept of Ma'at could be defined as "the theory of integration of every element in the world."[23] If such was the case, and it does appear as a tempting interpretation, then the Amarna concept of Ma'at, although somewhat more abstract and certainly no longer a mythic symbol, was not so far removed from the traditional thought of the Egyptian mythic systems. It was, however, a sign of the movement of Akhenaten's thought towards a stronger ability for abstract formulation.[24]

To conclude this discussion of Ma'at, it will be sufficient to state simply that because of this peculiar Egyptian concept the universe was seen as essentially benevolent to man. It was ordered, regular and dependable, under the rule of the divine, the earth being governed on behalf of the celestial gods by the good god, the Pharaoh. Insofar as the world and the whole of the cosmos was ordered by Ma'at, man could be assured of the stability of an eternal and on-going universe. Ma'at bound all things together in an indestructible unity. The universe, the natural world, the state and the individual were all part of the order of Ma'at. The result was the concept of a perfect universe which could not be totally destroyed. Although occasionally this order might be disrupted and thrown out of balance, Ma'at provided the assurance that it would eventually be restored.

Notes

[1]For a detailed comparison and contrast of the Greek and Egyptian ideas, see my article "Ma'at and ΔIKH: Some Comparative Considerations of Egyptian and Greek Thought," *JARCE* XXIV (1987): 113-121.

[2]There is a possible eschatological reference in Chapter CLXXV of the Book of the Dead, but this reference appears as an isolated one whose meaning and significance are highly vague and uncertain.

[3]J. Wilson, *The Culture of Ancient Egypt*, 48.

⁴*CT* II, 32b-c: *sꜣt pw Ꜥnḫt Tfnt*
  wnn.s ḫnꜤ sn.s Šw
  Ꜥnḫ rn.f
  MꜢꜤt rn.s.
⁵*CT* II, 35c-g: *sn sꜣt.k MꜢꜤt*
  di.n.k s(t) r fnḏ.k
  Ꜥnḫ ib.k
  n ḫr st r.k.
  sꜣt.k pw MꜢꜤt
  ḫnꜤ sꜣk šw Ꜥnḫ rn.f
  wnm.k m sꜣt.k MꜢꜤt.
⁶*The Eloquent Peasant*, B1, 320-321: *ḏd mꜢꜤt ir mꜢꜤt*
  ḏr ntt wr.s ꜤꜢ.s wsḫ .s.
⁷*ibid.*, B1, 304: *ir m ꜢꜤt n nb mꜢꜤt*
  nty wn mꜢꜤt n mꜢꜤt .f.
⁸See H. Frankfort, *Kingship and the Gods* (Chicago, 1948): 9.
⁹W. Helck, *Die Prophezeiung des Nfr.tj* (Wiesbaden, 1970), XVe (p.57):
  iw m ꜢꜤt r iit r st.s
  isft dr.ty r rwty.
¹⁰In a world such as is described in the *Iliad* of Homer it was considered wrong for a commoner to attempt to assert himself against a member of the aristocracy. Homeric thought demanded that each man keep to his proper place which had been assigned to him and that he act in a manner which was consistent with his station. For example, see the episode of Thersites in Book II of the *Iliad*.
¹¹C.J. Bleeker, *Egyptian Festivals*, 8.
¹²Translation in M. Lichtheim, *Ancient Egyptian Literature*, I, 163ff.
¹³J. Wilson, *op. cit.*, 50.
¹⁴I. Shirun-Grumach, "Remarks on the Goddess Ma'at," *Pharaonic Egypt, the Bible and Christianity*, 173.
¹⁵C.J. Bleeker, *De Beteekenis van de Egyptische Godin Ma-a-t* (Leiden, 1929).
¹⁶*LÄ* II, s.v. "Gott".
¹⁷J.H. Breasted, *The Dawn of Conscience* (New York, 1933), 369.
¹⁸R. Anthes, "Die Maat des Echnatons von Amarna," Supplement to the *JAOS* XIV (1952): 1-36.
¹⁹*di mꜢꜤt m ḫt.i* (Sandman, *op. cit.*, 60.2).
²⁰*bwwt.i grgw* (*loc. cit.*).
²¹*ibid.*, 93.2.

[22] S.I. Groll in *Pharaonic Egypt, the Bible and Christianity*, 366.
[23] *loc. cit.*
[24] Dr. Roland G. Bonnel has recently completed an interesting study of Ma'at in the Amarna period entitled "The Ethics of El-Amarna" which is due to be printed in a forthcoming Festschrift in honour of Miriam Lichtheim to be published in Jerusalem in 1988 or 1989.

VI. The Egyptian Kingship

An Eighteenth Dynasty papyrus, now known as the Papyrus Millingen, contains a text commonly called *The Instruction of King Amenemhet I*.[1] This text, written as if addressed by Amenemhet to his son Senwosret I, both of the Twelfth Dynasty, records the murder of the former king by members of his own bodyguard, an event which took place at about 1962 B.C.E. Such an assassination was a highly unusual occurrence when one considers the Egyptian tradition of the divine kingship. The event is recorded also in the famous story of Sinuhe, but there the account of the actual murder is somewhat vague and uncertain. The text in Papyrus Millingen is the only account from ancient Egypt which deals so precisely with the theme of regicide.[2] This latter fact points to the obvious abhorrence in which such an action would have been held by the ancient Egyptians, at least from the viewpoint of the official theology of the monarchy. The assassination of another ruler of ancient Egypt is recorded in the Africanus version of Manetho, where it is said that Teti I of the Sixth Dynasty was murdered by his bodyguard.[3] Hence, it is obvious that, despite the official teaching about the person and position of the Pharaoh, there were certainly occasions when they were forcefully despatched.

At least in theory, one would expect that the official theology which surrounded the King of Upper and Lower Egypt would have rendered such events impossible, and such is normally the general situation. Hence, the assassination of a ruler can only indicate a very extreme state of emergency. *The Story of Sinuhe*[4] provides a very graphic illustration of such an emergency situation. Sinuhe, having accidentally overheard the report of the murder of Amenemhet, was so frightened that he immediately fled the country, his whole demeanour during his flight reflecting his state of dire panic.[5] From even a quick perusal of the text, it is obvious that Sinuhe expected serious consequences to result from the death of Amenemhet, the official upholder of the principle of Ma'at. His sudden and violent disappearance meant that law and order could no longer be expected to prevail in Egypt, at least not until the restoration of such order under the new ruler, Senwosret I.

What men could expect of the ruler in accordance with the Egyptian theory of the kingship is very well summed up in a quotation from the tomb autobiography of the Eighteenth Dynasty vizier Rekhmire:

> What is the King of Upper and Lower Egypt? He is a god by whose dealings one lives, the father and mother of all men, alone by himself, without an equal.[6]

The powers and ability of the ruler to function in accordance with such high expectations were not, however, purely arbitrary nor dependent upon the capacities of the individual king. Rather this function of the king was based on two things: the fact that he was the 'good god' (*nṯr nfr*) by nature and position, and that, in virtue of this position, he was the basis and upholder of Ma'at. The king, therefore, ruled by divine right, his office having come into existence at the time of the creation itself.[7] He was the Son of Ra (*s ꜣ Rꜥ*), the Son of Isis (*s ꜣ ꜣst*) and the Horus incarnate. From this divine nature of the king, thus expressed by mythic symbolism, was derived both his authority to be the upholder of Ma'at and his ability to be so. We have already in the preceding chapter seen how the Eloquent Peasant could appeal to this responsibility and office of the ruler and could, moreover, expect satisfactory results because of the nature and function of the ruler. Moreover, *the Instruction for King Merikare*,[8] a document dating from the First Intermediate Period, strongly stresses the duty of the king to live and act in accordance with Ma'at. The ruler did not have the right to act in an arbitrary fashion; his actions had to be controlled by the proper principles.

The Instruction for King Merikare mentioned above did not have within it any intention of diminishing the status and position of the monarch. The official nature of the kingship remained what it had been ever since the mythical time of its establishment. The kingship of Upper and Lower Egypt, which historically was created at the beginning of the First Dynasty, had been in actuality founded (according to the mythic symbolism surrounding it) at the time of the creation, when the sun god Atum-Ra first became king of the universe.[9] The kingship was thus an integral element within the cosmos, the king being in both theory and fact, at least to the Egyptian mind, the legitimate successor of the creator deity. This very strict connection between the kingship and the creation was of paramount importance in the Egyptian mytho-theology of the royal office. From this theory there derived the conviction that the principle role of the king was firmly to maintain the unchanging order of Ma'at, the order which had been established in conjunction with the kingship by the creator god. The creation myth made it evident that the universe was from its very inception a monarchy, and that the first king of the created universe also became king of Egypt.[10] The mythic succession of the Egyptian kingship may be graphically portrayed as follows:

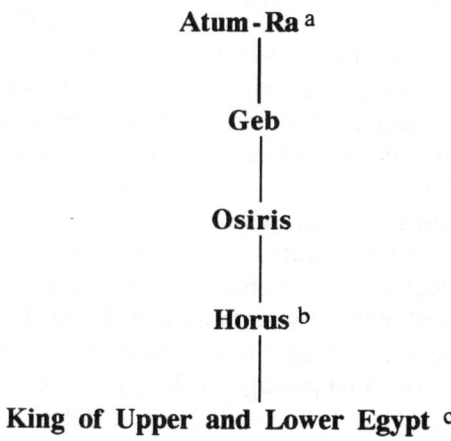

a = creator, founder of kingship
b = succeeding by right to the throne after his victory over Seth
c = mortal successor and incarnation of Horus

We may note here the two primary ancestors of the Pharaoh: the creator sun god Atum-Ra, and the earth god Geb, both symbolic of the process of procreation and the regeneration of life. It was this mythic symbolism of the divine origins of the monarch which justified the privilege and ability which he held in his office. (During the Amarna period Akhenaten placed strong emphasis on his own descent from the sun god, calling himself "the son of eternity who proceeds from the Aten" [$s3 n ḥḥ pr m Itn$][11] and "the one whom the Aten begets" [$p3 msy p3 Itn$].[12] By these, as well as by other numerous mythic expressions, Akhenaten sought to establish his identity according to the traditional mythic customs, and thus to justify his hold on the throne despite his rejection of the official state cults.) Both state and monarchy, therefore, had not only an earthly basis but also a cosmic one. The state, having been established at the time of creation, was part of the universal order of Ma'at, and the monarchy and person of the king likewise. We may recall here the mythic imagery of the creator deity appearing ($ḫ‛i$) on the primaeval mound and by so doing creating the light which was to be the symbol of creation and of the destruction of the principle of disorder and chaos. So also the succession of each new Pharaoh to the throne was described as an 'appearance', using the same term as was applied to the newly emerged creator sun god, the verb $ḫ‛i$. The accession of each new ruler to the throne was thus a mythic and cultic repetition of the original creative action of the sun god. In such a manner the state, the abstract kingship and each individual ruler were all seen as integral parts of the eternal and unchanging order of Ma'at. The rights, privileges and prerogatives of the king, therefore, were given a solid basis in the official state mytho-theology.

The divine birth and succession of the Pharaoh from his primary ancestors Atum and Geb created a kind of topological myth intended to express the concept of divine order, an order manifested in the perfect political order, and which was, moreover, handed on by a legitimate process of inheritance. The fact that between the Atum/Geb level of the royal ancestry and the final passage of the throne from Horus to the mortal monarch there was placed the symbol of the defeat of Seth served even further to emphasize the defeat of chaos and disorder which was characteristic of the monarchy.[13] This defeat having already taken place in a mythological manner, the Egyptian state and kingship could be said to have existed in a state of teleological perfection. There was no doctrine of a final struggle which would take place between the forces of good and evil as there would be later in the Judaeo-Christian tradition, for such, in Egyptian religious thought, had already taken place. Hence, the Egyptians did not look forward to an ideal king who would come in the future, a phenomenon found in Hebrew Messianism. Nor was the real task of the monarch that of accomplishing a final defeat of the forces of evil and chaos. The latter had in effect been already accomplished in the Horus/Seth mythic pericope. Hence, the main function of the earthly monarch was to maintain the order which had been already established. What in later religious thought (Hebrew and Christian) would belong to the realm of the teleological and eschatological had, in Egyptian thought, already been brought about. The Pharaoh was the symbol both of the original establishment of the perfected order and also the strength and power of its continuation. The Egyptian kingship thus expressed in reality what Christian mythic symbolism hopes for in its eschatological doctrine of the final establishment of a 'Kingdom of God'.

The symbols which we have seen above in the mytho-theology of the kingship were obviously originally derived from two separate and distinct sources. On the one hand there was the Osiris/Horus cycle of mythic symbols, and on the other hand the mythic symbols centred around the figure of the sun god. The Pyramid Texts provide ample evidence that the two traditions were originally separate, since in these texts the myth of the deification of the monarch is more frequently associated with the solar deities, references to the Osiris/Horus tradition being to a great extent separate and apparently belonging to a different mytho-theological system. It has been suggested, and does seem to be a likely probability, that the theological foundation of the kingship was finally connected more strongly with Ra than it was with Osiris.[14] In all likelihood this was the final result of the rise to prominence of Ra of Heliopolis (On) and the Heliopolitan tradition which gained the high point of its power at the beginning of the Fifth Dynasty. It is further likely that the Osiris/Horus mythological tradition of kingship was the result of the connection between the two deities at a relatively early period in history. Thus, the mythic picture of the complex royal succession (Atum/Geb/Osiris/Horus/Pharaoh) seen above was the result of a careful amalgamation and synthesis of mythic symbols from at least two different traditions.

The most common designation of the king in the earliest periods of Egypt's history was the title Horus,[15] a fact evident from the names even of the early kings of the First Dynasty. This Horus, who gave his name as a title to the monarch, was not originally the Horus who became the son of Osiris and Isis, but was rather Horus the Lord of Heaven,[16] his identification with Horus son of Osiris and Isis being only a later development. Even before this latter identification had taken place, the royal Horus had early been identified with the sun god Ra of Heliopolis.[17] The earliest royal mytho-theology was, therefore, the portrayal of the monarch as Horus/Ra, a solar deity, during which time Osiris retained as one of his chief characteristics the aspect of an underworld demon who was actually hostile to the spirit of the dead king. It was from the Horus/Ra mytho-theology that there eventually emerged the title Son of Ra which became a standard designation of the monarch during the Fifth Dynasty, although certainly in use before that time. The Horus myth of the kingship appears to have been formulated as a result of the unification of Egypt at the beginning of the First Dynasty,[18] when the Horus king of Upper Egypt became the ruler of the newly united kingdoms. Anthes has made the suggestion that it was from this earthly monarch that the deity Horus was then projected outwards as a sky deity, the earthly monarch then becoming in the mythic formulations the embodiment of the celestial deity.[19] If such was indeed the actual manner of the development of the myth, then we see in this phenomenon an important example of at least one way in which historical events were able to exert their influence on the development of Egyptian mythic expression.

At a later point in Egypt's history, although still within the boundaries of the early dynasties, the mythic symbols of Osiris and of Horus were merged into one system. Thus, the Horus who had defeated Seth, a possible reference to the wars of unification between Upper and Lower Egypt,[20] became also Horus the son of Osiris, the one who had vindicated his father against the enemy of the latter, Seth, the god associated with chaos and the opposite of creative life. In the new mythic pericope of Osiris/Horus/Seth we see an artful combination of politically based myth and nature based myth. The result of such a synthesis could only have been a further strengthening of the position of the divine kingship, for it had by now become associated not only with the solar religious tradition but also with the natural fertility cycle of the earth, the original concern of the Osirian tradition. The cosmic nature of the kingship was thus expanded to its fullest possibility, taking into itself the major mythic symbols of both traditions as they were combined in the Heliopolitan system. According to this new synthesized mythic system, Horus the Lord of Heaven, identified also with the sun god Ra, was incarnate in the earthly monarch, ruler of the Two Lands. The rule of the latter reflects the divine kingship of Atum which had first been established at the time of the creation, and was, therefore, indicative of the perfect order of Ma'at. The reigning king, the earthly Horus, at his death became Osiris in virtue of having been, during his earthly life, Horus son of Osiris. In such a system it appears that the earthly Horus (the king), as well as being an incarnation of the celestial Horus, the son of Ra, was also another hypostatic expression of Osiris. Osiris and Horus the son of Osiris were thus in essence different mythic expressions of the same divine power, two hypostases or *personae* of the mythic symbol of divine kingship. In accordance with his divine nature, therefore, the king was one personage, whether living or dead. As the living king, he was Horus the son of Osiris. As the dead king, he was transfigured into the figure of Osiris, thus passing from one level of deity to another, the mythic divinity of the monarch thus not being destroyed or made unreal by the obvious fact of his mortality.

The successor to the throne also fitted into the mythic pattern insofar as he became the ruling Horus on the death of the old king. Such accords very well with the myth of the conception and birth of Horus the son of Osiris after the murder of his father at the hands of Seth.[21] The birth of Horus is vividly dramatized, with perhaps a touch of intentional humour, in Spell 148 of the Coffin Texts.[22] (The institution of the coregency, it should be remembered, did not make its appearance until the Twelfth Dynasty with Amenemhet I and Senwosret I.[23]) The mythic device of making the king to be also the Son of Ra has already been discussed at an earlier stage in this work.[24] With this final step in the formulation of the royal mytho-theology, the basic mythical justification for the monarchy was completed. It is, however, somewhat ironic that shortly after this, during the Sixth Dynasty, the power and authority of the central monarchy began to weaken. It is as if the theory of the divine kingship began to lose its appeal once it had been established. This would be all the more certain if the tradition is accurate which relates the assassination of Teti I at the beginning of the Sixth Dynasty. Despite this, however, the myth of the divine kingship continued as the basic structure of royal mytho-theology throughout the rest of Egypt's history. The theological formulations of the Old Kingdom were obviously able to make a strong impact. Perhaps the reason for this is that the theology of the kingship provided a system which satisfied the religious needs of the state and the political organization by providing a mytho-theology which allowed for the existence of a deity who was transcendent in his celestial hypostasis and yet manifest in the earthly personage of the king.

A question arises at this point as to the actual nature of the divinity of the Egyptian monarch. Was he in fact a full god, equal to the major deities of the Egyptian pantheon and sharing totally in the divinity which set them apart from mortal men? Or did the divinity of the Pharaoh mean something else? Was he perhaps a god of a lesser nature, not to be compared with the celestial deities? Certainly the concept which the 'heretic' Akhenaten attempted to promulgate concerning his own position appears to have been one which claimed for him true divinity, possibly even total identification with the Aten himself.[25] Cyril Aldred has maintained that Akhenaten attempted a return to ideas of the divine kingship which belonged more to the age of Djoser, *i.e.*, the Third Dynasty, than they did to his own.[26] Nor can one deny that the place which Akhenaten and his family occupy in Amarna art seems to indicate that a strong hint of the actual divinity of the ruler was being given there. Akhenaten, however, cannot be taken as indicative of the normal Egyptian interpretation of the divinity of the king, his own position being one which was greatly exaggerated.

From the Middle Kingdom comes a cycle of six hymns addressed to Senwosret III, the last two of which have been largely destroyed. The first four,[27] however, are intact and may serve to present a good picture of the Middle Egyptian concept of the divine kingship. In these texts the monarch is praised for his strength, his victories and his goodness to the Two Lands. However, he appears to be regarded in the texts as more of a human hero than an actual deity. So also we must consider the aforementioned *Instruction for King Merikare* and *The Instruction of Amenemhet*. Both of these texts openly admit the fact that the king is mortal, perhaps all too mortal. Even such rulers as Thuthmose III and Ramses II do not appear to have been the actual equal of the gods. It is true that the cult of the king was very important in ancient Egypt and that thereby divine honours were paid to him. We must balance this, however, by the recognition that it was the duty of the Pharaoh to make the offerings to the traditional gods of Egypt, and at times he was even portrayed as kneeling before them, a relatively unusual position for the king, but nevertheless one which does occur. Even in the Amarna movement there is some indication that Akhenaten, although himself a deity, was still inferior to the god of the Amarna cult, the Aten.[28] Also the Pyramid texts seem to imply that it is only after his death that the true divinity of the king becomes a reality, many of the texts having been designed as rituals intended to effect the ascent of the monarch to the heavens where he would be subsequently deified. Such evidence seems to say that for the Egyptians the king could not have been seen as an actual deity equivalent to the great cosmic gods of the cult.

What then are we to make of the royal mytho-theology which seems to have been so carefully formulated in the Old Kingdom? Such expressions seem to indicate the full divinity of the monarch as the Horus incarnate and the Son of Ra. The answer here must surely lie in the very mythic nature of such symbols. Mythically speaking and as expressed in the cult there can be no doubt that the king was regarded as a deity. His very presence was the effective means of maintaining Ma'at and even mediating to the land the blessings of the great gods. Such, however, was and remained a mythic expression. For the Egyptian mind the power of the divine was in some mysterious way inherent within the person of the Pharaoh. He was in fact the 'good god' (*ntr nfr*), but he was not the 'Great God' (*ntr ꜥꜣ*). Such a title was reserved only for the gods who resided in the heavens and who were not seen by man, only apprehended in their manifestations in nature or their revelations in the cultic ritual. The king, himself a mythic expression of the divinity of the realm of the beyond, was not himself one of the great gods of Egypt. He was a symbol of their presence; he was a "token of the efficacious power of the creator god in the world."[29] In himself, however, the monarch was a mortal human being, the mythic symbol of the divine presence, and even one who after his death might well hope to join the gods. Nevertheless, even after death the Pharaoh could never hope to become the equal of Amun-Ra, Ra-Horakhtey or Ptah. Not even Thuthmose III or Ramses II, despite their much vaunted achievements would ever be a full member of the Egyptian pantheon. The king in the Pyramid texts was called the son of Nut and son of Isis,[30] but such was only in virtue of his mythic function. He himself was, and would remain, a mortal human being until the day of his death. It was only then that he could hope to be deified and to become united with the immortality of the divine life of the universe. After the end of the Old Kingdom, however, such a boon was available to all men, and was not only the prerogative of the monarch and of those on whom he was gracious enough to bestow it. During his earthly life the king was as mortal as the lowest of his subjects. Not even the mythic symbols of the Egyptian religious synthesis could change that fact.

The suggestion has been made that at an early point in the history of Egypt the ruling monarch was ritually put to death once his physical powers had waned or he had become too old to be any longer an effective symbol and agent of fertility.[31] (Such a practice might even lie behind some of the myths of early Greece, for example, the murder of Agamemnon by his wife Clytemnestra or the killing of his own father by Oedipus.) In all likelihood it would be possible to find in the mythology of most ancient cultures some examples to which this interpretation could be applied, and it is possible that in some cases such an interpretation might well be justified. There appears, however, not to be in ancient Egypt any real indication that such a *mise à mort* was ever practised,[32] and it is unlikely that many scholars would now take such a suggestion too seriously. Nevertheless, such a practice could have been in keeping with the mythic signification of the king, particularly in his role as a mediator of divine blessings to the land, most specifically the blessing of fertility. For evidence of such a practice one might suggest that the tradition of the scattering of the pieces of the dismembered body of Osiris by Seth could be seen as a mythic symbol of the sowing of the earth. (The imagery of the various parts of Osiris' body buried throughout the length and breadth of the land certainly does seem to bear this signification.) This need not, however, have implied the actual killing and dismemberment of the aged monarch as a necessity for the performance of such a ritual. The *mise à mort* of the ruler should, therefore, probably be taken as a myth in the modern popular sense of the term, *i.e.*, as fictitious.

If such a ritual killing of the king in the early, *i.e.*, predynastic, period were a plausible theory, it would probably add little, if anything at all, to our understanding of the mytho-theological significance of the Pharaoh. It might, however, offer a possible explanation for the origins of the famous Sed Festival, often called, although wrongly, the Jubilee, the Sed Festival thus being a substitution for the actual ritual killing. An older interpretation of the Egyptian term *ḥb-sd* presented it as being a *dreissigjährige Jubiläum des Königs*,[33] a thirty year festival. However, it now appears unlikely that the Sed Festival was such a thirty year festival or any type of regnal jubilee.[34] The instances of rulers celebrating a Sed Festival at times other than after a thirty year period are too numerous to support the theory of a 'thirty year festival'. For example, we find that the Sed Festival was celebrated by Mentuhotep V in his second regnal year, by Hatshepsut in the fifteenth year of her reign, by Akhenaten in his sixth year, and by Osorkon II in his twenty-second year.[35] The frequency with which Ramses II kept the Sed Festival is too well known to require any further comment, but it does strongly militate against the idea of such a festival being a thirty year celebration.[36]

C.J. Bleeker, basing his opinion on the fact that the term *sd* may mean a garment or a piece of clothing (and such is the case if the term is determined by the sign 𓋴 [37]), maintains that the purpose of the Sed Festival was the renewal of the priestly office of the king.[38] In such an interpretation, the term *ḥb-sd* might be translated as 'the festival of the clothing' or 'the festival of the investiture', with the significance that the putting on of the Sed garment indicated a renewal of the royal priestly powers. This interpretation of the Sed Festival is an interesting one and may well be a possibility. However, it appears that the term *ḥb-sd* does not have the hieroglyph 𓋴 as its usual determinative, but is rather determined with the sign 𓈀 [39] which has the significance of a tongue of land. Hence, the priestly nature of the Sed Festival may be perhaps somewhat tenuous, although the possibility need not and should not be entirely rejected. More likely, however, is the older interpretation that the Sed Festival signified the king's action of renewing his tenure of the rule of the Two Lands, and that it may have been celebrated by the monarch carrying out a ritual circumambulation of the Sed Festival court in token of assuming his kingship. I am further tempted to suggest that the actual origins of the festival may have been in remote antiquity as a graphic means of the king actually demonstrating that he still had the physical stamina to rule Egypt. Whatever the case may be, further speculation on the Sed Festival would probably be fruitless, its full signification being buried too far in antiquity.

If perchance the suggestion of Bleeker is correct and the Sed Festival was indeed a re-investiture of the priestly power in the king, it would be in accordance with one of the royal functions. In theory it was the king himself who was the true priest of the Egyptian cults. In actual practice, however, the duties of carrying out the daily rituals of cultic worship were deputized to the priestly class, the king himself conducting the rites only on certain festive occasions. Nevertheless, the reality and the source of priestly power lay within the king. It was the monarch alone who was the genuine intermediary between man and the gods, and hence only he who had the priestly character within him in virtue of his very nature and his office. His priestly character stemmed directly from the fact that he was the Son of Ra. Hence, he was the one individual who could properly stand in an intermediary position between man and the gods. In his position of a mortal who was also in a mythic fashion the real and effective symbol of the divine presence on earth, *i.e.*, since he was the 'good god', the divinity which was within him functioned as the element which made it possible for him to stand before the gods, thus bridging the gap between the earthly world and the divine. He was in fact the actual bridge by which contact could be made between the two worlds. That he rarely functioned liturgically in reality made little difference, for the royal priestly power was delegated to the priestly classes who were thus authorized to stand in his stead. Moreover, the very presence of the king in the Two Lands indicated that the priestly power within the state was indeed a reality. Hence, when the state cults were celebrated, it was sufficient that the priestly power be seen as present in the person of the monarch as a symbol and proof of its presence within the state. He himself was not required to be present at each cultic celebration in order to make the priestly power effective and operative. As long as the king was alive in the land, the priestly power was there as well. The mythic nature of the king, therefore, permitted the proper efficacious functioning of the state cults, and they in turn were able to accomplish the function for which they had been instituted.

All of this discussion concerning the nature of the monarch can be summed up in one brief remark: the Pharaoh was the sole effective means whereby Ma'at was maintained on the earth and in the state. When he ascended the throne as ruler, Ma'at was again re-established as it had been originally at the time of creation. Throughout the duration of his life he was the living and ever-present symbol of the continuation of Ma'at. When the order of Ma'at was threatened or disturbed, it was the king who would take positive action, by whatever means were necessary, to restore that order to its proper place. In this one individual there was summed up the true basis for the security of both the Egyptian state and even the universe itself. Insofar as he was the legitimate heir of the gods, the rights of his divine kingship could hardly be challenged. As the son of Ra and as Horus the son of Hathor, the Pharaoh brought into tangible and visible reality the celestial powers of the sky gods. As Horus the son of Osiris, he was further the embodiment of the fertile power inherent within the earth. As Osiris himself after death, the Pharaoh continued to exercise the power and influence which he had had while alive in his mortal form. The Egyptian Pharaoh was thus an integrating symbol, drawing together and actualizing within his person all aspects of existence, the earth, the sky, the political realm, human society and nature itself. He was the embodiment of the order of Ma'at which was in all of these. The fact that as late as the Twenty-Fifth Dynasty the same essential interpretation of the Pharaonic power was again put forward in the text known as *The Memphite Theology* bears witness to the essential importance and indispensability of the royal throne and its occupant.

Notes

[1] Translation in M. Lichtheim, *Ancient Egyptian Literature*, I, 135ff.
[2] *ibid.*, 135.
[3] A.H. Gardiner, *Egypt of the Pharaohs*, Oxford, 1961, 436.
[4] Translation in M. Lichtheim, *op. cit.*, I, 222-135.

[5] *Sinuhe*, B,1-19.
[6] A.H. Gardiner, "The Autobiography of Rekhmire," *ZÄS* 60 (1925): 69.
[7] It will be remembered that the creator deity, the sun god, had established himself as the first king at the time of the creation. The Egyptian Pharaoh had inherited this position by direct descent according to the mythic formulations.
[8] Translation in M. Lichtheim, *op. cit.*, I, 97ff.
[9] H. Frankfort, *Kingship and the Gods*, 15.
[10] H. Frankfort, *Ancient Egyptian Religion*, 53.
[11] M. Sandman, *Texts from the Time of Akhenaten*, 91.9.
[12] *ibid.*, 91.4.
[13] The theme of the defeat of disorder stands out in the Heliopolitan tradition by means of two symbols: Atum's first imposition of order on the chaos of Nun by the creation of light, an obvious cosmic symbol; and the defeat of Seth by Horus, a symbol which has more evident political overtones. As the direct successor of these mythic actions, the Pharaoh held an office which was both cosmic and political, effective over the natural world and over the realm of human government.
[14] C.J. Bleeker, *Egyptian Festivals*, 110.
[15] A.H. Gardiner, *Egyptian Grammar*, 72.
[16] C.J. Bleeker, *op, cit.*, 117.
[17] A.H. Gardiner, *loc. cit.*
[18] R. Anthes, *JNES* XVIII (1959): 179.
[19] *loc. cit.*
[20] It is possible that in the myth of the struggle between Horus and Seth some reflection of the wars in question may be seen. Such an interpretation, however, is by no means certain, and it is entirely possible that the myth may have a more natural background.
[21] R. Anthes, *op. cit.*, 175ff.
[22] *CT* II, 209c-226a.
[23] W.J. Murnane, *Ancient Egyptian Coregencies* (Chicago: The Oriental Institute, 1977), 1.
[24] See Chapter III above.
[25] C. Aldred, *Egyptian Art* (London, 1980), 174.
[26] *ibid.*, 180.
[27] Translation in M. Lichtheim, *op. cit.*, I, 198ff.
[28] J. Baines, "'Greatest God' or Category of God," *GM* 67 (1983): 21.
[29] E. Hornung, *Conceptions of God in Ancient Egypt*, 142.
[30] *PT* 1703a-c.
[31] A. Moret, *La mise à mort du dieu en Egypte* (Paris, 1927), 50. See also G.A. Wainwright, *The Sky Religion in Egypt* (Cambridge, 1938), 5.
[32] C.J. Bleeker, *op. cit.*, 114.
[33] *Wb* III, 59.

[34] H. Bonnet, *Reallexikon der ägyptischen Religionsgeschichte* (Berlin, 1952), 963.
[35] *ibid.*, 160.
[36] Insofar as there seems to have been no set pattern of regular intervals at which the Sed Festival was celebrated, one may well ask why any one particular monarch would have decided to celebrate this festival at a specific time. For this there can be no definite answer, the Egyptian sources themselves being silent on the meaning of the ritual, as they are on most aspects of religious practices. An interesting suggestion, however, has been put forward that the various celebrations of the Sed Festival may have been prompted by some "critical phase" in the lives of various kings (C.J. Bleeker, *op.cit.*, 122). There is, of course, no way to determine what sort of event or occurrence would have been considered to be such a "critical phase". However, if such was indeed the criterion for the decision to celebrate the ritual, it could explain the action of Akhenaten in celebrating a Sed Festival in the sixth year of his reign. This year, being the date of his move to his new capital of Akhetaten, a Sed Festival held at that time would have served as a token to mark the inauguration of what Akhenaten himself must have considered a new period in the history of Egypt.
[37] *Wb* IV, 365.
[38] C.J. Bleeker, *op. cit.*, 120ff.
[39] A.H. Gardiner, *Egyptian Grammar*, Sign List, N20.

VII. Osiris

Of all the Egyptian gods, Osiris is by far the most familiar to us. We know him in essentially three different, although related, aspects: as a deity of vegetation and fertility, as a god of rebirth after death, and as the divine judge and king of the dead. The myth surrounding Osiris appears to be the best known and the most highly developed and extended of all the Egyptian myths. The full saga of Osiris reaches almost epic proportions, forming a legend marked by numerous details and woven into a tightly constructed plot. It is thanks to the account given by Plutarch that our knowledge of the Osiris tradition is so complete. Unfortunately there is a tendency simply to accept the information transmitted by Plutarch at its face value and not to question the accuracy of his version. It is essential, however, to remember that Plutarch was a Greek writing against the background of Greek traditions and concepts of myth, and fully expecting to see in the Egyptian traditions mythic formulations of the same nature as those of Greece. It is, therefore, quite possible and altogether probable that the Osiris myth as related by Plutarch represents a construction of a somewhat new and non-Egyptian myth out of the original elements of the Egyptian tradition, resulting in a final product which treats these elements as if they all could be fitted together in a neat and finished literary format.

Such a treatment of the Osiris traditions totally neglects and even misunderstands the true nature of the original mythic symbolism. In theory, each element of the original Osiris traditions should be able to stand independently from the others as an expression of some mythic truth and reality. Once, however, these elements have been combined and made into component and related parts of a wider narrative, they stand in danger of losing their original mythic significance and becoming subordinated to the broader and more extended fictional creation.[1] Thus, a reliance on the account of Osiris as it is given in the work of Plutarch implies the acceptance an interpretation of the myth which has been made on the basis of non-Egyptian thought and non-Egyptian methods of comprehension. Such an understanding can do nothing but hide the signification of the early mythic values of Osiris, perhaps even superimposing new meanings on them, and the result will be a misconception of the theological values of the original traditions.

The question which arises from all of this is: Was there really such a thing as a single authentic Egyptian myth of Osiris? Should the mythic elements be combined and connected into a larger narrative framework, or should they be seen only as separate and disconnected symbols, each one standing in its own right to signify a particular apprehension of reality? Such questions cannot easily be answered. To be certain, we would be mistaken if we were to ignore the original signification of each of the elements within the Osiris tradition. Whatever theological values these various mythic elements may have had must be recognized and given their proper places within the Egyptian synthesis. Each element, in other words, must be seen for what it originally was, and not as it was later fitted into a wider pattern. This, however, is no easy task, and we are forced to admit that even for the Egyptians themselves many of these elements must have lost at least some portion of their original values. At the same time the extended structured version of the Osiris myth also had its value. With the conjoining of the originally separate Osiris and Horus traditions by the Egyptian mytho-theologians, a certain narrative tradition was formed from the pristine mythic elements, a narrative which served a specific political and theological ideology. Nevertheless, the work of the Egyptian myth-makers did not totally conceal the original meaning of the various mythic elements which went into the final product, nor was there ever any real intention of concealing such. The flexibility and more open attitude of the mythopoeic mind did not demand the suppression of seemingly contradictory or undesirable elements found in the primary sources. Thus, the Osiris traditions may be legitimately considered in two ways: as a collection of separate mythic symbols, and as an extended mythic narrative which was formulated out of these symbols. We must, however, bear in mind that there appears to have existed no official orthodox Egyptian narrative account of the Osiris myth. Whatever understanding of an extended pericope there may have been was quite obviously flexible and changing in accordance with the needs of the cultic setting in which it would have been expressed and articulated.

The myth of Osiris may be categorized in two different ways. From one point of view it may be seen as a mythic symbol which underlined the basic stability of the Egyptian kingship. This is evident in the symbol of the final defeat of Seth by Horus and the establishment of the latter in the position of King of Upper and Lower Egypt. As has been seen in the previous chapter on the Egyptian kingship, Horus and Osiris may be viewed as two different hypostases of the same divine being, the personification of kingship. From another point of view, the Osiris myth may be seen as an affirmation of the positive principle of life and the continuity of the same despite the inevitable fact of death. Death in the Osiris myth, since it was brought about by the murder of Osiris at the hands of Seth, may even be seen as a perversion of the perfect order of life. One ought not, however, attempt to adopt exclusively one of these interpretations of the myth, for certainly the Egyptians do not appear to have preferred one over the other, nor in fact are the two contradictory or mutually exclusive. The Osiris myth rather combined both of these two themes into the one single pattern.

Viewed from a somewhat wider perspective, specifically that of its mythological content, the myth of Osiris may be characterized as a myth of the dying and rising god. Such a theme was not an uncommon one in Near Eastern mythology. To quote but two examples from the ancient world, we have the myth of Tammuz who died in the heat of summer, and the myth of Ba'al who was slain by Mot, the god of death, the latter myth being known most clearly from the Ugaritic texts. In the case of the latter two myths, the principle of resurrection was quite vivid and dramatic, the deities actually returning to life on the earth. With the figure of Osiris, however, the situation was quite different. Osiris did not have an actual process of resurrection, not, at least, in the land of the living. While Osiris was definitely revitalized and reborn, this took place only in the underworld, the realm of the dead. He in no way returned to the original fullness of his earthly physical self. Instead, the place of Osiris in the land of the living was taken over by his son Horus who, as we have seen, may be considered as another hypostasis or expression of the deity symbolized by the mythic figure of Osiris. This mythic expression of the divine figure in two distinct hypostases was, no doubt, the result of the historical development of the myth, that is, the conjoining of the Horus myth with the myth of Osiris. We may note that the fact that Osiris was not resurrected to his original state of life was possibly an Egyptian way of recognizing the reality of death and the totally different quality of eternal life. The reality of death could not simply be made non-existent by the mythic symbol. Life which emerged from death had, according to the mythic pattern, to involve a type of transformation such as was seen in the rebirth of Osiris in the next world.

At the risk of over-interpreting the myth of Osiris and imposing upon it categories which would have been foreign to the Egyptian mind, we may subdivide the myth into three basic levels which correspond exactly to the three divisions of mythic action contained in the tradition. These three divisions are as follows:

1. The existence of Osiris as ruler of Egypt and creator of order in the kingship of the Two Lands;
2. The murder of Osiris by Seth;
3. The defeat of Seth by Horus, the vindication of Osiris and his establishment as eternal ruler and judge in the land of the dead. Also contemporaneous with this latter event was the final establishment of Horus in the position of his father.

Interpreting these three divisions of the mythic action, we may place them into the categories of topological mythology (the description of a state or order), historical mythology (the narration of events which took place at specific mythic times), and again topological mythology wherein is described the ideal state which has been realized as a result of the historical mythology. The expression 'historical mythology' as used here does not imply that the mythic content itself was based on actual historical fact, although there may well have been some historical elements which had contributed to it, possibly the Wars of Unification in the Pre-dynastic era. 'Historical mythology' in this case refers to a pattern of sequential actions, one or more specific events which were seen as having occurred within the mythic pericope and, once they were completed, had no more lasting effects on the topological situation. Their significance lay in the fact of their specific occurrence rather than in any wider or eternal setting.[2] Viewed in such a manner, the myth of Osiris appears as a purposely constructed narrative, one which in its scope was more extensive than any other of the Egyptian myths. Even in this latter fact the Osiris myth appears to be somewhat different than the normal Egyptian myth, the latter being usually non-detailed and relatively non-dramatic.

The figure of Osiris can be contrasted with the other Egyptian deities in yet a second aspect. For the most part the deities of Egypt appear as transcendent gods, to a great extent removed from the world of men. This, however, does not imply a total rift between those deities and the creation. We have seen already how that in creation mythology the power of the creator deity was very much manifest in the universe, and was in fact the very source of the being and existence of that universe. At the same time it was the transcendence of such deities which gave them the power to act and to manifest themselves in the natural order and in the political order. Osiris, by way of contrast, does not appear to have had the same degree of transcendence as the other gods. He was rather, in his basic essence, immanent within the world, specifically within the world of nature, being the actual power and force of fertility.[3] His immanence is even further underscored by the fact that it was primarily with him that the dead were identified in their resurrection in the next world. In these his aspects as both a deity of fertility and one of resurrection, Osiris was intimately connected with men, their dependence upon him being more immediate and more vital than was their dependence upon any other deity. Osiris had a very direct effect on the existence and well-being of each and every individual. He was related to men in a manner which was highly pragmatic and practical, representing far more than just a theory of universal and political stability, as important as such may have been in the wider context of the state and humanity. What Osiris offered was connected with the existence and prosperity of individuals, both in the present world and in the next. He was the source of personal and individual existence even beyond death. It is little wonder that his cult had such wide appeal.

Our understanding of the nature of Osiris would be greatly enhanced if it were possible to see his origins and development with certainty. Opinions on even his place of origin have varied from one scholar to another. Some have seen in Osiris a god who was brought into Egypt from a foreign source, although J.G. Griffiths has argued that Osiris was a native Egyptian deity who had originated in Upper Egypt.[4] The complex scholarly debate over the origins of Osiris has not, however, yielded any definitive results. Nevertheless, it is tempting to suggest that, given the early Egyptian resistance to foreign influences, a native Egyptian source for Osiris may well be a strong possibility. The writing of the name of Osiris[5] does not give any real indication of the meaning of the name itself (*Wsir* in Egyptian). Attempts to reconstruct the meaning of the name out of the hieroglyphs used to represent it seem to be relatively indecisive. The best that any scholar can do in this regard is to offer an opinion which may or may not be correct. If the name and person of Osiris were in fact foreign imports, no interpretation of the name in accordance with Egyptian linguistic roots will be of any benefit to our understanding of the personality of the god. If, on the other hand, Osiris originated from within Egypt, then an interpretation of his name as a native Egyptian one would be of definite value. In this connection Griffiths, who does maintain an

Egyptian origin for Osiris, has suggested that the name may derive from the root *wsr*, 'to be strong'.6 Although his arguments may not be entirely convincing to all, Griffiths does at least present a plausible suggestion. By interpreting the name of Osiris to mean 'The Strong One", we would at least have a definition of his name which would be in accordance with the nature he shows throughout Egypt's history, for their can be no doubt that Osiris was indeed a powerful religious force. If the Osiris/Horus mytho-theology of the kingship originated as a result of the unification of Egypt, then Osiris himself must have been already well-established by the beginning of the First Dynasty. Even if he was not native Egyptian, he definitely had become by that time firmly Egyptianized.

In considering both the origins and nature of Osiris one important characteristic of the deity must be remembered, namely that, in at least some early traditions, he was considered as a type of demon, one who was hostile to the dead, at least to the royal dead. In Utterance 534 of the Pyramid texts we find the following prayer for the protection of the dead king against Osiris and his entourage:

> May Osiris not come with his evil coming;
> Do not open your arms to him.7

In the context of the same Utterance, this prayer is used against the hostile attacks of other deities as well, against Horus (obviously as the son of Osiris), against Seth, Thoth, Isis and Nephthys. All of these gods appear as deities who were not originally connected with the solar religion of Heliopolis. Hence, the existence of prayers against them must indicate an early hostility between the solar religious system and the chthonic religious system connected with Osiris. It was obviously from this hostility that Osiris, at least in the circles which professed the solar religion, received his demonic character. At the same time, and even within the context of the same Utterance, Horus and Osiris are presented as being favourable to the dead king, as are also, Seth, Thoth, Isis and Nephthys. The Utterance in question thus displays an obvious blending of the two traditions and a willingness of the part of the solar tradition to accept the symbolism of the chthonic Osiris, a good example of the Egyptian willingness and ability to accept eventually two opposing sets of mythic symbols. In yet another Pyramid Text we see the opposition between Ra and Osiris, an opposition which had obviously existed before the general acceptance of Osiris and his entourage into the normal Egyptian pantheon:

> Atum-Ra has not given you to Osiris,
> And he shall not possess your heart.[8]

Immediately following this[9] we find the same prayer made against the power of Horus (Son of Osiris) to seize the soul of the dead king. In the same vein we find also the following affirmation:

> O Osiris, you are not powerful against him;
> Your son is not powerful against him.
> O Horus, you are not powerful against him;
> Your father is not powerful against him.[10]

We can thus detect in the Pyramid Texts clear evidence for an early hostility against Osiris on the part of the solar religious system. At the same time we see the results of a later synthesis of the two traditions, a synthesis in which the deities associated with Osiris have now become favourable to the dead monarch. Most important, however, is the fact that the deities of the Osiris tradition could be used even in the same text as symbols to express both good and evil powers, powers which even by Egyptian religious logic should only be totally opposed to one another. The fact that such opposing symbols could thus be used together in the same text with two opposing meanings seems to provide clear evidence that the figures of Osiris and the other gods were being used in such texts purely for their symbolic value and that they did not necessarily represent specific personal deities.

By the time of the Coffin Texts (Middle Kingdom) when Osiris had long since been accepted as a legitimate mythic symbol, we still occasionally find this same demonic aspect associated with him. For example, in Spell 229 of the Coffin Texts we find the following prayer offered against the might of Osiris:

> May you rescue me from the fishermen of Osiris,
> Those who cut off heads, those who sever necks.[11]

The terror and fear inspired by Osiris and his followers are also expressed in Spell 236 of the Coffin Texts where Osiris and his entourage appear as essentially demonic being who are hostile to the spirits of the dead and who are obviously to be avoided in the next world if possible. The following description of those who belong to the entourage of Osiris makes the undesirability of their presence quite obvious:

> O you who are terrible of face, agents of Osiris,
> You who close the mouths of the spirits because
> of what is within them...[12]

The text then proceeds further to state that these demons are to have no power over the deceased. Spell 498 also presents Osiris and the gods which surround him as hostile to the dead, the intent of the spell being that the dead should ascend to the sky with Ra and thus escape the realms of Osiris.[13] Of such a nature also are Spells 499 and 500.[14] Even during the New Kingdom the Book of the Dead, although much of its symbolism depends upon a positive view of Osiris, does not avoid this demonic representation of him:

> Cut down those who are in the following of Osiris.
> May they not be mighty against me;
> May I not go down before their knives.[15]

I have stressed the various images of the demonic nature of Osiris not in order to give the impression that such a nature was one of his chief characteristics, but to underscore the impact which it had made during at least one stage of Egyptian religious history. For the most part it was the positive and beneficial concept of Osiris which survived into the official corpus of Egyptian mythic symbolism. However, one may use these demonic presentations of Osiris as a means of recalling that to the Egyptian experience, death, despite the promise of immortality, still retained about itself something of the terrible, the fearful and the awesome. Of this negative aspect of death Osiris made as good a symbol as he did of the positive blessed state awaiting man in the next world. The many recollections of the demonic nature which Osiris once held bear testimony to the hostile attitude against him in the very early periods of Egypt's history. The fact that Osiris was eventually accepted into the general pantheon points to the normal Egyptian way of tolerance in matters of religious symbolism.

We shall see Osiris more fully in his aspect of a god of rebirth and resurrection when we consider the Egyptian idea of man's immortality in the following chapter. For the present, let us briefly define the general nature of Osiris before proceeding to a more theological consideration.

Osiris, as is evident in so many of the mortuary texts,[16] was manifest in the phenomena of the life of nature. He was seen in the growing grain and the vegetation of the land; he was seen also in the waters of the Nile, for it was these waters, the 'great efflux of Osiris', which brought fertility to the land and allowed it to produce its crops. A Pyramid text provides a very beautiful description of this manifestation of Osiris, the theological and mythic value of the passage being underscored all the more by the poetic format of the passage:

> O you whose *'b* tree is green, the one who is upon
> his field,
> O opener of the blossom, the one who is upon his
> sycamore,
> O brightness of the banks, the one who is upon his
> *im'* tree,
> O Lord of green fields...[17]

It would be difficult to find a more striking description of the vivid manifestation of the deity in nature and the revelation of his power of creation and regeneration. It is not at all surprising that the Egyptian, observing the yearly return of the life of the world of nature, became convinced that the same deity who accomplished this must also bring about the rebirth of the dead. True enough, there was no visible or physical resurrection in the present world, but the Egyptian none the less knew, or perhaps apprehended by the non-intellectual faculty of his personality, that the dead were reborn in another world, the same world where the mythical action of Osiris had taken place. Thus, from an observation of nature, the manifestation of the power of Osiris, the Egyptian conceived the idea of human immortality, and this became naturally the domain of Osiris.

In the manifestation of Osiris in the Nile and in the vegetation, the Egyptian did not see some form of pantheism, nor did he comprehend that the deity was actually the earth and the Nile itself. Osiris was not the actual inundation, not the actual flood waters which rose each year to cover the land. Rather he was the life force which was stimulated by the flood,[18] or which was in the flood itself as a hidden and mystic power. Osiris was not the actual water, but rather a particular function of that water, the source of the fertility and life which was inherent within it.[19] One might thus be tempted to say that, for the Egyptian, Osiris was the abstract principle of life. This may be partially true, but he was even more than that. The principle of life, represented in the figure of Osiris, was symbolized in the concrete imagery of the water and in the concrete image of the personalized deity. For the Egyptian, therefore, life was not an abstraction; it was a force which was real and almost tangible. Life was not simply the result of certain mechanical actions of the human body or of the workings of the natural world. Life, in other words, was not automatically produced. Life, in the Egyptian outlook, was something which was real and perceptible. Not produced by a force ulterior to itself, it was itself its own source, and its production was in fact reproduction, self-reproduction and self-generation. Life was continuous and eternal for the simple reason that such was its nature. It was in essence a living organism, indestructible, as the Egyptian experience of nature proved. Life was none other than Osiris himself. Such was the position of that deity within the Egyptian mytho-theological synthesis, a position which was both central and all-encompassing.

The central shrine of the rites of Osiris was at Abydos, where the mysteries of the deity were performed annually. There can be no doubt that these mysteries had a set form of liturgy, although such must surely have changed and developed over the course of the centuries. Unfortunately we possess no written document giving the text of the ritual, and hence we are unable to see clearly the full cultic representation of the Osiris myth. There does, however, exist a very important and interesting document from the Middle Kingdom, the stele of Ikhernofret,[20] which gives a few hints of the content of the ritual. There is in this text a sufficient, although vague, description to indicate that the central stress of the ritual was the conflict which led to the death and rebirth of Osiris. There can also be no doubt that with the connotations of the continuing divine life represented in such a ritual there was combined the significance of the stability of the earthly monarch, the Pharaoh. It is probably in such a context that there occurred in the ritual the raising of the Djed column. The exact origin of this symbol is again a matter which is somewhat uncertain, although the root $\underline{d}di$ from which its name was derived appears to have signified stability or steadiness (*Beständigkeit*).[21] The association of the erection of the Djed column with the action of the Pharaoh would have implied that the latter thereby strengthened his own rule and the kingship in general by participation in the rites of Osiris, the resurrection of the god being the mythic occurrence which rendered possible the cultic erection of the column. There is in the Book of the Dead an expression which directly reflects the connection of Osiris with the kingship of the Two Lands. Here Osiris is called 'Lord of the *wrrt* crown, the Lofty One of the white crown' (*nb wrrt k3 ḥd*).²² In the Papyrus of Ani the word *wrrt* is written with the determinative of the double crown, while the term *ḥd* is determined with the figure of the white crown of Upper Egypt. Hence, the expression *nb wrrt* seems to refer to Osiris (and to the Pharaoh) as ruler of the Two Lands, while the title *k3 ḥd* gives a possible reference to the historic conquest of the North by the South. The Abydos ritual thus appears to have combined historical memory, political ideology and the symbolism of the resurrected life of Osiris.

The fullest Egyptian account of the myth of Osiris occurs on the stele of Amenmose,²³ and takes the form of a hymn to the deity himself. While the text makes reference to many of the elements of the Osiris myth, it in no way gives a full and ordered account of that myth. The final section of the hymn expresses the praises of Horus, thus indirectly lauding the ruling Pharaoh who was himself the incarnation of the latter deity. The hymn has its value insofar as it confirms that many of the mythic elements of Osiris were in actuality conjoined in the Egyptian tradition to produce, if not an actual continuous narrative, at least an extended concept. Moreover, it confirms the fact that many of our modern theological interpretations of the Osiris myth do agree with the Egyptian concept. However, it must be noted that the hymn is the type of text which can justly be called theological, and one which was probably not intended for recitation during a cultic re-enactment of the myth. Thus, while the hymn of Amenmose does contribute something to our understanding of the Osiris myth, it illustrates even more strongly the growth of a deep theological tradition of Osiris, a theological tradition which had taken shape out of the original mythic symbols. Finally, since the text dates from the Eighteenth Dynasty, we may regard it as a product of the theological acumen which was becoming prominent at that period. The text of the hymn clearly shows that even in connection with Osiris there was now emerging a keen sense of universalism. That universalism would become most strongly emphasized and developed through its connection with Amun-Ra of Thebes, thus forming one of the chief characteristics of Egyptian religion during the Eighteenth and Nineteenth Dynasties, and constituting a possible influence on Akhenaten. The connection of universalist ideas with Osiris serves all the more to underline the importance with which that deity was viewed within the context of Egyptian religious thought. The most striking feature of the hymn of Amenmose, however, is the fact that it illustrates the constantly growing importance of the Osirian theological tradition. It is with a consideration of the theological values of the Osiris myth that we shall bring this section of our study to a conclusion.

The first division of the Osiris myth which has been designated above by the expression 'topological mythology' has as its main function the articulation of the perfect order. Herein there is a mythic portrayal of the nature of both cosmos and kingship. In this mythic articulation the ordering force of the universe is portrayed as:

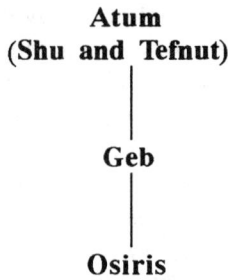

The signification of such imagery was the expression of the concept of cosmic order (Ma'at) in the three levels at which this order was apprehended by the Egyptian experience. The mythic figure of Atum points to the existence of a totally abstract, intangible and undefined principle of order. This principle then serves as the basis for a more concrete expression of order, one which is articulated in the visible and the specific. The figures of Shu and Tefnut, with their marked characteristics of masculinity and femininity, serve as transitional figures, articulating the undifferentiated procreative principle inherent within the male/female Atum, although they do not as yet signify the emergence of an actual tangible created order. Nevertheless, they point towards the real potential for such a creation. The creation itself becomes visible in the figure of Geb, the offspring of Shu and Tefnut, the separate and distinct male and female elements within the general creative principle, Tefnut herself being a personification of Ma'at.

The descent of Geb from the mythic figures Shu and Tefnut is in essence his descent from Atum, Shu and Tefnut being the manifestation of the full procreative power represented by the more abstract Atum. As such, they signify the actual ability of the generative force of Atum to be active as opposed to the pure potentiality which lies in the male/female Atum. The natural result of this is the mythic symbol of Geb who, along with his female counterpart Nut, is indicative of the created structure of the universe. At such a level the principle of order (Ma'at) is expressed in the visible and tangible creation of the physical cosmos, and in the latter the creative principle finds its full expression. In the creative act, the creative principle has produced something specific as seen visibly in the universe and expressed mythically in Geb. For the Egyptian mentality, it was important to give an actual personification to this tangible creation, for such a personal expression, in the absence of a scientific world view, was the only means of expressing the logic and rationality of the created cosmos. The figure of Geb, therefore, appears as a statement of the actualization of the divine creative principle, providing a concrete rationale for specific existence, a rationale which modern theology has expressed in terms of 'the Ground of Being', to use the words of the late Paul Tillich. In the figure of Osiris, the third level of this 'topological mythology', the principle of cosmic order (Ma'at) is extended into the political realm, the realm of the actual governance of human and state affairs. Again, for the Egyptian mind, this extension of Ma'at into the political had to be expressed through the presence of a mythic symbol, in this case Osiris, such an expression constituting a mytho-theological justification of the political order. Hence the mythic portrait of Atum/Geb/Osiris as given above may be interpreted in more abstract terminology as:

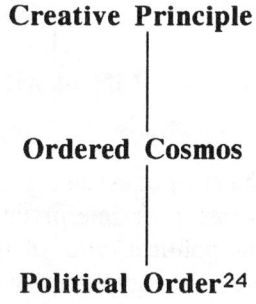

Creative Principle

Ordered Cosmos

Political Order[24]

One must, however, beware of falling into the misunderstanding of thinking that to the Egyptian mind the symbolism of Atum/Geb/Osiris was no more than an allegorical expression of something which could be intellectually comprehended by the more abstract means presented here. The central point is that the Egyptian mind was not capable of comprehending in an abstract manner a rationale of the natural and political cosmos. Hence, the Egyptian would not have seen the mythic configuration of Atum/Geb/Osiris as a simplistic symbol which could be translated into other terms. It was rather a *mythic* symbol, a symbol, that is, which was in actual fact that which it symbolized. Hence, no distinction was made by the Egyptian between Atum and the Creative principle, between Geb and the Ordered Cosmos, or between Osiris and the Political Order. In each case the symbol and the symbolized were but one real existent entity, and the mind was not expected to differentiate between them.

This theologization of the Atum/Geb/Osiris symbolism is specifically concerned with a 'political' expression of the universe. However, there was also in the Egyptian consciousness the knowledge or at least apprehension of the living nature of the universe, of the principle of life itself expressed in the cosmic order. Hence, the mythic symbolism of Atum/Geb/Osiris may also be given a theological interpretation as:

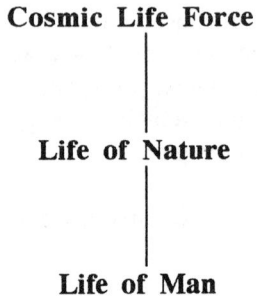

Cosmic Life Force

Life of Nature

Life of Man

Again, let us not make the error of assuming that for the Egyptian mind the above was another expression or interpretation of the Atum/Geb/Osiris mythic symbol. As in the political order of the cosmos, so in the natural order of the cosmos as well, the Egyptian would have been able to make no distinction between the Atum/Geb/Osiris symbol and the living organism signified thereby. The symbol and the symbolized still remained identical. As a result of the above theologization, we may see the Egyptian expression of the topological division of the myth in question as having the following signification:

Atum = Creative Principle = Cosmic Life Force

Geb = Ordered Cosmos = Life of Nature

Osiris = Political Order = Life of Man

The simplicity of the mythic symbolism of Atum/Geb/Osiris, with its three levels of perception, thus expressed for the Egyptian the complexity of the existential universe as both a living organism and a political reality, no distinction being made (or even being necessary) between the latter two aspects. For the Egyptian mind these were one and the same reality. Atum/Geb/Osiris was the reality which was experienced and apprehended, its mythic expression being the non-intellectual spiritualization of the cosmic system. It will be noted that in the above interpretation of the mythic system in question no mention has been made of the feminine principles expressed in Tefnut, Nut and Isis. The reason for this is the simple fact that these feminine deities had their mythic function and significance in their relationship to the three male deities. This does not imply any sense of subservience on the part of the female deities, for, at least in the case of Tefnut and Nut, they were integral components of Atum and Geb. Tefnut, insofar as she was the female counterpart of Shu, was in effect the feminine principle inherent within Atum, of whom both she and Shu were hypostatic extensions. Nut, being the female counterpart of Geb, was likewise the feminine complement of the tangible expression of creation within the latter deity. Geb, the earth, was equally and logically balanced by Nut, the sky. Isis also held a significance similar to that of Tefnut and Nut, although not within the topological division of the myth. Isis at this stage should probably be seen as no more than a personification of the royal throne which was in itself the basis for the kingly power. It was she who 'created' or 'bore' the king, these expressions again being understood in a mythic fashion. As such, the creative aspect of Isis takes its importance only with the emergence of

Horus into the mythic symbolism. At such a point, however, the maternal aspect of Isis equally balances the paternal aspect of Osiris so that the conjunction of the two deities produces the fullness of the procreative potential which is then actualized in Horus/Pharaoh.

The mythic symbolism as it is here interpreted creates the concept of an order which is basically unified despite the fact that it is given its expression through a plurality of deities. If these deities are considered from the point of view of mythic symbolism, we must state that they stand as individual hypostases. However, when seen from the viewpoint of theological interpretation, that is, as symbols in a mytho-theological synthesis, it is possible to maintain that they were not so much hypostatic beings as they were personifications of the complex aspects and manifestations of the creative force. The cosmos and the deities which mythically represented that cosmos thus produced a concept and perception of the universe which was in essence monistic. Hence, one cannot legitimately apply to this mytho-theological system either of the terms 'monotheism' or 'polytheism'. Such terms would have been totally irrelevant to the Egyptian conception of God or the gods, and hence neither one can be used as an apt description of Egyptian religious thought as it was expressed in the Atum/Geb/Osiris myth. Moreover, the terms 'monotheism' and 'polytheism' are even irrelevant to the theological interpretation of the myth. This results from the fact that none of these deities were fully representative of a theistic manner of thinking. They were not personal deities who were the subjects of a specific revelation and who would have, therefore, stood in a personal relationship to men. The Egyptian gods were rather representative of a type of deistic system, a system in which the divine is not manifest in a personal god. Hence, one may not define the Egyptian mytho-theological system as either polytheistic or monotheistic. One may more correctly speak in terms of 'monism', that is, an expression of the oneness and unity of both the divine creative force and the universe which is created through its agency. At the same time, however, it is important to avoid any suggestion that such monism implied pantheism in Egyptian thought. Creator and creation were for the Egyptians distinct and separate although closely connected through an intricate pattern of cause and effect.

The creation theology inherent within this mythic symbolism implied the concept of the perfection and completeness of the created order, a concept which is not unusual in theories of divine creation.[25] This concept of perfection was very heavily stressed in Egyptian thought through the figure of Ma'at, whose existence, as we have already seen, was a symbol of the perfect order of the cosmos. At the same time, however, any mythological or theological system must give some recognition to the existence of the negative force of evil or disorder. (Biblical theology does this through the symbol of the Fall of Man brought about by human disobedience to the divine will and through human free will which makes such disobedience possible.) The Egyptian mytho-theological system of Atum/Geb/Osiris also recognized the existence of the force of evil and chaos through the figure of Seth. (The Hermopolitan system affirmed the reality of chaos through its symbolism of the eight Heh gods, the chaos gods inherent within the primaeval state.) The figure of Seth in the Heliopolitan system gave a stronger and more graphic affirmation of the forces of chaos through the symbolism of Seth's rebellion against Osiris.[26] By the action of Seth the force of chaos disrupted the perfect order and caused a rupture within the system. It is noteworthy also that the Egyptian myth-makers described this disruption as coming from within the system, from one who was a member of the Heliopolitan Ennead. In such a way the Egyptian mythopoeic mind gave due recognition to the actual existence of the force of evil. Given the monistic nature of the creative force and the created order, such a disruption of the order could not, even in terms of mythic logic, come from without, the existence of an ulterior power being a total impossibility. Hence, in the Heliopolitan system, Seth played a role which is mythically similar to, although far more aggressive than, that of the serpent in the Adam and Eve pericope: Seth was the force of disorder, disobedience and chaos. This mythic action on the part of Seth required that the myth advance to its second main division, that of the 'historical mythology'.

The transition from the topological level of the myth to that of the historical is clearly marked by the killing of Osiris by Seth. This action then gave rise to the further events of the historical mythology, the birth of Horus, the conflict between Horus and Seth, and the eventual defeat of Seth and the vindication of Osiris. The signification of this level of the myth is clearly evident and requires little comment. It is nothing else than the defeat of the forces of disorder, chaos and evil, which results in the final teleological restoration of order. The major events within the process of the historical mythology are relatively simple: the murder of Osiris, the birth of Horus, the defeat of Seth and the rebirth of Osiris. The rebirth of Osiris and his vindication are probably best understood not as distinct elements within the sequence of the mythic narrative. Both the rebirth and vindication are essentially symbols which have the same signification as the conquest of Seth by Horus. All represent the wider concept of the victory of the force of order (Ma'at) over the force of chaos. On the other hand, the vindication and rebirth of Osiris, if viewed as separate mythic elements, are in reality the outcome of the victory of Horus. They thus become a mark of the third division of the myth where the symbolism returns back to the level of the topological.

Other elements also found their way into the historical process of the myth, for example, the tradition of Seth's dismembering the body of Osiris and scattering the fragments, the search of Isis for the parts of the body, and the lamentation of Isis and Nephthys over Osiris. The scattering of the fragments of the body, the σπαραγμός, is an element which obviously entered the mythic tradition through the nature aspects of the Osiris myth, the sowing of the grain, while the lamentation of Isis and Nephthys appears to reflect a ritual of cultic mourning. As important and interesting as these elements may be, they do not have a direct bearing on the signification of the mytho-theological system as a whole, being rather extensions of that system and additions to it. Moreover, since the historical process of the myth implies the occurrence of some specific dramatic actions, such events may be taken as individual steps within the dramatized process of the myth. One should not, however, attempt to force upon these elements some type of symbolic or allegorical significance. To do so could well result in a distortion of the mythic symbolism.

Within the context of the historical process of the myth, there appears the figure of Horus.[27] Unlike the other deities of the system, Horus appears to have had a certain theistic character. He was revealed as a god,[28] and in his aspect of being incarnate in the living Pharaoh he did have a certain personal relationship with men. The transition to the point of bringing such a theistic deity into the mythic system appears to have been necessitated by the political implications of the myth. The deity who is incarnate in the ruling monarch had of necessity to be a personalized god, a god, moreover, who had been revealed, the monarch himself being a type of revealed deity. Through the figure of Horus the mythic system was given a direct and practical relevance to the world of men and to the realm of the political. Moreover, it was through the person of Horus that the institution of the monarchy was eventually handed on to the earthly rulers. Horus thus became the deity who formed the actual connection between the world of the divine and the world of men, a connection which was visible in his incarnation in the Pharaoh. Horus/Pharaoh was, as it were, the concrete revelation of the gods within the realm of human history.

As well as belonging to the process of the historical mythology, the themes of the defeat of Seth and the vindication of Osiris belonged to the third division of the myth, the return to the topological level. With the occurrence of these mythic actions the perfection of the order of Ma'at was restored, resulting in the re-establishment of the original status signified by the Atum/Geb/Osiris symbol. At the same time this order was expanded by the eventual passing on of the earthly kingship to mortals, the Pharaohs, who now became responsible for the maintenance of Ma'at within the political and earthly orders. The victory of Horus over Seth, as well as his taking of the kingship, was also in essence the victory of Osiris, Horus having acted in the place of his father. As we have seen earlier, Horus and Osiris may be understood as two hypostases of the one concept of deity, and hence the victory of Horus was ultimately the victory of Osiris. By the separation of Horus and Osiris, however, Osiris was enabled to take on a new function as ruler and judge of the dead. Thus, the order expressed in the Atum/Geb/Osiris myth was extended into the afterlife, and Osiris, now having become a transfigured god, was further suited to be the deity of continuing life as well as the deity of natural life. In such a manner the life force of nature was personified in Osiris to a greater extent that it was in Geb. Geb, of course, still retained his capacity as the god of the earth and, as such, was still a deity of regeneration; but the figure of Osiris created a more tangible and defined deity, one who gave a stronger reality to the life force of the earth. Geb himself remained the earth, with Osiris being the personified life within the earth. At the same time, the function of Osiris as the god of individual resurrection was no less an important aspect of that deity. This function became realized as concerned each individual mortal by the identification of the deceased with the figure of Osiris, an identification in which the deceased actually participated in the mythic role of Osiris, and thus gained the same benefit of immortality. Such will be in part the subject of the following chapter.

The above study makes apparent the full signification of the Osiris mythic symbolism. In the figure of Osiris/Horus the eternal order of the divine became evident to the Egyptian and manifest in both the natural order and the political order. Insofar as these two, the natural and the political, were conjoined in the one mythic pattern, they were seen as being not two separate and distinct realms, but a total fusion into one single order of life and existence. The cosmic outlook thus presented, although it was expressed through a plurality of symbols, remained nevertheless a unity and a monad, the plurality of symbolism pointing to the fact of the complexity of existence. The Egyptian mytho-theologians made no attempt to create a simplistic view of the universe. They did indeed recognize the fact that the cosmos was highly intricate and composite, mysterious and hidden. The willingness and ability to admit and accept this mystery of the cosmos was perhaps one of the most positive points of Egyptian mytho-theology. At the same time, the Egyptians were also unwilling simply to resort to the bare statement that the universe was a mysterious and unknowable entity. What could not be understood by the intellect was still made accessible to human perception through the mythic symbolism expressed in the Egyptian cult. While such could never provide a scientific description of the universe, what it did provide was something much more important, a spiritual apprehension of the basic realities of the order of being. Such was perhaps more vital than a mere intellectual and scientific approach, for the spiritual apprehension of the universe was something into which man could enter fully and perceive himself as an entity which was somehow integrated into the whole. Through such a system of mythic symbolism, the individual was enabled to find a significance and meaning for his own existence, for he saw himself as part of the order of Ma'at which bound all things into one. In essence, all of this was the gift of Osiris.

Towards the end of the Eighteenth Dynasty the Pharaoh Akhenaten attempted to abolish the old ways of Egypt and to put in their place the 'purified' worship of his sole deity, the Aten. Evaluations of Akhenaten's movement are many and varied, and a discussion of them would exceed the interest and purposes of the present work. Whether Akhenaten was a monotheist, henotheist, political reformer or totally inept ruler makes no difference to our present study. However, his movement failed after less than two decades. One of the reasons for Akhenaten's failure in his new faith was the fact that he refused to recognize "the marvellously complex world of the Beyond,"[29] a world which had been for centuries expressed through the medium of Egypt's mythic traditions. Having taken this away from the Egyptian religious experience, Akhenaten left little that could appeal to the spiritual sensibilities of men. With the disappearance of Akhenaten, the old traditions with their mythic symbols returned, and Osiris was again able to satisfy the spiritual needs which Akhenaten had denied.

Notes

[1] Such is comparable to what was later created by the Roman poet Virgil in his famous epic of Aeneas. In the latter work, however meritorious and attractive its literary qualities may be, Virgil created an epic designed to serve a particular political ideology and its aspirations. The ancient traditions of Aeneas were thus used for an entirely new purpose and were made to reflect concepts and ideas which had never been contained in the original sources. The final result, although a literary work which has value in its own right, does not accurately reflect the true mythic values of early Roman civilization. The same criticism may be directed towards the literary works of Classical Greece, all of which were based in their content on much earlier mythic symbols. To be certain, however, we cannot correctly claim that the Homeric epics provide an accurate account of the mythic and religious traditions of the Mycenaean world from which they had drawn much of their source material. They were rather fictional narratives set against the background of the Mycenaean world which was thus interpreted through a much later mentality.

[2] My first occasion of using the terms 'topological mythology' and 'historical mythology' as applied to the Osiris myth was in the article which I co-authored with R.G. Bonnel, "Christ and Osiris: A Comparative Study," *Pharaonic Egypt, the Bible and Christianity*, 1-29.

[3] R.T. Rundle Clark, *Myth and Symbol in Ancient Egypt*, 97.

[4] J.G. Griffiths, *The Origins of Osiris and his Cult*, 99.

[5] The name Osiris was generally written as 𓊨 but appears in the Pyramid Texts as 𓁹.

[6] J.G. Griffiths, *op. cit.*, p.94.

[7] *PT* 1267a-b: *im iw Wsir m iwt.f tw dwt*
    m wn.k ꜥwy.k n.f.

[8] *PT* 145b: *n di kw Itm-R ꜥ n Wsir*
    n ip.f ib.k.

[9] *PT* 145c.

[10] *PT* 146a-b: *Wsir n s ḫm.n.k im.f   n s ḫm.n s ꜣ.k im.f*
    Ḥr n s ḫm.n.k im.f   n s ḫm.n it.k im.f.

[11] *CT* III, 295h-296a: *n ḫm.t wi m- ꜥw ḫ ꜥw Wsir*
    ḥs ḳw tpw snnw wsrwt.

[12] *CT* III, 304f-g: *i n ḥꜣw ḥrw wpwtyw Wsir*
    ḫtmw rw šḥw ḥr imyt sn.

[13] *CT* VI, 79-81.

[14] *CT* VI, 82-85.

[15] *BD* XVII, 30: *ḥs ḳimyw ḫt Wsir nn s ḫm.sn im.i nn h ꜣi.i r ktwt.sn.*

[16] It must be remembered that for the most part the myth of Osiris appears to have been strongly tied in with funerary practices, possibly as a ritual of sympathetic magic, a renewal of the original action of the myth applied now to the dead. (See J.G. Griffiths, *op. cit.*, 2f.)

[17] *PT* 699: *i wḏ ꜥb.f tpy sḫt.f*
  i wbs wḫyḫ tpy nht.f
  i tḫn idbw tpy im s.f
  i nb sḫwt wsdt...

[18] R.T. Rundle Clark, *op. cit.*, 100.

[19] J.H. Breasted, *Development of Religion and Thought in Ancent Egypt*, 20.

[20] Berlin Museum 1204. Translation in M. Lichtheim, *op. cit.*, I, 123-125.

[21] *Wb* V, 628.

[22] *BD, Pap. of Ani*, Pl.II, 2.

[23] Louvre Museum C286. Translation in M. Lichtheim, *op. cit.*, II, 81ff.

[24] In the present context the expression 'Political Order' also includes the world of nature, the latter also falling under the control of the Pharaoh.

[25] Compare, for example, the statement made at the end of the Hebrew Priestly creation narrative in Genesis 1:31: "And God saw everything which he had made, and, behold, it was very good." Even the Biblical narrative (despite the fact that Biblical theology is highly conscious of human evil and sin) expresses the fundamental belief that the created order was perfect, at least in its inception.

[26] It is tempting here to make a comparison with the disobedience of Adam and Eve as narrated in the Book of Genesis. However, Seth's rebellion against Osiris appears as much more purposely carried out. In the Biblical myth, Adam and Eve cannot be said to have willfully tried to do wrong in the sight of God.

[27] It is interesting to note that Horus, despite his importance in the system, was not part of the Heliopolitan Ennead. J.G. Griffiths, (*op. cit.*, 19) has suggested that the reason for his absence from the Ennead may have been the fact that he was so closely identified with the living king.

[28] See especially Spell 148 of the Coffin Texts, *CT* II, 209-226.

[29] D.B. Redford, *Akhenaten, the Heretic King* (Princeton, 1984), 169.

VIII. Immortality

Despite the complexity of the Egyptian mytho-theological system and its attempt to give a unified expression to the created universe, the Egyptians in their myths paid very little attention to man and showed no great concern to articulate the manner in which he had come into being. Such, however, should hardly be any cause for surprise, for most creation myths give relatively little space to the formation of a doctrine of the emergence of humanity. Even the Hebrew creation myths state little more than that God had created man in his own image (Genesis 1: 27) and that man had been created out of the dust of the earth (Genesis 2: 7). Both of these Biblical statements say only that man was created by God and that he received his life from God. In actual effect very little more needed to be said. Such was sufficient in any creation mythology to give mankind a significant place within the created order.

The normal Egyptian symbolism of human creation appears to have been the mythic image which stated that man was created from the tears of Atum-Ra. According to one account, Shu and Tefnut had become separated from Atum in the primaeval waters of Nun. Atum sent out his eye to search for them and they eventually returned to him. Upon seeing Shu and Tefnut, Atum wept for joy, and from his tears there came humanity. Such an account of the creation of humanity says virtually the same thing as the Hebrew myths, although its does not give man the same dignity which he enjoys in the biblical account. The Hebrew theologians, at least in the so-called the P source, took care to stress the importance of man by placing him at the climax of creation and affirming that man's creation had been in the image and likeness of God (Genesis 1:27). Thus man appears to have been the result of a deliberate decision on the part of the divine creator. It was also from that same creator that man received the breath of life (Genesis 2: 7). In the Heliopolitan system, however, where man was sprung from the tears of Atum-Ra, he appears to have been something of an accident, no thought or deliberation having been given to his creation. Nevertheless, in the Egyptian system man was at least seen as the direct product of divine activity, even the tears of Atum-Ra having within themselves the creative and generative ability to produce life.

Ptah and Khnum in the Egyptian tradition were also seen as creators of mankind, Khnum, the potter god, fashioning each individual on his potter's wheel. In the theology of the Amarna movement strong emphasis was placed on the dogma that men had been created by the Aten, their life and being coming into existence by the power of his rays:

> The one who fosters the foetus in women,
> The one who creates the seed in men,
> The one who gives life to the child in his mother's womb.[1]

However, beyond the active power of the Aten's rays, which in the Amarna texts are the sole means of the deity's activity on the earth, there was no mythic symbolism of the creation either of man or of any other entity. The actual means whereby man had come into being was in fact of very little interest to the Egyptian mind in general. The Egyptian seems to have been content with the knowledge that man had been created as part of the divine order of the cosmos. Mankind, for the Egyptian, was thus part of the order of Ma'at, the concept which most strongly held his main religious interest.

Man, however, despite the paucity of information on his origins, was in the Egyptian conception a complex being, far more complex than the 'living soul' (נפש) of the Hebrew tradition (Genesis 2: 7). In the Egyptian concept, man consisted of a physical body, a heart (*ib*) which was the seat of physical life and of morality, a heart (*ḥʾty*) which contained the ability of thought and understanding, and a spirit or ba (*bʾ*), the source of spiritual strength and vital energy. In addition, man also possessed, although separately from his bodily existence, a type of guardian spirit, a second self, the ka (*kʾ*), which was the true creative energy of a person.[2] The ka came into being at the time of the birth of the individual, but always existed apart from him. It was considered to be a type of protecting genius which assisted man throughout his earthly life. It was only at death when the individual was said to 'go to his ka' that the two were actually united. The ka symbolized for the Egyptian the transmission of the divine life to a man; it was the essence of his power,[3] that element of the divine life which had been provided for man and which was the principle which infused him with his own life. Even after his death when a man had gone to his ka, it was this same ka which continued to assist him in the next world.

To be united with one's ka was in fact the true end and purpose of man. Just as Egyptian mythology was silent on the reason for the actual creation of the world, so it was also silent on the ultimate reason for the existence of man. There was no hint that the gods had created man for the express purpose that he might enjoy immortality. Nevertheless, having come into existence and possessing a divine ka, man could look forward to joining his ka and becoming immortal. The lot of a man after his death, provided that his life had been lived in accordance with Ma'at, was to become an akh (𓅜), a glorified spirit. In such a state he would live forever, sharing the divine life of the gods and becoming totally identified with them. This is in sharp contrast with the Hebrew concept of the end of man, for in the Hebraic system man's life ended totally with the death of the body. Such was not the case in the Egyptian system. In Egypt, due mainly to the agency and person of Osiris and what he represented, man was able to look forward to a continuation of his life beyond the tomb and into eternity itself.

The question might be asked as to whether a study of Egyptian theological principles is the proper place to discuss the concept of the afterlife. Strictly speaking, the idea of afterlife is not an actual point of theology or even of mythology. The hope for life after death was in reality a *belief*, almost even an official dogma, of the religious systems of ancient Egypt, but there was no real theology which attempted to elucidate and justify such a belief. Nevertheless, it was expressed through a number of mythic symbols and was founded on the principles which had been so strongly developed in the mytho-theological traditions. It was in effect a natural outgrowth of the traditions of Ra and Osiris, almost a type of naturally revealed truth. The mythic systems which expressed the existence and activity of these deities were of such a nature that they had inevitably to give support to the hope of the continued existence of human life. Such deities, as we have seen, were in fact the very power of life itself, and, given the clear manifestations of the potency of the life force, manifestations which could be experienced in virtually every aspect of nature, it must have appeared to the Egyptian mind that the continuation of life was even a necessary aspect of existence. Hence, from a relatively early period in Egypt's religious history a belief in the afterlife was an essential factor. Indications of it are found well before the dynastic era in the early burials. Hence, it was by natural means that there soon developed complex expressions to affirm the reality of this hope, and these expressions soon became almost a mythic system in their own right. Certainly by the time of the composition of the Coffin Texts in the Middle Kingdom and the Book of the Dead in the New Kingdom, the afterlife had been illustrated by numerous and often very strange and formidable portraits. Many of these were not true mythic symbols. But rather pictorial representations designed to express the unknown world which lay beyond the tomb. They do, however, bear witness to the impact which the hope for eternal life had made. Because of the importance of that hope, we must consider in some detail the next world as the Egyptians saw it.

It is a common idea that the chief goal and purpose of all Egyptian religious practices was the attainment of the afterlife on the part of the individual. The religious texts which are most widely known to us do indeed seem to support this idea. The Pyramid Texts, the Coffin Texts and the Book of the Dead all have this aim as their main concern. Even the tomb inscriptions from the Amarna period are not lacking in the hope that the occupant of any given tomb will live forever, not, however, due to the agency of Osiris, but due rather to the fact that the deceased had faithfully followed the teachings of Akhenaten. The attainment of everlasting life was in the Amarna period to be the reward of the individual for his loyalty to Akhenaten. Two things, however, must be kept in mind with regard to such texts as have here been mentioned. These texts had been composed solely for the purpose of assuring the continued existence of the individual after death. Hence, one should not base any general evaluation and assessment of Egyptian religion on them. Secondly, the desire to overcome death is surely a universal human hope and aspiration; very few individuals are willing to be totally and utterly annihilated. Hence, it is understandable that, if any culture conceives of even a remote possibility of an afterlife, the hope of that afterlife will usually be given a religious basis and expression.

One must seriously question the idea that the Egyptian mytho-theological systems had evolved solely for the purpose of satisfying the hopes and aspirations of the individual. The answer to such a question may appear to be affirmative when we consider that the chief role of Osiris in his final form seems to have been the preservation of the individual to eternity. Also the festivals of the dead, which were often centred around gods other than Osiris, had as their purpose the assurance of the continuation of life beyond the tomb. These observations, however, must be balanced by the realization that, although Osiris at an early stage took over the function of providing eternal life, a function originally associated with Khentiamentiu, the god of Abydos, this was not indeed his original function. First and foremost, Osiris was the god of life in general, the continuous life of nature and the fertility of the earth. His function of assuring the survival of man beyond death was in essence an outgrowth, albeit a natural one, of this original function. Egyptian religion appears to have started not with the hope of eternal survival, but rather with the recognition of the power of life itself. The cults and myths of Egypt functioned as an affirmation and recognition of this principle which was so evident in the natural world. It was only as a result of this that a more pragmatic purpose, that of the immortality of man, made its way into Egyptian religious thought. The hope of immortality was indeed important in ancient Egypt, but that hope had arisen out of a much more basic experience and realization, and was not itself the cause of that experience and realization. At the very heart of the Egyptian religious consciousness there lay the experience of the power and stability of the life of the cosmos with its divine origin, and this power and stability eventually became the foundation of the more personal hopes of the individual. The hope of immortality was the fruit of Egyptian religious experience, but it was certainly not the root of that experience.

The Egyptian did indeed, like most people, fear death, but his experience and instinct had taught him that death was not the utter and final end. The great mortuary texts of Egypt were all produced in order to provide the proper rituals by which a man might escape death and to give him the means whereby he could be guided through the perils of the next world, the latter being particularly formidable once there had emerged the ideas of the dangers of the underworld and the complex journey which the soul of the deceased had to make in order to reach its eternal bliss. Such texts could not totally obliterate the fear of death, a natural fear of an unknown experience. They could, however, provide the assurance that death would be overcome, and this assurance was given because such deities as Ra and Osiris showed themselves both in myth and in nature to be triumphant over death. In the mind of the ancient Hebrew, only his God, Yahweh, was immortal, and man could not expect to share in that immortality, for there was too great a distinction between God and man. Such was not the case for the Egyptian. For him there was not this great gulf fixed between himself and the gods. This is not to say that there was absolutely no distinction. The gods were by their very nature immortal, while man was mortal. Even the Pharaoh himself was mortal despite his divinity. Frequently, however, the mortuary literature shows the deceased as actually identified with the various gods. Such seems to indicate that the deceased had within himself something of the divine nature which enabled him to conquer death.[4] One might also suggest that such an identification gives further evidence that for the Egyptians these various gods were in essence symbols of the power of life over death, mythic symbols which could be used to affirm the natural hopes of mankind.

To the end of affirming man's hope of immortality, the Egyptian texts often appear to deny the reality of death itself. The dead are even spoken of as being 'the living ones' (ʿnḫw). For example, Spell 36 of the Coffin Texts says of the deceased: "Today he has arrived in the land of the living."[5] In like manner, Spell 76 has in one version the title of "Becoming a living god" (ḫpr m nṯr ʿnḫ).[6] Other texts also quite clearly deny the very fact of death, Spell 144 having two such denials within its text:

> You have departed living; you have not departed dead.[7]
>
> Rise up to life, for you have not died.[8]

This denial of the effective power of death indicates that in the mind of the Egyptian death was in fact the beginning of life. In this connection we may see an interesting relationship between the symbolism of Sokar and that of Osiris. Sokar, the god of death, whose abode was in the underworld and who, like the Greek god Hades, had connected with himself nothing of the symbolism of life, was still a deity who had within himself the potential for life, for from death (symbolized by Sokar) came the actuality of life (symbolized by Osiris). In this relationship we may even see a mytho-theologization of both the reality of death and also the fact of its eventual ineffectiveness. The figure of Sokar stressed the fact that death was the real absence of life. Yet even this absence of life was still the source from which renewed life would emerge in the person of Osiris. Despite the obvious attempts to deny the actuality of death, the Egyptian was forced to admit its reality, but this reality did not prevent the deceased from becoming a glorified spirit and dwelling in the Western Land with, or as, Osiris:

> ... when he travels in peace on the beautiful paths of the West in his form of a divine spirit.[9]

The deceased, thus spiritualized, was thought to exist in a non-corporeal state, his eternal existence having no need of a physical mortal body. Spell 45 of the Coffin Texts describes the soul as ȝḫ.ti and bȝ.ti,[10] 'spiritual' and 'soul-like'. The deceased was thus transfigured into a new state of being, transformed into a deity, just as Osiris has been transformed after his death at the hands of Seth. Thus, life beyond the tomb appears to have been perceived as totally different from life on earth, for it was a life lived in a new and indestructible manner.

In general this boon of life after physical death was open to everyone who was able to have provided for himself the proper burial rituals. Such an afterlife, however, had not always been available to the entire Egyptian populace. During the Old Kingdom it had been reserved only for the king and his chosen nobility, individuals who, having been given the privilege of burial in the vicinity of the royal tomb, were thus also permitted to share in the royal afterlife in the next world. Even the early systems of burial, pit graves for the commoners and constructed tombs for the nobility, illustrate different expectations and hopes (as well as different economic resources). The general theory in the Old Kingdom, at least as it is illustrated in the Pyramid Texts, was that immortality in virtue of one's nature belonged only to the king.

The Pyramid Texts, which were obviously a compilation of earlier and often contradictory symbols, do show some evidence that the dead king was associated with, and even identified with, Osiris. This tradition, however, appears to have been the latest one to enter the Pyramid Texts. In general, the place of the royal afterlife in the Old Kingdom was in the sky, where the dead king crossed the heavens with Ra in the sun boat.[11] Such a setting for the royal afterlife appears quite natural, for in the developed mytho-theology of the Old Kingdom the king was the actual son of Ra. Not only was the dead king associated with Ra in the afterlife, he was even identified with Ra:

> O Ra, O *Wšḫty*, O *Wšḫty*,
> O *Pndty*, O *Pndty*,
> Teti is you and you are Teti.[12]

The titles *Wšḫty* and *Pndty* were used here to identify Ra in his aspect of a cosmic deity, the former being a title of the sun god as a power of fertility and regeneration in nature, and the latter signifying Ra in his aspect of a primordial serpent. Hence, the dead king was seen in effect as being united and identified with the actual life force of nature itself. His own being and life had been absorbed into the being and life of the universe, thus becoming one with cosmic reality. The identification between the dead king and the sun god is described even more graphically by the statement of an identification which is, at least symbolically, physical:

> Hear, O Ra, this word which Pepi speaks to you.
> Your body is Pepi, O Ra;
> Your body will be nourished as Pepi, O Ra.[13]

The identification between the sun god Ra and the dead monarch thus appears to have been total and complete, the text itself stressing the fact that there was no distinction between them. They were one even in their bodily form or image (*ḏt*).

Not only did the dead monarch become Ra, but he was seen also as a Heh god,[14] one of the deities of the primaeval chaos described in the Hermopolitan cosmogony. So also he could be identified with the original primaeval mound which had first appeared at the time of creation:

> This Pepi is the (primaeval) mound of land
> in the midst of the sea.[15]

Herein the dead king was identified with the actual emergence of the created order, and by such an identification he would have partaken in the mythic action of the creation, thus becoming united with the cosmic life of the universe itself. So too the dead king is called the 'Sole One':

> Pepi is the Sole One of heaven,
> A potentate at the head of the sky.[16]

The king was further described as "the one who has become the Great God."[17] This latter symbol as well as the title of the 'Sole One' appears to be solar in nature and implies the transformation of the dead king into the sun god Ra.

Perhaps the most beautiful and peaceful symbols of the deification of the dead king in the Pyramid texts are those which describe his transformation into a star:

> This Unis is enfolded by the Duat [the underworld],
> Pure and living on the horizon.
> It is well for him and for them [the other stars],
> It is pleasant for him and for them,
> In the arms of his father,
> In the arms of Atum.[18]

> You shall go out with Orion from the east of the sky,
> You shall descend with Orion in the west of the sky.[19]

Those who are familiar with the principles of Egyptian grammar will recognize in the geminated verbals forms *prr.k* ("you shall go out") and *hꜣꜣ.k* ("you shall descend") an indication of repeated and continual action. The dead monarch was thus identified as part of the natural cycle, moving eternally in the constant motion of the stars. His life had thus become united with the eternal cycle of nature, being absorbed into the actual force of cosmic life.

The mythic symbolism of the Osirian system also made its way into the Pyramid Texts, and we often find that the dead king was thought to become immortal by identification with Osiris:

> O Osiris-Pepi, you have risen as King of
> Upper and Lower Egypt.[20]

In this identification between Pepi and Osiris we may note also the use of the royal title King of Upper and Lower Egypt (*niswt-bity*), indicative of the political ideology which was by this time in Egypt's history also expressed in the Osiris/Horus symbolism.

For the most part in the Pyramid Texts the deification of the king after death appears to have been almost automatic. He gained his position in the cosmic life cycle in virtue of the position and nature which he had held on earth. Nevertheless, even in the Pyramid Texts there did start to appear some indications that immortality was also dependent upon the monarch having lived his earthly life in a righteous and just manner in accordance with the principles of Ma'at. Such indications are not numerous, but they do at least start to emerge at this time. For example, we find:

> Pepi is the son of Khnum;
> There is no evil which Pepi has done.[21]

Later in the history of Egypt, as convictions of the necessity of moral living became more pronounced, the condition of having lived a righteous life became an important prerequisite for the attainment of eternal happiness. The Pyramid Texts, however, show at least the beginning of the development of such a concept. Nevertheless, it does appear that at this stage of Egyptian religious thought the requirements of moral living as a condition for gaining eternal bliss were still in their infancy. The actions of the king, in virtue of the position which he held as the embodiment of Ma'at, could hardly be considered other than just and righteous. It was only with the opening up of the hereafter to all men that the performance of Ma'at became such a necessary condition for survival beyond death. It is understandable, of course, that such ideas of morality were slow in developing, moral convictions not being a necessary innate characteristic of the human personality.

Before leaving the Old Kingdom symbols of the deification of the king, we may note in passing that in the Pyramid Texts the death of the king was sometimes portrayed as being accompanied by natural phenomena of such magnitude that they can be described only as virtual cosmic upheavals. Such is the opening of Utterance 273, the famous 'Cannibal Hymn', a text which would lose its somewhat barbaric nature if read in the light of mythic symbolism. The interpretation of this particular text, however, is not our present concern. What is important is the vivid description of the storms and earthquakes which accompany the passing of the king from this world into the heavens. The symbolic significance of such a picture must be immediately evident: the death of the king, with his resulting transformation into a god, was seen as an event of cosmic dimensions and importance. As such it may well have been seen, for in the Egyptian concept of the royal deification there was in effect implied the coming into being of the Great God himself. In this text the king is showing as emerging into the next world as the very acme of divine power and strength. His transformation in death was thus a revelation of the actual cosmic power of the divine life in the celestial realms. In a word, the death of the king is portrayed here as a violent recurrence of the emergence and manifestation of the divine. In such a portrait of the royal passage from earth to the heavens we may easily comprehend the overwhelming impact which such an event was thought to have made. The earthly monarch had been transformed and transfigured into the actual essence of the divine power. His passing was thus perceived as the moment on the divine conquest of all possible celestial powers. In very brief, he had become God.

After the collapse of the Old Kingdom the hope of immortality began to spread first to the nobles and then to the commoners of Egypt. This seems to have been due to the failure of confidence in the monarchy and to the general discouragement which must have set in as a result of the breakdown of centralized authority during the First Intermediate Period. Men began perhaps to realize that, if they could not hope for the ideal and stable kingdom on earth, then they would have to seek it in the more enduring world of the beyond. Whatever the actual cause of this religious phenomenon may have been, the aspiration to eternal life now became one of the mainstays of the ordinary Egyptian populace. As a result of this there gradually grew up the corpus of mortuary texts now known to us as the Coffin Texts. Based to a great extent on materials embodied in the Pyramid Texts, the Coffin Texts were no longer the property of the royal and noble classes. Their usage was open to anyone who could afford to have a coffin inscribed with one or more of the texts. From such texts we have gained much of our knowledge about the symbols used by the Egyptians to express their hope of immortality and even to transform that hope into a reality. From them we also learn that the world of the beyond was no simple place, nor was it even expressed as one definite and particular location. The complicated and complex descriptions of the next world indicate that it was a highly intricate world, one which was very frequently filled with dangers, perils and obstacles which the spirit of the deceased had to overcome in its journey towards immortality. Nor was there any one expression of the ultimate place to which the soul would make its journey. Sometimes it appears that the deceased continued to live simply in the tomb, coming forth and going in according to his will. At other times it appears that the abode of the dead was in the Duat (the underworld) into which the sun sank to rest every evening. So also it could be located in the Hotep fields, in the sky where the soul continued to live on as a star or in the sun boat with Ra, or in the Western Land where the deceased became one with Osiris and shared his immortality throughout all eternity. In actual fact, however, it made very little difference where the land of immortality was located. In keeping with the Egyptian usage of symbolism, a plurality of such symbols was better suited to express the place of eternity. What man could not know for certain was best articulated under as many different forms as possible. This plurality of symbolism only served to enrich and enhance the concept of the place of man's final beatitude.

From the Pyramid texts it is easy to take the impression that the transition from earthly life to the realm of eternity was one which was made with little or no difficulty. There appears to have been at that stage of Egyptian thought no perilous or dangerous journey which the soul had to undergo. However, during the Middle Kingdom there developed the idea that the soul had to pass through a series of dangers and trials before it finally reached its goal. In order to equip the soul to confront and overcome such dangers there were evolved those particular spells and rituals which, in virtue of the power of magic contained within them, would have that very effect, such rituals being embodied in the Coffin Texts and later in the Book of the Dead. The Pyramid Texts had also contained a few such formulae, but for the most part these consisted of simple prayers and recitations, as, for example, the statement that the power of Osiris in his aspect of a demon would not overcome the dead monarch. The dangers and difficulties described in the Coffin Texts and the Book of the Dead, however, were much more complex, and the soul had now to be prepared by means of a variety of spells and recitations to overcome these. Even the geography of the next world, the actual route which the soul had to take, was a complicated one. Various gates and portals had to be passed and rivers crossed in order to reach beatitude. For example, Spells 1107-1111 of the Coffin Texts[22] were designed so that the soul might easily pass the First, the Middle and the Third Gates as well as the Gate of Darkness. These are but a few examples of the extremely intricate and often very perilous features of the next world, the descriptions given in the Book of the Dead being even more vivid.

The question arises as to the importance and significance of such descriptions. Were they taken literally? Such a question probably requires, at least to a certain extent. an affirmative answer. There can be little doubt that many must have quite simply accepted such texts at their face value and provided themselves with the proper spells to overcome the dangers and difficulties. This acceptance of the literal value of religious symbols is common in virtually every tradition in both the ancient and modern worlds. This kind of interpretation, however, must unfortunately be seen as a rather simplistic understanding of religious symbolism and implies the inability or even the unwillingness to comprehend the basically symbolic nature of all such forms of expression. Such an acceptance of religious symbolic expression may result in a type of very deep faith, trust and security within certain individual believers, but it may also obscure the real essence and deeper significance of a religious tradition. To put it very briefly, and perhaps somewhat cynically, such an interpretation may turn religious symbolism into little more than a system of cheap magic practices designed to obtain the pragmatic and personal ends of individuals.

A better understanding of the nature of such expressions is obtained when one sees them in the light of the principles of symbolism. As symbols their literal value is of relatively little importance. Moreover, one should not attempt to impose upon each symbol a specific meaning such as can be expressed in other equally graphic terms. To do so would be to reduce the symbols to the level of mere allegory, thus in essence making them unnecessary. A symbol which can be thus interpreted is not in reality a symbol, but rather a literary device. The symbolism surrounding the passage to the next world, therefore, should not be interpreted as an attempt to express the specific characteristics or complexities of that world. The most acceptable interpretation which may be given is to say that the details of such descriptions underscore the very magnitude of the transition from death to life. We have already remarked that the Egyptians did indeed have a very definite fear of death and the passage to the unknown world which lay beyond the grave. Hence, mythic symbols, used to give a graphic sense of realism to such a process, were quite appropriate. The fear of the actual death process emphasizes the critical nature of the event itself. It was not seen as a mere natural occurrence; it was rather the climax of one's existence. Hence, the elaborate portrayals of the passage to the next life were suitable and even necessary, for they stressed the realty of death and its consequences as constituting almost a type of personal eschatology. Such an event could not be lightly or simply expressed, and the more elaborate and fantastic the symbols surrounding the event, the greater was the realization of its very magnitude and importance. Death was not merely a movement from one place or mode of existence to another; it was a total transformation of the being of the individual. Hence, the awesome and terrible tableaux presented in the symbolic representations of the mortuary literature was the Egyptian way of articulating what could not be expressed through the imagery of normal experience. An understanding of the symbolism surrounding death in this manner makes the Egyptian genius for the mythic expression of the mysterious all the more evident.

One may also approach such symbolism in a somewhat more cynical way, and suggest that the fantastic elaborations concerning the next world may well have been products of the priestly organizations and designed for the purpose of increasing the influence and power of these same organizations by creating a dependence on the part of the populace on their esoteric knowledge and skills. Such also would have been no small source of revenue for the temple organizations as well. This assessment will no doubt appear to be highly negative in its evaluation of the aims and ambitions of the temples and their clergy, but one must admit that similar situations have occurred within the context of all organized religions. We should not, therefore, be so blind as to deny that such motivations were found in ancient Egypt, at least to some degree, nor should we be so negative as to maintain that these motivations were paramount. While such must surely have existed, they did not necessarily detract from the more spiritual values which the texts in question could hold. The highly elaborate and fantastic symbolism surrounding the transition from death to eternity did retain its value within the Egyptian tradition and became a significant part of the mythic expression of Egyptian spiritual values.

The concept and conviction of personal resurrection in ancient Egypt was expressed most commonly through the mythic figure of Osiris. Very briefly but nonetheless correctly stated, the usage of this myth affirmed that just as Osiris had died and was raised again to life so also would the mortal individual be raised to life by participating in the Osiris experience. In death, therefore, each individual basically underwent the same process as the deity had undergone, becoming through this experience Osiris himself and hence attaining the same position of eternal life in the Western Land. In Spell 74 of the Coffin Texts,[23] for example, Isis and Nephthys are portrayed as calling upon the dead Osiris to rise again to life. We may detect in this particular text a process of ritual mourning for the dead, and there can be no doubt that it was such. Beyond that, however, such a text was further a cultically dramatized myth, probably re-enacted as part of the funeral ritual and intended to effect by its actual performance and recitation the same fact and reality which it portrayed. The ritual mourning expressed here in the figures of the two goddesses was intended as more than a mere recitation of what had happened. It was rather a re-creation and renewal of this same event, a symbol which was intended to make an equation between the burial of the ordinary individual and that of Osiris himself. Isis and Nephthys would have been seen as being cultically, mythically, symbolically and actually present in such an action, and by their presence they would have brought about the resurrection of Osiris who, in each individual instance, would have been the deceased person for whom the ritual was performed. The basic principle which underlay this practice was one of total ritual identification in which the unseen reality of Osiris and his revitalization was again made real in the mythic and cultic setting, the reality manifesting itself in the deceased who became one with the dead and subsequently resurrected Osiris. The deceased, however, did not simply become another Osiris. He was in effect the original Osiris, the power of life and regeneration, the power of the resurrection of the specific individual. The mythic symbol of Osiris thus had its most common impact when it was expressed in concrete terms, in this case in the specific person of the deceased. This total identification between Osiris and the deceased is seen in numerous places in the Coffin Texts and in the Book of the Dead, the title 'Osiris' being prefixed to the personal name of the deceased. One example from Spell 36 of the Coffin Texts will suffice:

> O Osiris, bull of the great ones, ruler of the living ones,
> Behold Osiris-(*Name*) is come unto you.[24]

The 'living ones' referred to in the above passage were of course the dead who, in virtue of now enjoying the life of eternity, were seen as being those who were truly alive in contrast to those whose life was still of a terrestrial nature. Thus, the deceased was able to go to Osiris in the West for the very reason that he (the deceased) had in symbol and fact become Osiris.

The symbolism of identification, however, was expressed in the Coffin Texts in an even richer and more complex fashion. The deceased, it is true, was usually identified with Osiris, but he could also at the same time be identified with Horus and in this role participate in the Osiris myth in order to gain his immortality. For example, Spell 303 has the following passage which would have been recited on behalf of the dead:

> My father Osiris, behold I am come before you,
> Having smitten Seth for you.
> For you I have killed his confederacy;
> I have smitten those who smote you,
> I have conquered those who conquered you.
> I am the one who conquers by strength,
> The total heir.[25]

The identification between the deceased and Horus was in effect nothing other than an identification between the deceased and Osiris, for, as we have seen in an earlier chapter, Osiris and Horus were in reality two hypostases of the same divine force. The focal point, however, in the above statement is the affirmation on the part of Horus (in this context the deceased) that he is "the total heir" (*i ʿw mi ḳd*). The deceased in his Horus role performed what would have been the legitimate function of Osiris in taking vengeance on Seth, in defeating the force of chaos and death. In virtue of this he became the "total heir," the legitimate successor of Osiris and was thus entitled to share in the eternal life of that deity. One must also see in the above passage the royal overtones of the rightful succession of the crown prince to the throne, he (the crown prince) having become the Horus after the death of his father through the proper performance of the funeral rituals. In the Coffin Texts, however, this regal function of the passage has been largely forgotten and the text could now be applied to the rebirth of the ordinary mortal.

The common identification of the deceased with Osiris did not prevent his association with other deities as well. In Spell 18 of the Coffin Texts we see an association between the deceased and Ra:

> Hail, Osiris-(*Name*)! You shall cross the sky,
> You shall traverse the firmament.
> Those who are in the lake of Kha shall adore you;
> They shall see you when you arise on the eastern horizon.[26]

> Hail Osiris-(*Name*)!
> You shall ascend on the great west side of heaven,
> You shall descend on the great east side of earth
> Among those gods who bare in the entourage of Osiris,
> In perfect peace with Ra who is in the sky.[27]

The above two passages do not explicitly speak of an identification between the deceased and the sun god, but they do describe a very close relationship between them. In the first passage it is stated that the deceased will be worshipped when he is seen rising in the sky, which may be interpreted to imply that he at least shares the divinity of Ra. The important point, however, is the conjoining of Ra and Osiris as symbols for the deification of the dead, the latter idea being the central one. The main stress here is on the transformation and deification of the deceased, the specific symbolism of the god by whom this is effected being of little real importance.

The deceased could also be transformed into Shu, as may be seen in the title to Spell 75.[28] He could be transformed even into Seth, the enemy of Osiris, the principle of symbolism being able to admit two logically opposing images:

> Hatred of you is in this my body;
> I have swallowed the powers of Osiris.
> I am Seth.
> I have tread upon her who was pregnant by you, Osiris.[29]

There may be contained in this text a possible reference to the negative and demonic aspect of Osiris, the aspect in which he had once been seen as hostile to the dead. Seth would, therefore, have been seen here in the positive role of overcoming the force which was hostile to man and would have prevented his eternal happiness. If such is the case, then the imagery of the transformation of the deceased into Seth could be taken as a symbolic way of affirming the escape of the soul from the destructive powers of the next world. Despite the details of the symbolism employed, the major point of such a text was still the basic concept of transfiguration, the imagery through which such is expressed again making very little difference. In actual fact, according to the mythic symbolism of the mortuary texts, the deceased could be transformed into virtually any deity, as can be seen in the end title to Spell 301 of the Coffin Texts, "Taking shape as any god a man wishes."[30] The result was that in the Coffin Texts the deceased was pictured as taking the form of Horus, Osiris, Shu, Thoth, Nehebkau, Atum, Neper, Ra, Isis, Anubis, Sokar, Kheperi, Min, Sobek, Soped, the Four Winds, the Eye of Horus, the Nile, Hu, Hathor, Seth, Hetep, Babi, Neith or the Double Lion. The deceased could, even within the same spell, become more than one god. For example, in Spell 423[31] we find the deceased as Seth, Soped and Atum, while Spell 649[32] represents him as Thoth, Ma'at, Horus, Geb, Min, Anti and Khons. It is difficult, if not impossible, to escape the conclusion that such images and symbols of transformation were never intended to have any type of literal value, nor were the deities who were used as such symbols intended to be understood as actual beings having hypostatic existence as personal gods, at least within the cultic context of the texts in question. They were rather to be taken as symbolic expressions of the power of the divine life which revitalized the dead and effected the spiritual transformation of all terrestrial life into the eternal and divine life of the cosmos and of the mystic power which vitalized that same cosmos. This interpretation does not deny the fact that in Egyptian thought these deities may have had a distinct hypostatic existence, but it also places their significance on a higher level.

The symbolism of transformation was also extended further than the gods alone. We find, for example, that the deceased could become the grain of Osiris in Spell 269:

> Becoming barley of Lower Egypt.
> (*Name*) is that bush of life which comes forth from Osiris,
> Which grows on the ribs of Osiris, which nourishes
> mankind.[33]

He could become the Nile, as described in Spell 317:

> I am Hapy, Lord of the water, he who brings vegetation.[34]

The same spell at a later point adds the following:

> Behold ye me as I shine in the rising of the sun,
> For I have become the efflux of the Bull of the West.[35]

The "efflux of the Bull of the West" is of course nothing other than the Nile itself, the nourisher of Egypt, and the imagery of the river shining in the light of the rising sun graphically underscores the transformation of the deceased into the river. Even here, however, the Nile signified more than the physical water of the river; it was rather the primaeval life force into which the life of the deceased had been transformed:

> Behold ye me, O gods! Come in my retinue!
> Give me worship! I am the primaeval god of the earth.[36]

The deceased in effect becomes nothing less than the actual divine source of all life and creation:

> I am he who gives power to Osiris.[37]

> I am he who created darkness,
> He who made his place at the limits of the sky.[38]

> I am the ba who created the primaeval waters.[39]

One wonders if the genius of any religious tradition could find more powerful and effective symbols to express the magnitude and eternity of the indestructibility of human life. The theme of transfiguration and transformation was not, however, expressed only in such grandiose terms. Chapter LXXXVI of the Book of the Dead, entitled "The beginning of the spells of making shapes," list various living entities of nature into which the deceased could be transformed. He could become, for example, a swallow (*mnt*), a falcon (*bik*), a crocodile (*msḥ*), a *šnt* bird, a phoenix (*bnw*), a lotus (*sšny*). As with other mythic symbols one must beware of the temptation to interpret these images of transformation too finely lest they lose their mythic and mystic signification and become only allegorical figures. Such was not the true purpose of the Egyptian expressions of transfiguration. From the most minutes images, such as those of the swallow or the lotus, to the most majestic and grandiose, such as those of the great gods, the Egyptian mythic symbols of the transformation of the soul of man attempted to affirm his eternal and indestructible relationship with the depths of the life force of the universe.

Despite this spiritualized and almost abstract concept of the afterlife, the Egyptian mortuary texts tended to speak in terms of an almost physical resurrection of the deceased as an individual who retained his own personal existence and whose new life was described in physical terms. Hence, we find in Spell 51 of the Coffin Texts the following ritual of resurrection:

> Raise yourself on your left side,
> Place yourself on your right side,
> So that you may receive the breezes of the shore,
> So that you may eat bread with the living ones.
> Travel in peace to the beautiful West,
> While the western deserts worship you.[40]

In such a passage we have a description of the actual and virtually physical, journey to the Western Land, the deceased being gradually revived by the cool breezes of the river, imagery obviously drawn from the experience of normal life. So also the deceased was described as having power (*sḥm*) over the physical parts of his body, the ability to move, act and function as was his normal custom on the earth. Chapter XXVI of the Book of the Dead has the deceased saying:

> I know my heart (*ib*),
> I am powerful over my heart (*ḥȝty*),
> I am powerful over my two arms,

> I am powerful over my two legs.
> I am powerful to do what my ka desires.⁴¹

The usage of the verb *sḫm*, 'to be powerful', implies the actual ability to control one's body and physical parts. An afterlife which was totally spiritualized, totally abstract, wherein the soul had become absorbed into the life of the gods, would have been too incomprehensible for the Egyptian mentality. Insofar as his own experience of life was based on the physical, such a life would have appeared unreal and unsubstantial. Hence arose the necessity to express the afterlife in the concrete terminology of the physical life of the body. Only in such a manner could eternal existence be seen as real and comprehensible. Such descriptions of the afterlife should not, therefore, be understood as actual concepts. They were rather mythical expressions of the unknown, corresponding in their nature and purpose to the myths of the gods.

Despite such physical expressions of the afterlife, the true Egyptian concept of life beyond death was one which may be seen as essentially mystic in its nature. It was in the greater and more transcendent powers of nature and the cosmos that the dead would survive in an eternal existence:

> I shall die and I shall live, for I am Osiris.⁴²

> I shall live and grow as Neper [the grain god].⁴³

> I shall live and I shall die, for I am emmer.⁴⁴

The force of human life, thus taken back into the wider reality of cosmic life, would continue to exist in the constant and continual cycle which was manifest in the universe, while the personal and individual expressions of this existence assured men that they would not cease to exist as the separate entities which they had been during the earthly life which they had enjoyed before death. Their names, the expressions of their individual personalities, would not be obliterated, as may be seen in a passage from Spell 45 of the Coffin Texts:

> Your are the son of the king, the heir.
> Your ba shall surely exist,
> Your heart shall be with you,
> And Anubis shall remember you in Djedu.⁴⁵

The concept of eternal life, if it was not a strict theological principle for the Egyptian, was nevertheless founded on sound mytho-theology and had itself evolved its own mythic expressions to articulate its reality. The afterlife was, therefore, a natural and a necessary result of the Egyptian concept of the nature of the universe. The Egyptian mind saw the unity of the creative force, the unity of creation and the unity of that life which pervaded the entire universe. All were contained within the essential order of Ma'at, the principle which bound all things together and assured their stability. Even the life of the individual was an integral part of this ordered unity, and, as such, it could not be destroyed or annihilated, just like the wider order of cosmic life. Human life had to be an eternal and continuous process. The exact manner and means of this process could not be comprehended and understood by the mortal mind, but, like all mythic reality, it could be apprehended by the one means of perception which was truly valid, that is, by experience. By all the logic of mytho-theology, the fact of human immortality was a necessary reality. The Egyptian perceived and gladly accepted this reality, expressing it in the symbolic and mythic statements and affirmations of his mortuary literature.

As natural as the transition from death to immortality may have been (natural, that is, in the sense that it was a normal and necessary event, demanded by the nature of life itself), eternal existence in the afterlife was not a boon which was automatically granted to all men. Man's life was an aspect of Ma'at, and hence, if the life of the individual was to continue, it had to be a life which had been lived in accordance with the principle for which Ma'at stood. Man's life had to be orderly, free from chaos and from the evil (*isft*) which was the contrary of what Ma'at demanded. In a word, immortality depended upon morality. Before a man was permitted to enter the realms of Osiris, his heart (*ib*), the seat of morality, had to be weighed in the balance and he himself pronounced as 'justified of voice' (*mɜʿ ḫrw*). Such a concept was the necessary result of the Egyptian perception of reality. In entering the world of eternity, the deceased was entering that realm where all was perfection, where evil and disorder did not exist; he was entering a world of eternal bliss and happiness. Hence, one who had not been vindicated and justified would not be able to find a place there, for his nature would have made him unsuitable for such an existence. The perfect life of eternity naturally demanded that those who enter it be also perfect.

Such a requirement for happiness after death had already begun, even in the Old Kingdom, to make its appearance in the Pyramid Texts, although it was not yet so highly developed as it was to become at later stages of Egyptian thought. Nevertheless, we see that even by the Sixth Dynasty the autobiographical inscriptions on the tombs of the nobles started to exhibit the affirmations that their occupants had lived their lives in accordance with Ma'at. This did not imply only a negative type of goodness, mere freedom from having done wrong. Men felt obliged to stress the fact that their lives had been positive forces for goodness, that they had acted in such a manner as to promote the welfare of those around them and of those in need. Whether such protestations can always be taken at their literal face value or not is another question. We may well assume, and probably rightly so, that many such statements of moral worth must have been placed in the tombs in the hope of realizing a moral life simply by the power of the spoken and written word. Be this as it may, such statements do at least underscore the fact that moral values of a relatively high standard were starting to emerge even in the Old Kingdom. The inscription on the false door of the tomb of Nefer-Seshem-Ra at Saqqara, dating from the Sixth Dynasty, has its owner stating that he had done Ma'at, had spoken the truth, had fed the hungry and clothed the naked, buried the dead and given due respect to his parents.[46]

With the collapse of the Old Kingdom and the subsequent disorders of the First Intermediate Period, men must have begun to realize all the more the necessity for moral and upright living. Only by such could good order and decency be expected in society, and hence morality began to be stressed even more as the mark of a good man and a good life. The result was an even greater emphasis on justification as a requirement for the enjoyment of eternal happiness. Hence, we find in the Coffin Texts constant statements that the deceased had been pronounced justified and was worthy to enter eternity. For example, Spells 7 and 8 have the following pronouncements:

> Hail to you, magistrates of the gods!
> Osiris-(*Name*) is justified before you on this day.[47]
>
> Vindicated is Osiris-(*Name*) in the presence of
>   Geb, prince of the gods.[48]

These are but two instances of protestations of vindication in the Coffin Texts where so much of the mythic symbolism of rebirth was based on the idea that the deceased would be vindicated in the next world just as Osiris had been vindicated. The dead were thus identified with Osiris not only in the fact of resurrection but also in the status of being true and just in both word and deed.

The Book of the Dead also abounds in protestations and affirmations of moral innocence and purity. In Chapter I, for example, we find a text which accompanied the action of Horus as he lead the soul of the deceased into the presence of Osiris:

> Words spoken by Horus, son of Isis:
> I have come into your presence, O Unnefer [Osiris],
> And I have brought to you Osiris-Ani,
> His heart being justified as it comes forth from the balance,
> For he has not sinned against any god or any goddess.[49]

The deceased, now in the actual presence of Osiris, further makes the following declaration of his innocence:

> Words spoken by Osiris-Ani. He says:
> Behold, I am in your presence, O Lord of the West.
> There is no evil in my body,
> Nor have I knowingly spoken falsehood.[50]

The protestations of moral innocence in the Book of the Dead are even more pronounced in the so called 'Negative Confession' found in Chapter CXXV. As the title implies, this particular passage places its stress on the fact that the deceased has refrained from committing certain moral offences which would render him unworthy of entering into the afterlife. It does not deal with the positive moral aspects of his life, the actual good which he had done. However, the point of such was to underline the fact that no evil existed in the heart of the deceased such as would make him unfit to enter into eternal life. What was important was the innocence of the individual, not the fact that he had been an active force for right or a worker for social justice. This does not imply that the Egyptians had no consciousness of the necessity for positive moral action. Such concepts did abound and were particularly evident in the type of writings which have been called the Instructions. These, dating from virtually every period in Egypt's history, are valuable in that they illustrate the evolution and development of positive moral values. However, such do not concern us at this point, nor were such positive values necessarily a religious requirement. In the rituals of the

Coffin Texts and Book of the Dead it was sufficient, it appears, for a happy afterlife that the deceased had simply refrained from disruptive and harmful actions. Even this was a positive moral position for the Second Millenium B.C.E. The Egyptian mind, at even an early period of history, had advanced to the stage where it had been able to develop an advanced system of mytho-theology. Its philosophical and abstract abilities were not yet sufficiently developed to enable it to evolve a complete and systematic synthesis of moral theology.

All of this discussion on the Egyptian afterlife has presented a few concrete images and symbols of that life as the Egyptians expressed it. Many more such portrayals of the next world are to be found in the Egyptian mortuary texts, but even a longer compilation of these would not result in any clearer picture of the exact nature of that world as the Egyptians saw it. What is important in all of these texts is to abstract from them a generalized understanding and comprehension of how the Egyptians perceived the afterlife. There can be no doubt that many must have taken at least some of the symbolic representations at their face value and thus constructed for their own satisfaction some concrete expectation of the future life. Others, however, must surely have seen the symbolic nature of the texts and accepted them as such. In both cases the Egyptian would have realized that his life would go on beyond the grave. He knew that in some way he could hope to continue his personal existence as he had known it on earth. Perhaps he could even hope to enjoy in some ways the exact pleasures and way of life which he had known on earth. The portraits of the dead in the next world such as are found on the tombs from every period of Egypt's history certainly portray the next life in a very terrestrial manner. To some, such portraits must have been an expression of the actual life to which they looked forward; to others, they must have been but symbols. In either case it would have made very little difference. Both interpretations would have said that the individual would live forever in his own personality and in his own being. Whether one defined the method and manner or not was essentially of no real importance. As well as a personal existence, however, the Egyptian was able to perceive or sense that after death his life would be conjoined to the wider and more cosmic life cycle of the universe. He would become one with nature and the very source of being. He would enter into the cycle of existence which would go on for "millions and millions of years."

Egyptian mytho-theology had given rise to what we can only call a living faith in the hope of immortality. Perhaps the most simple, but also the most elegant, expression of this faith is found in Spell 1162 of the Coffin Texts where it is said that the dead "shall eat bread among the living ones, and they shall never die."[51]

Notes

[1]M. Sandman, *Texts from the time of Akhenaten*, 94.10-11:

    s ḫpr mȝyw m ḫmwt
    ir mw m rmṯ
    s ꜥnḫ sȝ m ḫt n mwt.f.

[2]C.J. Bleeker in *Historia Religionum* I, 97.
[3]R.T.R. Clark, *Myth and Symbol in Ancient Egypt*, 231.
[4]C.J. Bleeker, *Egyptian Festivals*, 128.
[5]*CT* I, 137b: *ii.n.f min m tȝ ꜥnḫw.*
    My own translation of this line differs from that of R.O. Faulkner who renders it as "He has come here *from* the land of the living," (*The Ancient Egyptian Coffin Texts*, I, 25.)
[6]*CT* II, 1i (on Coffin G1T only).
[7]*CT* I, 187e: *šm.n.k ꜥnḫ n   šm.n.k mt.*
[8]*CT* I, 190a: *ꜥḥꜥ rk n   ꜥnḫ n mt.k.*
[9]*CT* I, 86B (Spell 30): *sdȝ.f m ḥtp ḥr wȝwt nfrwt nt Imnt m irw.f n šḥ nṯry.*
[10]*CT* I, 194e.
[11]*PT* 517b.
[12]*PT* 703a-b: *i Rꜥ i Wšḥty i Wšḥty*
        i Pndty i Pndty
        Tti pw tw tw pw Tti.
[13]*PT* 1461a-b: *sḏm sw mdw pn Rꜥ ḏdw Ppi n.k*
        ḏt.k m Ppi Rꜥ
        s ꜥnḫ ḏt.k m Ppi Rꜥ.
[14]*PT* 1390a.
[15]*PT* 1022a: *Ppi pn pw ḥw n tȝ ḥry-ib wȝḏ-wr.*
[16]*PT* 2041: *Ppi pw Wꜥ n pt sḫm-irf ḫnty nwt.*
[17]*PT* 272b: *ḫpr m nṯr ꜥȝ.*

¹⁸PT 151c-e: šni wnis pn m Dwʒt
  wʿb ʿn ḫ m sḫt
  sḫ n.f n.sn
  ḳbb n.f n.sn
  m-ḫnw ʿwy it.f
  m-ḫnw ʿwy Itm.
¹⁹PT 821b-c: prr.k ḫ n ʿ s sḫ m i ʒbty n pt
  h ʒʒ.k ḫ n ʿ s sḫ m imnty n pt.
²⁰PT 776a: Wsir Ppi ḫʿ.n.k m niswt-bity.
²¹PT 1238a: Ppi pw s ʒ Ḫnmw
  n ḏwt irt.n Ppi.
²²CT VII, 437-440.
²³CT I, 306-313.
²⁴CT I, 135a: i Wsir k ʒ wrw s šmw ʿn ḫw
  mk Wsir-(Name) pn ii.w r.k.
²⁵CT IV, 56c-i: it.i Wsir mk wi ii.kwi ḫr.k
  ḫwi.i n.k St ḫ
  sm ʒ.n.i n.k sm ʒwt.f
  iw ḫwi.n.i ḫww ṯw
  ḳni.n.i ḳnw ṯw
  ink it m wsr
  i ʿw mi ḳd.
²⁶CT 53d-54a: h ʒ Wsir-(Name) pn ḏ ʒi.k pt
  nmi.k bi ʒyt
  dw ʒ ṯw imyw š n Ḥ ʒ
  m ʒʒ.sn tw wbn.k m sḫt i ʾbtt.
²⁷CT I, 54f-j: h ʒ Wsir-(Name) pn
  prr.k ḫr imy-wrt ʿʒt nt pt
  h ʒʒ.k ḫr t ʒ-wr ʿʒ n t ʒ
  m-m nw n nṯrw imyw šmsw Wsir
  m ḫtp sp sn ḫr Rʿ imy pt.

The mention of the rising of the sun in the west and its setting in the east is a reversal of the natural situation. Such may be due to a scribal error (R.O. Faulkner, *The Ancient Egyptian Coffin Texts*, I, 11), or it may refer to the rising and setting of the sun in the underworld where, from the point of view of those living on the earth, the directions would be reversed.

²⁸CT I, 314a.

29CT V, 267d-268a: iw bwt.k m ḫt.i tn
                    iw ꜥm.n.i wsrw Wsir
                    ink St ḫ
                    iw šʾs.n.i iwrt.k Wsir.
30CT IV, 53e: irt ḫprw m nṯr nb mrrw s.
31CT V, 265-268.
32CT VI, 271-272.
33CT IV, 6b-f: ḫprw m it M ḥw
                (Name) pn bʾt tw nt ꜥn ḫ prt m Wsir
                rdt ḥr sprw nw Wsir s ꜥn ḫt r ḥyt.
34CT IV, 115d-e: ink Ḥꜥpy nb mw in wʾddt.
35CT IV, 130c-d: mʾ wi ir.ṯn wbn.i m wbnt
                   ḫpr.i m rdw n kʾ imnt.
36CT IV, 135c-f: mʾ wi ir.ṯn nṯrw my m šmsw.i
                   dy n.i iʾw ink pʾwty tʾ.
37CT IV, 62r: ink ddi ʾḫ n Wsir.
38CT IV, 63 e: ink ḳmʾ kkw
                 ir st.f m drw ḥrt.
39CT IV, 63p: ink bʾ ḳmʾ nwn.
40CT I, 234a-f: ṯsi ṯw ḥr gs.k iʾb
                  dy ṯw ḥr gs.k imn
                  šsp.k ṯʾww mryt
                  wnm.k t ḥn ꜥ ꜥn ḫw
                  ḫpi m ḥtp r imnt nfrt
                  dwʾ ṯw smwt imntt.
41CT Papyrus of Ani, Pl. XV, 7f.:   r ḫ.i m ib.i
                                    s ḫm.i m ḥʾty.i
                                    s ḫm.i m ꜥwy.i
                                    s ḫm.i m rdwy.i
                                    s ḫm.i m iryt mrrt kʾ.i.
42CT IV, 168b-c: mt.i ꜥn ḫ.i ink Wsir.
43CT IV, 169c: ꜥn ḫ.i rd.i m Npr.
44CT IV, 169, f-g: ꜥn ḫ.i mt.i ink bdty.
45CT I, 197f-198a: ntk sʾ niswt rp ꜥ
                     wnn wnnt bʾ.k
                     wn ib.k ḥn ꜥ.k
                     s ḫʾ ṯw Inpw m Ddw.

⁴⁶*Urk.* I, 198-200. Translation in M. Lichtheim, *Ancient Egyptian Literature*, I, 17.
⁴⁷*CT* 1, 22a-b: *ind ḫr.tn srw ntrw*
  mꜣꜥ ḫrw Wsir-(Name) ḫr.tn m rꜥ pn.
⁴⁸*CT* I, 25b: *mꜣꜥ ḫrw Wsir-(Name) m bꜣḥ Gb rpꜥ ntrw.*
⁴⁹*Papyrus of Ani*, Pl. IV, 1-2: *dd mdw in Ḥr sꜣ ꜣst*
  ii.n.i ḫr.k Wn-nfr
  in.n.i n.k Wsir-ꜣny
  ib.f mꜣꜥ prt m m ḫꜣt
  n btꜣ.f ḫr ntr nb ntrt nb.
⁵⁰*ibid.*, Pl.IV, 5-8: *dd mdw in Wsir-ꜣny dd.f*
  mk (wi) m bꜣḥ.k nb imntt
  nn isft m ẖt.i
  nn dd.n.i grg m rḫ.
⁵¹*CT* VII, 506.

IX. Universalism and Monotheism

Egyptian myth, as is especially evident in the Heliopolitan mythic symbolism of creation, gave vivid and graphic articulation to the concept of order. In the Heliopolitan system, the basis of this order was the life force contained within Atum, who, as is evident in his very name (*Itm*), was seen as being in himself completion and totality (*tm*). Furthermore, and also according to the Heliopolitan system, the reality of life as an active and vital force was given concrete expression in the figure of Shu, while the reality of order in the created universe was expressed in the person of Tefnut, herself an embodiment of Ma'at with whom she was identified, as we have seen above. Interpreting this mythic symbolism in a more abstract fashion, we may state that for the Egyptian mind the whole of the cosmos was dependent upon the divine life force which was controlled by the laws inherent within nature itself.[1] In this brief statement of the signification of the Heliopolitan creation mythology we may see the true value of such a myth, a value which is totally and entirely symbolic. The Heliopolitan mythic system was in actuality a true myth; it was not simply a saga or folktale of creation. Nor was it really intended to be understood in a fundamentalist manner. The actual method of the creation, the way in which it had actually been brought into being, was not articulated in any kind of comprehensible fashion. Intellectually the latter fact could only remain a mystery. More important was the underlying significance of what was said by the myth: the whole of the cosmos was dependent upon the divine creative and ordering force. It was this force which had originally called it into being, and it was this force which continued to support and maintain it. The universe was, therefore, the on-going and continuing expression of the divine life.

The important question may be asked at this point as to whether or not such an expression of the creation implied the concept of a universal deity. General logic would obviously state that a deity who is the creator of all, or the creative force upon which all depends, must by his very nature be seen as a universal deity. At the same time, however, it must also be asked to what extent the Egyptian mind would have been able, at least at the period of this mythic formulation, to think in terms of such a wider order of being. R. Anthes[2] has seen even in the Pyramid Texts evidence of a concept of a universal deity, articulated in such expressions as *nb tm* ('Lord of all')[3] and *nn dr.f* ('he who has no limit').[4] This, however, is not necessarily monotheism, for it does not exclude the existence of other gods, other deities even being indicated and given an essential role in the Heliopolitan system. Moreover, such terms are far from sufficient in themselves to indicate a true concept of universalism. The somewhat parochial attitude of the Old Kingdom would surely have done much to prevent the Egyptian consciousness from looking beyond its own geographical boundaries and seeing a unified world order outside the borders of Egypt. With regard to intellectual comprehension, the Egyptian mind of the Old Kingdom would probably have been unable even to comprehend such a wider outlook, Egypt's interests in the outside world being confined only to a certain expansion of her political interests, and that mainly for self-protection. It seems impossible that the Egyptian mind of this early period could have conceived of an all-encompassing order and a deity who maintained it, a unity of the human and political into which all things were bound into one. Such a concept of the world did, of course, exist, but it was confined within the borders of Egypt, but could hardly have been able to extend beyond them. Egypt at this early period saw herself as the centre of the world, and, in effect, she *was* the world, at least to her own way of thinking. Nothing outside of her own boundaries really mattered, and hence the gods of Egypt had no real interest outside the Two Lands. To posit the existence of universalist ideas in the Old Kingdom, therefore, appears impossible. Such ideas appear to have arisen only after the growth of the Egyptian empire during the New Kingdom. Indeed universalist ideas seem to have depended directly upon the establishment of this empire. To a great extent the religion of Egypt held a strong nationalistic bias, a bias which never really fully disappeared even under the rule of Akhenaten. The theological position of the king would have contributed to such a nationalistic sentiment. Amarna theology shows very strong tendencies to regard the foreign lands (*ḫswt*) as being somewhat inferior to the land of Egypt, Egypt and her position being obviously the favoured domain and interest of the Amarna deity.

It is, however, in the religion of the Amarna movement that one most frequently sees universalist tendencies. It has been suggested that the sun temples of the Amarna movement strongly reflected this concept of universality.[5] This assertion, however, has no inherent implication that such universalism actually took its beginnings from the Amarna movement. On the contrary, it appears to be an unconditionally accepted fact that the religion of Akhenaten owed much of its content to the earlier worship of Amun-Ra in his aspect of a sun deity, and this tradition too shows strong marks of universalism.[6] The sun hymns from the tombs of the Eighteenth Dynasty, texts which were very much typical of the piety of the period, show heavy tendencies towards a universalism centred around the sun god. Exceptionally worthy of note are the two sun hymns of the brothers Suti and Hor,[7] both of whom bore the title Overseer of the Works of Amun, the two hymns being inscribed on a stele now in the British Museum (No. 826). These two texts express the adoration of Amun in his aspect as a sun god, praising him under the names of Ra, Kheperi, Horakhtey, Khnum, Amun and Aten. In these texts, which date from the reign of Amenhotep III (c. 1391-1353), the period immediately preceding the Amarna movement, we see an excellent example of the tendency to syncretize a number of deities in the person of the sun god. More important than such syncretism, however, are the marks of the universalism which is associated here with that same sun deity. The god appears as holding universal rule, as being the source of universal order and creativity, and as constituting the source of all life. The position held by the Aten in the Amarna movement was no wider in its dominion than was that of the sun god in the texts in question. Hence, it appears obvious that the characteristic of universality in the deity was something inherited by Akhenaten from an already existing theological position. At least in this regard, the religion of the Amarna movement appears not as a novelty in Egyptian theological thought, but as part of a much wider development in theology. This wider theological outlook must in turn be seen in the political context from which it emerged, for there can be little doubt that it was the natural outgrowth and extension of the Egyptian empire which had been gradually built up during the Eighteenth Dynasty following the expulsion of the Hyksos, an event which may well be the source of the Hebrew myth of the Exodus.

That the growth of the Egyptian empire was bound to have an effect on religious thinking and expression is axiomatic. We have seen the suggestion that it was the emergence of the kingship in the First Dynasty which gave rise to the concept of the heavenly Horus. Such an interpretation, whether or not we accept it as a valid reading of the historical situation, points to the very real probability that historical developments did affect the development of religious concepts. Insofar as the Pharaoh was considered the reflection and incarnation of the heavenly deity, it was only to be expected that as the concept of the earthly monarch expanded, so also would the concept of the heavenly monarch grow in proportion. As a result of the expansion of Egypt during the Eighteenth Dynasty, the Pharaoh had grown from his position of King of Upper and Lower Egypt (*niswt bity*) to a point where the same title implied a universal domination. He had in effect become an emperor, ruler of a far wider dominion than that which was enclosed within the boundaries of Egypt. The natural corollary of this is that the position of the chief national deity of Egypt would also have grown in proportion to that of his earthly counterpart. Hence, Amun-Ra, who by this time had become the leading god of Egypt (due to the growth of the Theban power), was now by the natural process of history expanded into a deity who held universal sway and dominion over the lands which had been taken into the Egyptian empire. Such a growth must have given a further justification to the imperialistic policies of the New Kingdom. J.H. Breasted has stated that "Monotheism is but imperialism in religion."[8] Such an assessment of monotheism obviously does something of an injustice to the full nature of that particular religious phenomenon, although it may well point to one aspect of the growth of monotheistic thought. We might do well, however, to adapt this assessment slightly and state that *universalism* is imperialism translated into and expressed in religious terminology. In brief, the growth of universalism in the Eighteenth and Nineteenth Dynasties was a natural outgrowth of political evolution.

The newly evolved imperialistic nature of Amun-Ra, combined with the association of that same deity with the sun disc, gave rise to the practice of writing sun hymns on the walls of the Eighteenth Dynasty tombs, a practice which became very widespread during that period.[9] The whole period between 1500 and 1200 B.C.E. was one of Egypt's most productive times for the writing of such sun hymns within the tombs.[10] These sun hymns appear as characteristic marks of the theological phenomenon which J. Assmann has called the 'New Sun Theology' (*Neue Sonnen-Theologie*).[11] The hymns were addressed to the sun disc at the time of its rising and of its setting and also throughout the day,[12] thus making it evident that the full cycle of daily time was seen as being under the rule and auspices of the sun god. Hence, the veneration of Amun-Ra as part of the personal piety of the dead became a further expansion of the universal power of the sun deity. It is perhaps for this reason that Assmann has seen in the so-called New Sun Theology a type of individual and personal religious experience which became, at least in part, the basis for the religion of the Amarna movement.[13] The theological details of the New Sun Theology appear to have constituted a relatively complex system, but two aspects in particular stand out. In the first place, the sun god was seen as interacting with other deities, thus providing an expression which was in essence polytheistic. The point here is that the New Sun Theology was not monotheistic in the sense of attempting to suppress or deny the other deities. Secondly, however (according to the interpretation of Assmann), this New Sun Theology did contain a type of monotheistic trend which was symbolized by the figure of the sun disc as evidence for the deity's uniqueness (*Einzigkeit*).[14] The New Sun Theology may thus be seen as a movement which followed in general the Egyptian practice evident in mythic symbolism, that of accepting two opposing symbolic expressions, in this case polytheism and monotheism. Both expressions of divinity were accepted in this new system, neither one invalidating the other. The combination of these two normally opposing religious ideologies was probably necessitated by the traditional mythic expressions of Egyptian religion, that is, by the accepted plurality of religious symbolism. This traditional plurality of deities, a polytheistic form of expression, would have made it virtually impossible for the myth-oriented mentality of Egypt to reject all other deities in favour of one sole god. Hence, although in effect the New Sun Theology may have recognized the essential singularity of the divine power, it did not, nevertheless, reject the plurality of expression. The chief deity within such a system, even though he may have been seen as acting alone without any dependence upon other deities, was still able to admit the mythic expressions of other divine beings. In actual fact, the existence or non-existence of other gods was probably of very little real interest or importance within this way of thought. What is important, however, is that the system known as the New Sun Theology did not have within itself any inherent necessity of actively excluding gods other than the sun god. Such a system may appear as a type of monotheism for all practical purposes, for it does seem to have recognized the singular power of a supreme deity, the sun god, who had no need of other deities for his actions or for his existence. At the same time, however, the system did not go to the full lengths which would normally be expected of a monotheistic system and actively deny the existence of all other gods. In this respect it is difficult to see the New Sun Theology as a full philosophical monotheism. At best it appears to have been a type of practical henotheism.

Insofar as the New Sun Theology showed no real interest in the traditional gods, the older mythological concepts which had belonged to those gods no longer held any important place. In the older mytho-theologies the other gods had been associated with the sun god as a constellation of deities, but in the New Sun Theology they were described in a cosmic dimension as actions of the sun.[15] If and when they did appear in the texts, it was as a species of creatures and living beings on a level with animals and men, but not as partners of the sun god in a constellation of deities as before.[16] The eventual result of this was virtually a new concept of God in which the traditional mythic dimension was replaced by a cosmic revelation. Hence, men were now able to relate to the deity by means of the natural phenomena which were visible to them. The iconography of the traditional mytho-theology no longer had any place,[17] for the New Sun Theology dealt only with phenomena which could actually be seen. The traditional religious expressions had been founded on myth, that is, on symbols which expressed concepts which were beyond human perception. (Hence, I have used for this way of articulation the term 'mytho-theology'.) As a result, although the gods were different from men, they were not totally remote. They were, at least to some extent, knowable through their mythic symbols. In the New Sun Theology, however, God could be seen through his manifestation in the sun disc, but his essence remained unknown. He was not an actual personification of the natural life force as, for example, Atum had been in the older Heliopolitan system. God was remote and unknown to man in his essence, but not totally inaccessible, for he could be known through his actions and revelation in the natural phenomena of the universe.

Such an interpretation of the religious atmosphere of the Eighteenth and Nineteenth Dynasties is a matter of personal opinion, and perhaps the interpretation of Assmann is somewhat too philosophical and too abstractly theological. What is clearly implied in this interpretation is a concept of deity which is highly spiritual, non-anthropomorphic and totally other. Such tendencies have already been seen in earlier stages of Egyptian religious thought. However, we must note that such were but tendencies, tendencies which are naturally inherent within any mythic system and which in fact make a mythic means of expression a necessity. At the same time, the mythic expression is usually kept in such cases for the simple reason that the human mentality is not yet able to reason in an abstract manner. If Assmann's view is in fact correct, then we would be obliged to see in the New Sun Theology a system of thought which had far surpassed the abilities of the older mytho-theological systems.

The opinion of Assmann on this subject may perhaps be seen in better perspective if it is balanced by the view of Hornung who holds that the Egyptian gods were by their very nature neither eternal nor transcendent.[18] If such in fact was the case, then it would be impossible to see in the New Sun Theology the type of abstract theological comprehension which Assmann proposes to detect there, unless of course the Egyptian mind had developed a sudden ability for such theological speculation, and was thereby enabled to discard the role played by the traditional mytho-theology of the past. One certainly does see that these traditions underwent a wholesale rejection by Akhenaten, although even he was forced to put in their place certain mythic symbols centred around the Aten. Nevertheless, one cannot maintain that there was any kind of complex Amarna mythology. What Akhenaten retained was a number of mythic symbols connected with the deity and the person of the king, but such symbols were obviously unable to compensate for the loss of the traditional mytho-theological systems. If they had been able to do so, then the Amarna movement may have had a better chance of surviving its founder. In both the Amarna movement and in the periods which preceded and followed it, one must admit the existence of certain ideas of the transcendent nature of the sun god. However, it is somewhat doubtful that such was sufficient to lead to a totally abstract concept of the deity such as Assmann sees in the New Sun Theology. The universalism of the Eighteenth and Nineteenth Dynasties appears to have developed to a certain extent, but not to the full extent of being able totally to replace the older mytho-theology with a new abstract theological comprehension. In brief, we may easily admit the existence of a universalist outlook at this period of Egypt's religious history, but it is difficult to see beyond this to a concept of a transcendent and spiritual god, one who can be totally divorced from the traditional mythic expressions. Even Akhenaten did not succeed in creating such a deity.

The question of universalism in Egyptian religion appears to present little problem. Such seems to have been an actual phenomenon which had evolved out of the international position of Egypt in world politics. Monotheism, on the other hand, represents a somewhat different question, one to which many answers have been given, and one on which it is highly difficult to make any definite judgement. The desire to see either monotheistic tendencies or full monotheism in Egyptian religion is one which has been common to many Egyptologists, one modern scholar having even spoken of "the underlying monotheism of the Egyptian mind."[19] Even in the Nineteenth Century a number of prominent Egyptologists stressed the idea that from a very early period the Egyptians had worshipped one deity who was "nameless, incomprehensible, and eternal."[20] The very highly philosophical and theological nature of this suggested early monotheism as it has been described by de Rougé[21] would have made of Egyptian monotheism a system which could hardly be surpassed by the most profound of modern theologians. Champollion-Figeac wrote in 1839 that "the Egyptian religion is a pure monotheism, which manifested itself externally by a symbolic polytheism."[22] Such a view is in keeping with the symbolic nature of the Egyptian mythic expressions which has been adopted in the present work, and this interpretation of these mythic expressions does appear to be consistent with their usage by the Egyptians themselves. However, to insist that the Egyptians were conscious of the monotheistic nature of their religion appears to impose upon the Egyptian mind a theological ability which was foreign to it. As we have seen earlier, terms such as 'polytheism' and 'monotheism' would have been irrelevant to the Egyptian way of thought. G. Posener has examined the usage of terms such as $n\underline{t}r$ ('god') and $p\,\mathcal{S}\ n\underline{t}r$ ('the god') in the pre-Amarna wisdom literature, and has concluded that such terms were not used to refer to any sole or unique deity.[23] Nor does Pirenne regard the Heliopolitan idea of one god as a type of serious monotheistic movement.[24] Budge, attempting to push Egyptian monotheism to its fullest possible extent, had stated that the Egyptian was "a monotheist pure and simple as a sun-worshipper. It avails nothing to call his monotheism 'henotheism'."[25] This view takes as its starting point the assumption that sun worship must imply, or at least naturally lead to, a monotheistic religion. Sun worship may indeed quite easily lead to the concept of a deity who is supreme above all others, but it does not necessarily contain within itself any inherent tendencies towards monotheistic thought.

Other scholars have thought to see evidence of a monotheistic belief among the Egyptians in the writings of the wisdom literature. For example, Drioton and Vandier have stated: "Le monothéisme est en fait l'apanage des livres de sagesse..."[26] As we have just seen, however, G. Posener has rejected the idea that the writers of the wisdom literature had any innate tendency towards monotheistic thinking. With regard to religious teachings in the wisdom literature we should also note that religion and the gods do not appear to have been the main concern of the writers of these texts. Such texts were not religious in nature, but practical. Their intention was to give advice on moral actions and etiquette, on good and proper behaviour. If one can derive any religious values from these texts, such values are of a secondary nature and are not the main purpose of the texts. Even when the wisdom writers use the term 'god' (*ntr*), it appears that it can stand for virtually any deity and that it makes no reference to any one supreme God of a monotheistic nature.[27] Even authors who used the term 'god' (*ntr*) in the singular were also quite capable of using the plural 'gods' (*ntrw*) on occasion.[28] Despite the number of opinions in support of an Egyptian monotheism, the evidence from the Egyptian texts themselves does not really provide conclusive proof that such a monotheism ever existed, and any clear statement that it did is probably based on too romantic an idea of ancient Egyptian religion. It appears that the safest conclusion which can be reached on the subject is that monotheism was not innate in the nature of Egyptian religion. This statement may be modified by the further suggestion that in the two centuries preceding Akhenaten certain tendencies towards a monotheistic or henotheistic belief were growing, but that these did not reach any definite monotheistic climax. Whether such a monotheism emerged with Akhenaten is a totally different question, one which must now be considered.

The assessment of Akhenaten's religion as a monotheism is one which has frequently been made, perhaps too often made without any attempt to consider carefully the full impact of such a statement or the total circumstances of the Amarna movement. It is a fact that Akhenaten applied to his deity, the Aten, the epithet 'one' (*w ʿ*), but such in itself cannot be taken as a total statement of monotheism. It is difficult to imagine that a full monotheistic faith could have emerged out of a background which was essentially polytheistic in its expression, unless that monotheistic faith had been preceded by at least some strong manifestation of similar thinking, or unless it had been the product of a mind which could be characterized as having a peculiar genius for religious perception. The latter possibility has indeed been suggested,[29] and may in fact have been the case. Against such an assertion, however, it is necessary to consider the fact that the Amarna writings contain little which is truly original or which reveals the influence of a religious intellectual giant, much of the content of the Amarna religion already being evident in earlier religious thought. As for precedents in monotheistic thinking, we have already seen the possibility of monotheistic or henotheistic tendencies in the movement which Assmann has called the New Sun Theology, but these possibilities must be taken only as such. To state categorically that a monotheistic trend had indeed existed before Akhenaten is perhaps to make too rash an assumption on the basis of the available evidence. It has, nevertheless, been maintained that before Akhenaten monotheistic ideas had been growing quite steadily, and that the main accomplishment of Akhenaten himself was to establish this monotheism as the official and only religion of Egypt.[30] Gardiner appears not to have hesitated to designate Akhenaten's new faith as a "genuine monotheism,"[31] even though his own estimation of Akhenaten's overall achievement was not the highest. Zabkar's evaluation of Akhenaten's faith is somewhat more cautious, as he points out that the Amarna faith was not philosophical monotheism. He prefers instead to characterize it as a form of solar monotheism,[32] a designation which implies an obvious identity between the deity of Akhenaten and the sun disc itself. Such a form of religion, however, could hardly be viewed as genuine monotheism insofar as it lacked a spiritualized and transcendent deity, and directed its worship instead to the physical disc of the sun. Breasted had seen the apparent lack of mythology in Akhenaten's movement as a positive mark, interpreting this lack as a sign of the monotheistic nature of the Amarna religion,[33] the same lack of myth also being noted by Hornung as a positive characteristic of the movement.[34] Hornung further sees Akhenaten's faith as remarkable insofar as it was a phenomenon wherein "henotheism has been transformed into monotheism."[35] Davies was also relatively positive in his evaluation of Akhenaten's achievement, seeing it as a positive advance that Akhenaten had banished the other deities and had taken steps towards a universal religion. At the same time, however, he stresses the fact that Akhenaten did not contrive either a monotheistic system or an ethical system, but no more than a "humanized henotheism."[36] Other opinions on the nature of Akhenaten's religion, some positive and others highly critical, could be cited here as evidence of the wide range of interpretation which is possible concerning the Amarna movement. Further discussion, however, would add nothing specific to our understanding of the problem. Let it suffice here to say that the presence or absence of monotheism in the Amarna system has been the subject of a long debate, and perhaps no definitive answer is possible to the question. At the same time, it is necessary to stress again that the true and genuine religious characteristic of the Egyptian civilization in which the Amarna movement occurred was polytheism or at least a polytheistic expression. It was the "multiplicity of approaches" and the "multiplicity of answers" which, according to H. Frankfort, was the true mark of the

Egyptian religious genius. In such a religious system, man was able to approach his god or gods in many different ways and through many varied symbols. The emergence of a monotheism in such an atmosphere would have obviously been viewed as a total destruction of all genuine and valid religious values, for it would have required a totally new way of approach to the divine. This is, of course, exactly what Akhenaten's movement did, and it may be that this was the main reason for its failure. It was, in a word, too totally non-Egyptian in its outlook and approach. Even the New Sun Theology had not gone so far in its innovations. In such a situation, one may argue that Akhenaten's movement was the totally revolutionary step which some claim that it was, namely a monotheism which had emerged out of earlier tendencies and had tried to overthrow the accepted system. On the other hand, it is also possible to maintain that the environment of traditional Egyptian religion was so far removed from any type of monotheistic thinking that Akhenaten could have done no more than realize the henotheism which Davies has seen in the Amarna movement. In either case, no final answer is given here to the problem of Amarna monotheism. Even a tentative decision concerning this question must rest on a much more detailed examination of the nature of the Amarna deity.

The Aten, the deity of Akhenaten's new religion, may or may not have been equated with the actual sun disc, and scholarly opinion is divided on this question. A number of scholars who have maintained the monotheistic nature of the Amarna deity, including Gardiner and Zabkar, have nevertheless maintained that in the Amarna system deity and sun disc are equated. The religion thus becomes a solar monotheism. The main basis for such an argument appears to be the fact that in the Amarna texts the god of the movement is designated as the Aten (*Itn*), a common Egyptian term for the physical sun disc. Zabkar's argument is that the texts do not show any specific evidence that there was in the Amarna system any unnamed deity who was simply represented by the sun disc and was obviously distinct from that disc.[37] The same position is taken by Lagier[38] and by Assmann,[39] although the latter qualifies his assertion somewhat by stating as an alternative that the sun disc was at least an incarnation of the deity.

In opposition to such opinions we must note the fact that the Amarna texts do make an apparent distinction between the terms 'the Aten' (*pꜣ Itn*) and 'the living Aten' (*pꜣ Itn ꜥnḫ*), the former of these two expressions referring mainly to the physical sun disc, and the latter used to refer to the actual deity himself. Such in fact was the opinion of Davies, who saw the real Amarna deity as being "the mysterious life which gave movement, energy, creative and beneficent power to the Sun."[40] In this interpretation, the actual sun disc was in reality no more than an instrument of which the deity made use, but the actual god, the 'living Aten', was superior to and distinct from the physical disc of the sun. The deity himself was named as essentially Ra or Ra-Horakhtey, depending upon whether any given text was composed before or after the ninth year of Akhenaten's reign. Before the ninth year we find that the normal titulary of the Aten was written as ʿnḫ Rʿ Ḥr-ȝḫty ḥʿy m ȝḫt m rn.f m šw nty m Itn ('The Living One, Ra-Horakhtey who rejoices on the horizon in his name as the Brightness which is in the Aten'). After year nine, however, when Akhenaten appears to have attempted a purification of the title of his god from any older associations, the name was changed to ʿnḫ Rʿ ḥḳȝ ȝḫty ḥʿy m ȝḫt m rn.f m Rʿ ii.ti m Itn ('The Living One, Ra, ruler of the two horizons, who rejoices in the horizon in his name as Ra who has come in the Aten').[41] We may note here in passing that the obvious purpose for the change in year nine was to drop from the titulary the references to Ra-Horakhtey and to Shu, which could have recalled the older deities of Egyptian tradition, and to substitute for them expressions which were more in keeping with the exclusive nature of Amarna religion. It is, however, of more importance at this point to recognize the fact that in both of these titularies the term Aten in used as a designation of the sun disc in which the deity has been made manifest. It does not appear as the actual name of the deity. Even the title 'the Great Living Aten' (Itn ʿnḫ wr)[42] appears to have been not a name of the deity, but rather a designation intended to differentiate the god from the sun disc. The deity of the Amarna movement appears to be best designated as Ra, the ancient solar god of Heliopolis whom Akhenaten had brought against the power of the Theban Amun, and whose nature went beyond the mere physical sun disc. It thus appears unlikely that any full identification should be made between the Amarna deity and the sun disc. The best we may say is that the sun disc was the instrument of the god, or at the very most an incarnation of him.

The citing of actual texts to illustrate the nature of Akhenaten's god would lengthen this section of our study too much. It is at this point sufficient simply to summarize the character of the Aten as he was seen in the Amarna system.[43] Akhenaten's god appears to have been sole creator (his creative activity being expressed through the imagery of the spoken word, light, the rays of the sun and parentage), universal deity and ruler, transcendent and immanent, source of all life, provider of sustenance, controller of the order of the universe, and revealed in nature and in the teaching of Akhenaten. Such a characterization indicates that Akhenaten desired to create a god who would be the equivalent of, and even more than, the universal power of Amun-Ra as he had developed in the Theban system. The theological nature of the Aten, representing a concept of a deity who was universal in his domain and whose powers were obviously very extensive, does appear to qualify him for the position of sole deity. Moreover, the texts themselves purposely avoid any kind of reference to other gods. The Aten was thus obviously the only god recognized and worshipped in the Amarna cult. Such implies at least a henotheistic position, if not a monotheistic one.

A number of scholars have pointed to the lack of myth in the Amarna system as being one of its main characteristics. Both A. Erman[44] and H.M. Stewart[45] take the attitude that the absence of myth, as well as the idea of one god, was the invention of Akhenaten. As we have seen above, however, Assmann points out the essential absence of mythology in the New Sun Theology. If Assmann's description of the latter movement is correct, then it is obvious that Akhenaten made no great innovation by his attempt to demythologize religion. This seeming lack of mythology may not, however, be taken as an strict indication of monotheism, for, due to the symbolic nature of myth, it is far from being incompatible with a monotheistic system. A lack of myth would have done no more than assure that the deity was less anthropomorphic and more spiritualized than the gods who were associated with the mythic systems. Moreover, to state that the Amarna system was entirely non-mythological is perhaps not totally correct, for it is possible to see in many of the texts certain mythic symbols, particularly statements relating to the creation and to the person of the king. These symbols do not constitute a highly developed system of mythic symbolism, and in this regard the Aten was less mythological than the traditional gods of Egypt. At the same time, however, mythic expressions are a virtual necessity for the articulation of any religious doctrine or experience, and they did find at least a limited usage in the Amarna system.

In order to assess the Amarna system as a strict monotheism, it would be necessary to provide evidence from the actual Amarna texts that the Aten was perceived as the sole God and that no other deity had any existence beside him. The texts do in numerous instances apply to the Aten the adjective-verb w^ci ('one', 'sole', 'unique'), but this term cannot really be taken as the exact equivalent of the Greek μόνος, for it does not contain the necessary inherent implication that the entity which it describes is totally and categorically alone or single in his essence. Moreover, the instances in which it is used in the Amarna texts to indicate the aloneness or uniqueness of the Aten as a deity do not by their context further imply the non-existence of other gods. An expression such as *iw.k w ʿ.ti*[46] ("You are alone") need imply no more than that the Aten was unique of his kind, but not that he was the sole existent god. So also the phrase *pȝ Itn ʿn ḫ nn ky wpw- ḥ r.f* [47] ("the living Aten beside whom there is no other"), which may be seen as a statement of monotheistic faith, may also be interpreted simply as an affirmation of the uniqueness of the deity. Finally, a variant of the last expression, *pȝ nṯr w ʿ nn ky ḥr ḥw.f*,[48] frequently interpreted as "the sole God beside whom there is no other," may also be given the meaning of "the unique God, who has no other face," with reference to the revelation of the deity in the universe which he has created. Such an interpretation may easily be supported by the writing of the line and by the context in which it occurs. Such uniqueness or soleness on the part of the deity need not imply an existential singularity. The usage of the term *w ʿ* ('sole', 'one'), therefore, makes no clear monotheistic statement about the Amarna deity. In fact, the term was frequently in earlier Egyptian writings applied to other gods with no reference to monotheism and no indication that such gods were alone in their divine existence. The usage of such a term may indeed be seen as no more than "flattering exaggeration."[49] Such statements may be seen as expressions of a type of practical henotheism, but hardly as indications of true monotheism. We see, for example, that the term *w ʿ* was applied to Amun in the Prayer of Paheri,[50] but it obviously had here no monotheistic overtones insofar as other deities are mentioned in the same context. The epithet 'unique god' appears as a common designation of many deities, a sound indication that no monotheistic statements were thereby implied. Even the palm tree could be called 'unique',[51] and the Asiatic deity Qudshu was described as being 'without equal',[52] as was Nefertem in the Pyramid Texts.[53] The epithet *pȝ nṯr w ʿ*, 'the sole [unique] god'), which was often applied to the Aten was also found in connection with Ma'at, Sekhmet and Mut.[54] The reference in such cases must surely be seen as pointing to the unique nature of the divine in general or as distinguishing between the various gods themselves. One should not, however, see the usage of such a term as implying any type of monotheistic overtones. So also in the Amarna texts such monotheism must be called into doubt, especially given the non-monotheistic nature of the whole background of the movement.

Despite the fact that the Amarna texts make no denial, either implicit or explicit, of other deities, we still have the evidence of Akhenaten's final persecution of the other Egyptian gods during the last years of his reign. In the absence of any written explanation for such an action, one can only guess at what motives may have laid behind it. Either it was prompted by a sudden outburst of zealousness for the monotheistic nature of his new faith, or it came about as a result of Akhenaten's desire to overthrow once and for all any opposition to his movement from other religious traditions. In the latter event, it may be seen as more of a political move than a religious one. Such an explanation appears as the most obvious and, therefore, most likely, and this leaves us with the highly likely conclusion that the Amarna movement presents no clear evidence that it was in fact an abstract philosophical monotheism. If one wishes to apply any label to Akhenaten's movement, the safest one appears to be that of henotheism. As concerning any monotheistic features, the best that we may say is that the Amarna movement appears to have been a type of practical henotheism, showing the one sign that it eventually attempted to destroy all other deities instead of just ignoring them. The basis for this, however, appears not to have been a theological one, but rather one which was political and perhaps even fanatic. In any event, it is unlikely that it was prompted by any genuine monotheistic convictions, the existence of which still appears highly questionable and perhaps even doubtful.

I have dealt with the movement of Akhenaten at some length, not because of any positive contributions which it may have made to the Egyptian theological achievement, but because of its highly unusual nature within the history of Egyptian religion. It is, moreover, necessary to see the monotheistic possibilities of the movement in a more realistic context than they have often been taken, for the attribution of monotheistic ideas to Akhenaten would imply the existence of a theological stance which could not have been achieved by the ordinary Egyptian religious mentality. A monotheism during Egypt's Eighteenth Dynasty would probably have been a totally improbable and even impossible anachronism. One must, therefore, exercise extreme caution when attempting to characterize the religion of the Amarna movement.

One may ask what the true significance of Akhenaten's movement was. What, if anything, did it contribute to Egyptian theological development?

To be certain, it did contain a high element of universalism, but this appears to have been an inheritance from the past, a concept which was a necessary development of both the political and religious evolutions of the preceding centuries. At the same time, however, we may suggest that the concentration of Akhenaten on his one deity, whom he stressed as a universal god, may well have exerted a positive influence on the further development of Amun-Ra in the centuries which followed the Amarna movement. Ironically enough, when the older traditions were again restored by the rulers who followed Akhenaten, it was Amun-Ra, the deity whom Akhenaten had been most intent of dethroning, who inherited the position of the Aten and became the Egyptian deity with whom universalism was most associated. Lest, however, we do Akhenaten the injustice of totally denying him any worthwhile achievement, let us note here that in the opinion of J. Wilson the concept of universalism in religion was the main achievement of Akhenaten.[55] Such may well be a possibility and it should not be absolutely denied. At the same time let us again recall the the hymns of Suti and Hor, dating from the pre-Amarna period, as well as many of the other sun hymns of the same period, show principles which were very similar to those of the Amarna system.[56] The most likely interpretation of the Amarna movement, therefore, is that is was the final outcome of a process which had been developing over a number of decades. It may be that the personality of Akhenaten himself contributed much to the specific way in which the movement evolved, but the basic foundation for the movement had already been laid.[57] If Akhenaten had not intervened with his particular hostility to Amun-Ra, the history of Egyptian religion could well have taken a somewhat different course. What the outcome of that would have been is, however, only a matter for speculation. The final outcome of Akhenaten's movement at least is quite clear: a firmer strengthening of the power of the Theban clergy, the results of which would eventually be seen in the Twenty-First Dynasty when Upper and Lower Egypt were in effect split into separate kingdoms with the High Priestly throne of Thebes in control of Upper Egypt.

As a final assessment of Akhenaten and his movement let us note two opposing opinions. Cyril Aldred has described it as being "a more joyous acceptance of the natural world, and a more rational belief in a universal sole god."[58] At the opposite extreme we have the opinion of Donald B. Redford who sees the movement of Akhenaten as being essentially, at least to the Egyptian mind, little less than atheism.[59] Such an opinion grows out of the fact that in ancient Egypt myth was the only true and possible means of revelation. Once mythology had been abolished, there would have remained for the Egyptian religious mind no means of knowing, perceiving or communicating with the divine. Hence, in a very real sense Akhenaten's 'practical monotheism' would have been in fact transformed into a type of practical atheism, at least for the Egyptian, whose concept of religion was far different from that of the 'heretic of Akhetaten'. The 'monotheism' of Akhenaten was totally opposed to the natural and ingrained Egyptian tendencies to respect the phenomena of nature and to accept these as a valid revelation of the divine. It denied the recognition of the multiplicity of the divine power. The Egyptian perception of reality, a perception which had been sanctified by centuries of mythic expression and mythic experience, made it impossible for a deity such as Akhenaten's to receive anything but the most superficial acceptance. Moreover, the demands made by Akhenaten for the acceptance of certain principles of dogma and doctrine were highly foreign to the Egyptian mentality which was accustomed not to accept dogmatic statements but to experience the reality of the divine in the mythic symbolism of the cult. Akhenaten's system destroyed the freedom to do this very thing, even though such was the basic essential of the Egyptian religious experience. In brief, Akhenaten's movement attempted to force upon Egypt a religion which could not possibly have been accepted by her myth-oriented mentality. Ironically enough, in such a situation the evolution of monotheistic thinking could not really be seen as any kind of religious advance or as a positive development in human understanding. Its effects would rather have been of a destructive and detrimental nature, for it would have attempted to force the Egyptian mentality into a way of thought which was still far beyond that mentality. In brief, the New Kingdom of Egypt was not yet ready to accept philosophical and ethical monotheism.

As a final statement, we must admit that, at least at the time of Akhenaten, the concept of monotheism would have been totally and completely irrelevant to the Egyptian religious experience. It would have made no sense even as a logical statement. It could have found no genuine intellectual assent, because it was a contradiction of the traditional Egyptian mytho-theological system and way of expression. As such it could have had no place in the principles of Egyptian theology. Above all else, the mytho-theology of ancient Egypt permitted to the human spirit a sense of religious freedom and tolerance. Akhenaten's dogmatism would have removed and even totally obliterated that freedom. Such a goal cannot be the legitimate objective of any true religion. Because, therefore, of its intolerant nature, and because it was so totally non-Egyptian in its outlook, the religion of Akhenaten and the Amarna movement was not able to survive its founder, nor was its 'monotheistic' ideology able to make any impact upon the mythic system which was so characteristic of Egyptian religious expression.

Notes

[1] R.T. Rundle Clark, *Myth and Symbol in Ancient Egypt*, 47.
[2] *JNES* XVIII, 191.
[3] *PT* 305a.
[4] *PT* 1434b, 1442b.
[5] A.M. Badawy, "The Symbolism of the Temples at 'Amarna'," *ZÄS* LXXXVII (1962): 79-95.
[6] See, for example, W.F. Albright, *From the Stone Age to Christianity* (New York, 1959), 219; J.H. Breasted, *The Dawn of Conscience*, 298; A. Varille, "L'Hymne au Soleil des architectes d'Aménophis III, Souti et Hor," *BIFAO* XLI (1942): 25-30.
[7] Translation in M. Lichtheim, *Ancient Egyptian Literature*, II, 86ff.
[8] *Development of Religion and Thought in Ancient Egypt*, 315.
[9] See, for example, H.M. Stewart, "Some Pre-Amarna Sun Hymns," *JEA* XLVI (1960): 83-90, and "Traditional Egyptian Sun Hymns of the New Kingdom," *BIA* VI (1966): 29-74.
[10] J. Assmann, *Re und Amun* (Freiburg, 1983), 1f.
[11] *loc. cit.*
[12] H.M. Stewart, *JEA* XLVI (1960): 84.
[13] J.Assmann, *op. cit.*, 18.
[14] *ibid.*, 22.
[15] *ibid.*, 100.
[16] *ibid.*, 99.
[17] *ibid.*, 103.
[18] E. Hornung, *Conceptions of God in Ancient Egypt*, 195.
[19] R.T. Rundle Clark, *op. cit.*, 69.
[20] E.A.W. Budge, *The Book of the Dead: The Papyrus of Ani*, New York, 1967, xci (reprint of the original 1895 edition).
[21] *ibid.*, xcii.
[22] *loc. cit.*

[23]G. Posener, "Sur le monothéisme dans l'ancienne Egypte," *Mélanges bibliques et orientaux en l'honneur de M. Henri Cazelles* (Neukirchen-Vluyn, 1981), 348-351.
[24]J. Pirenne, *La religion et la morale dans l'Egypte antique* (Paris,1965), 89.
[25]E.A.W. Budge, *From Fetish to God in Ancient Egypt*, London, 1934, 3f.
[26]Drioton & Vandier, *L'Egypte*, 63.
[27]See H. Kees, *Der Götterglaube im alten Ägypten*, 2nd edition (Berlin, 1956), 273.
[28]E. Hornung, *op. cit.*, 53.
[29]L.A. White, "Ikhnaton: The Great Man versus the Cultural Process," *JAOS* 68 (1948): 91-114.
[30]J. Baikie, *The Amarna Age*, London, 1926, 313ff.
[31]A.H. Gardiner, *Egypt of the Pharaohs*, 227.
[32]L Zabkar, "The Theocracy of Amarna and the Doctrine of the Ba," *JNES* XIII (1954): 93f.
[33]J.H. Breasted, *Development of Religion and Thought in Ancient Egypt*, 339f.
[34]E. Hornung, *op. cit.*, 248.
[35]*ibid.*, 246.
[36]N. de G. Davies, "Akhenaten at Thebes," *JEA* IX (1923): 132ff.
[37]*JNES* XIII, 93.
[38]C. Lagier, Le Pharaon du Disque Solaire," *RSR* IV (1913): 297-341.
[39]J. Assmann, *op. cit.*, 100.
[40]Davies, *Amarna*, I, 45.
[41]On this change of the titulary of Akhenaten's god see B. Gunn, "Notes on the Aten and his Names," *JEA* IX (1923): 168ff.
[42]M. Sandman, *Texts from the Time of Akhenaten*, 93.9.
[43]For a more extensive discussion of the nature of the Amarna deity, see my article "Amarna and Biblical Religion," *Pharaonic Egypt, the Bible and Christianity*, edited by S.I. Groll, (Jerusalem, 1985), 231-277.
[44]A. Erman, *Die Religion der Ägypter*, Berlin, 1934, 66.
[45]H.M. Stewart, "Some Pre-Amarna Sun Hymns," *JEA* XLVI (1960): 90.
[46]M. Sandman, *op. cit.*, 95.11.
[47]*ibid.*, 7.4-7.
[48]*ibid.*, 94.17.
[49]J. Wilson, *The Culture of Ancient Egypt*, 225.
[50]M. Lichtheim, *op. cit.*, II, 16.
[51]I. Wallert, *Die Palmen im alten Ägypten*, (*MÄS* 1), 1962, 134.
[52]M. Tosi & A. Roccati, *Stele e alteri epigrafi di Deir el Medina*, Turino, 1972, 103, no.50066.
[53]*PT* 483b-c.

[54] L.A. Christophe, *ASAE* 51 (1951): 349.
[55] J. Wilson, *op. cit.*, 107.
[56] A. Varille, *op.cit.*, 25-30.
[57] J.N. Oswalt, *The Concept of Amun-Re as Reflected in the Hymns and Prayers of the Ramesside Period*, Ph.D. Dissertation, Brandeis University, 1968, 37.
[58] C. Aldred, *Akhenaten and Nefertiti*, New York, 1973, 79.
[59] D.B. Redford, Akhenaten, *The Heretic Pharaoh*, Princeton, 1984, 244.

X. Egyptian Morality

The great gods of Egypt were essentially state gods, just as the Egyptian cults were state cults. The central aim of Egyptian cultic actions and religious symbolism, therefore, was normally directed towards the broad, and even cosmic, concerns of the nation. This did not mean that the individual was able to find no place for himself and no satisfaction through these deities and their cults, for the individual was himself part of the cosmic order which the gods upheld and which the cults effected. Furthermore, the life of the individual depended to a very great extent on the regular order of the seasons and of the phenomena of nature, and therefore his interest in the mythic rituals and their results must have been far more than minimal. Even if one makes a distinction between personal religion and state religion, this does not nullify the fact that the official religion of Egypt was significant for the private individual as well as for the wider order.

Frequently, however, personal piety was centred on other minor deities, deities who may perhaps have had no temples and no major shrines, but who were worshipped and venerated in the homes.[1] Our understanding of Egyptian personal piety is bound to be less than our comprehension of the official cults, for it is the official religion of Egypt which has left behind the greater volume of remains. Moreover, it is this official religion which was marked by the high development of the mytho-theology which we have seen. Nevertheless, we do have instances of individuals praying to various gods and making intercession both on behalf of others and on behalf of themselves. While intercessory prayer for others was no doubt quite important to personal piety, in all likelihood the major emphasis of such piety must have been the desire to be free from evil and to live one's life in accordance with the principles of Ma'at. In other words, the individual Egyptian was conscious of the fact that it was possible to act in an unrighteous manner, to sin and thus to incur the disfavour and anger of the gods. That is to say, moral considerations were not totally absent from Egyptian religion, even though the official myths and state cults had not laid down specific rules, codes and commandments of moral conduct. The specific details of moral and righteous living were rather the interests and domain of the writers of the wisdom literature, and the relationship of the individual to morality was essentially a matter of personal piety and of his personal conscience.

To a certain extent, at least in the experience of the ordinary individual, considerations of morality must have been largely of a pragmatic and practical nature. Men would have refrained from committing wrong for a variety of self-interested reasons: in order not to incur punishment from the authorities, in order not to bring upon themselves the wrath of the gods, or in order to ensure that after death they would be judged sinless and thus be enabled to enter the next world. In brief, as in most cultures, morality was promoted through both fear of punishment and hope of reward, the hope for personal immortality being the most obvious boon which men could expect in return for leading an upright life.

As we have already seen, such a reward was not the lot of the ordinary individual in the Old Kingdom where immortality was reserved for the monarch and his chosen favourites. With the rise of the Middle Kingdom, however, the hope of immortality became the property of all men, and as a result a greater awareness of the importance of leading a righteous life came into existence. The Middle Kingdom Coffin Texts, like the later New Kingdom Book of the Dead, make it evident that the fact of having lead a proper life, of being judged as 'justified of voice' ($m3^c$ $ḫrw$), was a prerequisite for entry into eternal happiness. Morality gradually became defined in a stricter manner, and the Negative Confession in the Book of the Dead implies the existence of generally accepted standards of correct moral behaviour, standards by which certain actions were seen as ones from which man had to refrain in order to be acceptable to the gods in the next world. Later in the New Kingdom, we see that men became more and more aware of their own sinfulness, more conscious of the wrong of specific actions which they may have committed. At the same time, however, they also became more aware of the possibilities of divine forgiveness; they became aware that the gods were merciful and would willingly absolve them of their sins once the wrong of their actions had been admitted and due repentance expressed. Personal piety and an ethical life were, therefore, inseparably connected.

The consciousness of sin and the subsequent and natural action of seeking forgiveness from a deity became especially marked in the period following the Amarna age. The religion of the individual had by this time become more personal, a phenomenon which may well have arisen out of the conflict between Amun and Aten during the Amarna period. The texts from Deir el-Medinah, for example, frequently provide evidence that man had by now a sense of his unworthiness when he was confronted by the moral demands of the gods. The same texts also show a realization of the merciful and compassionate nature of the gods and the confidence that man can confess and repent of his sins and thus find pardon and forgiveness. The mercy and compassion of the gods may be seen in the text of the stele of Nebre from Deir el-Medinah (Berlin Museum no. 20377).[2] Herein Amun of Thebes is praised by Nebre for his kindness and compassion not only in forgiving sins, but also to those who in any form of distress call upon him. The consciousness of the mercy and kindness of Amun illustrated in this text is highly comparable to the sense of divine mercy which is shown in many of the penitential psalms of the Hebrew Old Testament. One sees in this text that, despite the fact that man is inclined to do evil, Amun is shown as inclined to forgive and not to persist in his anger. Amun is, moreover, shown as one who has compassion for the poor and for the one who is in distress and trouble; he is described as a god who comes at the call of human need. It is interesting to note here that, although Amun-Ra bore the exalted position of king of the gods in the official state religion, he was nevertheless able and willing to hear even the lowliest and humblest of the people. It is obvious that the mytho-theologization of the gods did not prevent them from becoming also the personal gods of the common people. In fact, it may have been the very greatness and exaltedness of the gods which caused men to realize that their cosmic goodness had of necessity to be extended even for the benefits and interests of the common man.

Another votive stele from Deir el-Medinah, that of Neferabu (Turin Museum no. 50058),[3] further shows the forgiveness and compassion of the gods. The text of this particular stele is addressed to Merit-Seger ('She who loves Silence'), the goddess of the Peak. In this text the forgiven penitent speaks of his foolishness and ignorance, his inability to discern between good and evil. As a result of such ignorance he had sinned against the goddess and she in turn had punished him. Her punishment, however, appears not as mere vindictiveness, but as having been imposed in order to teach the sinner wisdom. When Neferabu called upon Merit-Seger in penitence, she was merciful to him and forgave him. This text illustrates a high level of comprehension of the true nature and purpose of divine wrath and anger and of subsequent forgiveness. The penitent Neferabu states not simply that he had done wrong, but that his sin had arisen from ignorance of right and wrong. Whatever his sin was, therefore, it was not considered by the goddess to be an intentional evil, but rather an unintentional mistake arising from human folly. In such a case punishment from the goddess came upon the sinner not as a mark of emotional anger and wrath, but as a means of chastising him and teaching him the difference between right and wrong. The goddess had thus acted out of kindness for him, out of a concern to correct his ways and to improve the quality of his life. The anger of the gods, which in this case appears to have been experienced in the form of some illness, was thus shown to be a manifestation of their love and care for mankind. It was Neferabu's realization that through human wickedness men see and experience the divine love as wrath and anger. Once, however, the sin was realized and confessed, the gods were willing and swift to forgive and to remove the punishment which they had sent upon the individual for his own benefit. As a result of this, Neferabu was able to call himself 'justified of voice', for the divine mercy had punished and chastened him, but it had also pardoned and forgiven him.

One may well take the impression that Neferabu's life was far from being as upright and righteous as it should have been, for he appears also to have offended the god Ptah by taking a false oath, a transgression for which he had been struck by that god with blindness. Neferabu's account of this event was also recorded on a stele which is now in the British Museum (no. 589).[4] Although the text does not make it clear whether or not Neferabu's sight was eventually restored to him, it does show that Neferabu was made to realize the wrong of his action and to repent of it. It is noteworthy too, and a mark of the high moral consciousness of the individual, that he puts no unjust blame on Ptah for his blindness, but rather acknowledges the righteousness of the manner in which the god had dealt with him.

The themes of sin, penitence and forgiveness as they were expressed in these texts were a later development in Egyptian personal piety, but they illustrate the moral qualities which eventually emerged out of the total Egyptian religious experience. That the gods could extend their care and their concern to the common individual who had offended them by the wrongness of his actions points to a high degree of consciousness of the beneficent nature of those same gods. Although such may have been a development of popular piety rather than one of official theology, reflecting a natural human aspiration for acceptance by the divine powers, it nevertheless added an important theological dimension to the mythic systems of ancient Egypt. The gods were now able to satisfy a basic psychological need of their worshippers, the need for forgiveness realized through proper chastisement, and thus those gods became a stabilizing force for the inner spiritual life of each individual. In this way they were able to provide man with a means of re-integrating his own life back into the universal order of the cosmos, the order sustained by Ma'at, even though his own actions may have caused him to see himself as having been separated from that order through his own wrongdoing. Although this may have been one of the latest achievements of the Egyptian religious mind, it was far from being the least of those achievements, for through it religion was able to touch the basic core of man's inner and spiritual life. It meant that in effect a way of redemption and restoration had been provided for the individual who had fallen into sin through his own blindness and folly.

Such moral consciousness was not, however, directly produced by the mytho-theological systems of early religion, although it did to a certain extent depend upon those systems. Judging from the content of the moral values of the Old Kingdom, and relying particularly on the text of *The Instruction of Ptahhotep*,[5] one may arrive at the conclusion that the moral consciousness of that particular period had evolved quite naturally out of the Egyptian love of the good and pleasant life. One of the chief aspirations which one detects in the writings of the Old Kingdom is that the individual would be able to live a long and happy life and be buried in 'great old age'. The Egyptians showed in their writings that they loved life and desired to see it prolonged so that they might enjoy its pleasures to the fullest. This does not, however, indicate only that the Egyptians were hedonists, seeking only after sensual satisfactions and joys. What they sought was a life which would be filled with happiness and the natural joys which come from passing one's life in contentment, peace and the prosperity which was to be gained from legitimate success and achievement. One finds in the Old Kingdom no striving to 'get ahead' by unceasing toil and effort, no ideologies which stress nothing but hard work in order to accumulate as much material wealth as possible. Life itself was the main concern of the Egyptians in this period, life with its normal activities and vitality, life with its natural joys and pleasures. In brief, the Egyptians sought to realize in their personal and individual lives all the possible goodness and happiness which was to be derived from a well balanced and well ordered existence. In this ideal of the good life, reverence for the gods and for the standards demanded by Ma'at naturally held a very high place, for the Egyptians saw that it was by these methods that they could ensure proper balance and happiness in their personal lives.

The mytho-theologies which had evolved early in Egypt's history gave support to the idea that life was by its very essence and nature good. It was good because it had been created that way by the deity who was the source of all things. At the same time, however, the Egyptians of the Old Kingdom did not rely totally on the gods to provide a good life for each individual. They were realistic enough to understand that success and happiness in this world depended to a great extent on their own abilities. Indeed a good life depended more upon man's own abilities than it did on the gods, and it would not to one who was content to remain in a state of passive inactivity. Men were not tied to the gods in some kind of absolute dependence or forced to accept whatever the gods might decide to send. Such may have been the case in the more fatalistic worlds of Mesopotamia and Homeric Greece, but it was not so in the world of the Egyptians. The Egyptian realized that success in life depended upon his own abilities and upon his own attitudes. He had no need of the constant support, help and guidance of the gods. He gave the gods their due reverence and respect, but he also knew that he had the ability to succeed in life without their constant favour and intervention. The Egyptian may have been dependent upon the ordered nature of the physical world, but he was not dependent upon the whims of the gods. He was in essence free to make his own life and his own destiny. He was free and self-reliant, not bound by the powers of fate and a pre-ordained destiny. Hence, he could be, especially in the positive atmosphere of the Old Kingdom, optimistic and hopeful about his future.

If life was to be good and pleasant for man, such could not be expected to occur automatically with no effort on his part. If the Egyptian had the ability to create his own happiness, this ability was also accompanied by a certain sense of responsibility. Happiness and contentment would not come to the man who did not live his life in such a manner as to produce them. Before life could be good, it had to be ordered, it had to be lived within the confines of those principles which could ensure goodness and happiness. Those principles were themselves contained and expressed in the wider and all-embracing principle of Ma'at, the cosmic order which had been created by the gods, which was integral to the life of the universe, and which was, therefore, an essential part of the life of every individual. In *The Instruction of Ptahhotep* we see that this force of Ma'at was regarded as firm and enduring, that it would prevail over any schemes and plans of human invention. Man could not with impunity exceed the boundaries and standards which Ma'at demanded, and, if he did attempt to do so, he would surely fail in his purposes and goals. According to the text of *The Eloquent Peasant*, all of man's actions and words had to be in accordance with Ma'at, for this was the enduring principle:

> Speak Ma'at, do Ma'at,
> For it is mighty, it is great, and it endures.[6]

This is not unlike the power of the Greek δίκη as it would be later expressed by Parmenides: "Justice does not release her fetters and allow anything to come into being or to be destroyed, but holds fast all things."[7] Such also was the case with Ma'at; it was the restraining and ordering force of the universe. If Ma'at was respected and followed by a man in his everyday life, then he could expect all things to go well for him. Ma'at, if properly observed, was thus the guarantee of the happiness and contentment which men sought in life. Hence, it was a principle of moral order and action, one which was an integral part of the totality and unity of both cosmic life and the life of the individual.

The reliance and hope which the Egyptian placed in the power of Ma'at to uphold the natural world and the moral order did not blind him to the reality of the evil and disorder which could and did occur from time to time in life. Evil, as may be seen from its common Egyptian designation as *isft*, implied not the wilful sin or transgression, but rather an upsetting of the natural order of things, be it in the universe, in the state or in the life of the individual. Wrong was nothing else than an aberration of Ma'at, the order which gave meaning and stability to all aspects of life. The Egyptian, especially after the events of the First Intermediate Period, was well aware that such disruptions could take place in the order of Ma'at, and that a man might experience trouble and unhappiness which were not necessarily the results of his own action. Texts such as *The Prophecies of Noferty*, *The Complaints of Kakheperre-Soneb*, *The Dispute of a Man with his Ba*, and *The Eloquent Peasant* all testify to the awareness of such a possibility in the order of life. At the same time, these texts, despite the reality of evil which they recognized, still expressed the assurance that Ma'at would eventually triumph over the disorder which had occurred in the Two Lands. The most pessimistic of all these texts, *The Dispute of a Man with his Ba*, shows very clearly and graphically how unworthy of living was a life which was marked by disruption and social corruption. So bad was it, that the unnamed individual who figures in the text actually contemplated ending his own life which had, as a result of such evil, become totally tasteless and unbearable.

Yet even here, despite the apparent lack of hope for anything better, it appears that the individual was finally persuaded away from his purpose by the arguments of his own ba. The force of evil and disorder was given an even more graphic personification in a figure such as Seth, who eventually, in the conflict between himself and Horus, was defeated, the result of which was the establishment of order and right. So also the Apep snake, the gigantic serpent whose abode was the primaeval waters under the earth, functioned as an embodiment of disorder, attempting each day to obstruct the solar barque of Ra during its journey. He too, however, was defeated each day, a mythic symbol of the assurance of the triumph of Ma'at.

The concept of Ma'at was for the Egyptian the basic foundation of his moral life, and it was coupled with his desire for happiness to produce the unwritten and undefined moral code by which he lived. Man desired a good, happy and prosperous life, and he knew that such could be realized only by living in accordance with Ma'at. Hence, the latter aspiration became the chief goal of one who sought happiness in his existence. Herein, however, we may also detect the basic element of freedom in the Egyptian moral life. Ma'at was indeed the foundation of human morality, and, therefore, it becomes immediately apparent that morality had a strong connection with the gods. Yet the gods were not such, nor was Ma'at such, as actually to dictate moral principles and rules, to lay down dogmatic codes of action which had to be strictly followed. Ma'at was in reality a general norm for morality, a principle against which human actions could be measured so as to reveal either the rightness or wrongness of such actions. Ma'at did not provide a detailed code of ethics. No rules, such as the Hebraic Ten Commandments of the Old Testament, had been laid down so that man could simply abide by them and so order his life in an acceptable manner. Morality and upright living were not that simple for the Egyptian, who was forced rather to rely on his own conscience and to interpret the general principle of Ma'at in the practical affairs of his everyday life. He did not have the easy solution of falling back on an already existing code of ethics as a guide to his life. He was free from such restrictions as would have been imposed by a moral code, but in this freedom he was expected to take the responsibility of developing his own moral system as well as the responsibility of assuring that his personal moral code was acceptable to the wider principle of Ma'at.

Such a requirement for moral living might well seem to be a total impossibility, for it would have implied that each individual had developed a perfect conscience and a perfect ability to distinguish between right and wrong. As we have seen above in the stele of Neferabu, however, such was not always possible. Few men had the ability to live without some type of moral guidance and instruction, and there could be no better means of such instruction than to listen to and heed the words and advice one one's elders, those who had come through the actual experiences of life. It is for such a reason that Ptahhotep stresses the duty of a son to heed the advice of his father, for such would be beneficial and useful to the son in his own life. The text of Ptahhotep even purports to have been written for the benefit of the writer's son. It was indeed for the very purpose of handing on useful, practical and beneficial advice about life that the various wisdom texts were written. For such a reason, texts of this nature were not philosophical or religious in their content and character; they did not attempt to speculate on the gods or on the abstract realities of the universe. They dealt rather with the simple facts of everyday life, giving advice on how one ought to behave in virtually any given situation. Such texts may not, of course, be regarded as strict moral theology, the latter concept being unknown among the Egyptians. Nevertheless, they do imply an important principle of such moral theology, for every detail of one's life had to be lived in accordance with Ma'at, and the wisdom texts attempted to translate such an ideal into practical action. The practical and pragmatic nature of the wisdom texts thus took on a more universal and abstract purpose. The life of the universe was in accordance with Ma'at, as was the life of the state. So also the life of the individual had to be lived in such a manner, and the aim of the wisdom literature was to see to it that this ideal was accomplished. If the wisdom texts were not moral theology, they were at least the first step in the direction of such a theology, for they tried to establish sound norms by which an individual might guide his actions and thus remain within the boundaries and ideals of the universal order of Ma'at.

In its actual origins the concept of morality had not been connected with the gods, for the gods had originally been, as we have already seen, powers of nature and personifications of certain aspects of the royal and political ideology. No special human conduct had originally been demanded by the gods. Man's duty towards them was rather to provide them with worship and offerings, and to perform the mythic cults in such a manner that there would be effected those principles for which the gods stood. Morality, on the other hand, appears to have arisen from human conscience, from the innate desire on the part of each individual to have a life which was good, pleasant, peaceful and ordered. If such a life were to be possible in a society of individuals, then it was necessary for members of that society to conduct themselves in such a way as to ensure that every individual would have the ability to live in this manner. First and foremost, therefore, morality was a practical and pragmatic concern, not necessarily based on inherent ideas of abstract right and wrong. What was right or wrong could easily be determined on the basis of what would benefit or hinder both the individual and the society as a whole. The state and human society were, therefore, the real roots of moral action, the practical end of that moral action being to assure good order within society. With the rise of the kingship, however, and with the connection of the kingship with the wider mytho-theology of the Old Kingdom, it was only natural that moral action would find some connection with the divine forces which sustained the state. Such a connection was readily and naturally provided in the concept which already lay at the basis of the universe and the state, the concept of Ma'at. The gods themselves were seen as living and acting by the principles of Ma'at, and hence it was an easy, and probably even necessary, step to conjoin human morality with the interests of the gods. Since the gods lived by Ma'at, they, therefore, would have hated any deed which itself was against Ma'at.[8] This does not imply that the gods themselves now became the basis of morality, for any wrong committed was a transgression not against the gods, but against the more abstract principle of Ma'at. Nevertheless, the gods as the guardians of Ma'at might well have been expected to take upon themselves the duty and prerogative of correcting the transgression. Strictly speaking, however, the gods did not punish simply for the sake of being vindictive and exacting vengeance for the wrong which had been done. Their purpose was far wider; they restored the order which had been disrupted by the evil and chastened and corrected the ignorant sinner. In such a sense the gods also may be seen as moral beings. They did not dictate codes of morality, for the elucidation and expansion of specific moral activity was left to the abilities of the human conscience. The gods did, however, expect that human conscience would have a sense of Ma'at and that it would guide the life of the individual accordingly. We have seen above that the wisdom literature had evolved for the very purpose of educating and instructing the human conscience so that man could indeed live in such a manner. At the same time, it must be remembered that the wisdom texts never gained the authority of sacred scriptures. No matter how high the esteem in which a particular text may have been held, that of Ptahhotep for example, such a text was never seen as being totally authoritative in its own right. Never would such a text have the same weight and authority as the Holy Scriptures of the Judaeo-Christian tradition. Ptahhotep's text may have been regarded as venerable and honourable because of its antiquity, because of the author to whom its composition was ascribed, and because of the inherent wisdom and value of its practical advice, but it remained no more than this. It was not the final word in morality.

That moral requirements were demanded by the gods was evident to a certain extent even in the Pyramid Texts. The growth of the power of the sun god Ra of Heliopolis during the Old Kingdom must have done much to aid in attributing to him the demand for the moral purity and righteousness expected of the dead king. The Pyramid Texts in fact show a tendency to make Ra the actual judge of the dead more than Osiris[9] who would gain this position only at a somewhat later period in the history of Egypt's religious development. The expectation and demands of morality in the Pyramid texts were not highly developed, nor do these texts show any strict code of moral laws. Nevertheless, their general principle in this regard was that the dead king had been the guardian and keeper of the order of Ma'at. The following brief selections from the Pyramid Texts will sufficiently illustrate this requirement:

> Unis has set Ma'at in it (*i.e.*, the Island of Fire) in the
> place of wrong.[10]

> Justified of voice is this Pepi;
> Justified of voice is the ka of Pepi.[11]

> This Pepi is the son of Khnum;
> There is no evil which Pepi has done.[12]

> Heaven is satisfied and the earth is in joy,
> For they have heard that Pepi has put Ma'at
> in the place of wrong.[13]

Such statements do not give us any clue as to what exact measures the dead king had taken in order to establish Ma'at or what transgressions he had refrained from committing. Such a fine description of the royal morality was hardly really necessary. It was sufficient for the compilers of the Pyramid Texts to state simply that the monarch had been, and still was, the embodiment of Ma'at itself. Insofar as he was such, it was hardly necessary to detail a code of moral action by which he had lived and for which he stood. That such moral expectations had arisen by the time of the Fifth and Sixth Dynasties is in itself sufficient testimony to the moral conscience and ideals of ancient Egypt and her religion.

Sin, in the sense in which it came to be understood as a result of Biblical interpretation, was unknown in ancient Egypt. Man did not sin as a result of an evil character or a corrupted nature. He was not seen as a being 'fallen' from some ideal situation. Rather it was the fact that man was foolish and ignorant, lacking in true understanding, which caused him to commit wrong actions.[14] Hence the wisdom literature, the Instructions (sb3yt) as they were called in Egyptian, had the function and purpose of educating and teaching man the way in which he ought to live and act so that his life might be in accordance with Ma'at and not be governed by folly. The Old Kingdom *Instruction of Ptahhotep* is not the oldest of such texts in ancient Egypt. Earlier there had been produced the texts which bear the titles *The Instruction of of Hardjedef* and *The Instruction for Kagemni*. Both of these, although of interest in their own rights, are relatively short and do not constitute any type of complete treatment of ethics and morality. Ptahhotep, on the other hand, provides a far more comprehensive treatise on ethics, morality, etiquette and proper behaviour, complete to the extent that we may accept it as a full description of the Old Kingdom concept of a virtuous man and a good life. A full treatment of the text is not possible here, but a brief summary of its major points will be useful in defining the Old Kingdom ideals of moral uprightness. In many ways this text presents a picture of morality which is highly valid even in the modern day and age, its maxims being such as would constitute an acceptable code of ethical behaviour in virtually any society.

Ptahhotep's ideal of the good man cautions strongly against human pride and arrogance, even if such seem to be deserved because of one's accomplishments, for, as he reminds his readers, no one is perfect, and there is always leeway to improve oneself. Truthfulness also appears as a high virtue in his ethical system, truthfulness in reporting what has been entrusted to one, and truthfulness in one's own actions and dealings. The good man does not gossip, he does not steal, he does not engage in schemes, for the scheming of men will come to nothing. It is the plans of the god which will ultimately prevail. Nor does he overlook the necessity for good table manners, especially when one is an invited guest. On such an occasion one should eat what is set before one and not show oneself a glutton. Greed and selfishness of all kinds appear to be abhorrent to Ptahhotep. Instead he recommends that a man should be beneficent and generous with his goods, treating his friends well and sharing his bounty with them. Trustworthiness in doing one's duty, and respect for one's superiors also appear as laudable virtues. Ptahhotep also counsels against being overly belligerent in the court-room; it is better, he says, to let one's opponent confound himself than to try to fight against him. With regard to the affairs of one's family, Ptahhotep recognizes the value of a good son, who should be recognized for what he is. A bad son, however, deserves and needs to be chastised, and such chastisement should not be withheld, insofar as it will benefit such a son. A wife who is satisfactory should be loved and well treated; she should be kept happy and content, but never allowed to get the upper hand. Finally, let us note that Ptahhotep cautions against the dangers which may arise should one become involved with the women of another's household. Nothing but evil can arise from such affairs. Ptahhotep's general outlook on life can probably be seen in the fact that he advises his reader to "follow his heart" throughout all his life, that is, to enjoy life and its pleasures, and not to exert too much labour and effort in one's profession. Life, in the opinion of Ptahhotep, is to be enjoyed for the natural goodness and happiness which it can offer to the one who approaches it in the proper attitude and manner. A man should show self-control, moderation, truthfulness, justice and kindness; he should be discreet in all his actions and attempt to live in peace. The rewards of such a manner of living will be the contentment and happiness which life has to offer. In brief, Ptahhotep advises that, if a man lives by Ma'at, then his life will be well and ordered and he will prosper in everything which he undertakes, for it is Ma'at alone which is strong and prevails in all things.

It is worth noting that Ptahhotep does not advise against specific actions for the reason that they have been absolutely forbidden by the gods, although he does recognize the power of the latter. The main reason for avoiding wrong actions in Ptahhotep's moral system is the fact that such actions will eventually bring their own punishment. The individual, in other words, may expect to reap what he sows. Hence, full responsibility for a man's fortune and lot in life rests with the individual himself; there are no forces of fate or destiny which will bring a man to either good or ill. For what happens to him he can give the blame or credit only to himself. Ptahhotep recognizes man's full freedom and responsibility for his actions, and sees each individual as the master of his own destiny. That destiny may be either good or evil, but by following and acting by Ma'at man has every right to hope for the best.

In *The Instruction of Ptahhotep* we can see the high point of the optimism of the Old Kingdom and perhaps even in the whole of Egypt's history. The same ideals of restraint and humility may also be seen in the earlier texts of Hardjedfef and Kagemni, although, as has already been stated, neither of these represents the same intricate and developed ethical system as does Ptahhotep. The earliest Egyptian treatments of morality appear, therefore, to have been wholly humanitarian and based on man's own abilities. No gods were required either to sanction moral codes or to enforce them. Nor did a man need the grace and support of any deity in order to be the upright individual which Ma'at required him to be. Man, in the thought of the Old Kingdom, had that ability within himself. There was no need for any god either to strengthen him or to redeem him from his evil situation. It is true that the gods demanded morality, but it appears also that those same gods had sufficient confidence in human ability that they saw no need to hand down moral codes to the world.

The great moral treatise to come out of the Middle Kingdom is the text commonly known as *The Tale of the Eloquent Peasant*. Although cast in the form of a piece of fiction, this text is essentially a treatise on the nature and power of Ma'at as the force which upholds order and righteousness within the world. The text itself requires little in the way of comment or interpretation. Its story is simple enough: a peasant who has been wronged by a nobleman eventually receives satisfaction and justice through his persistent efforts at importuning the steward of the king. The main point which is constantly stressed and repeated throughout the text is that Ma'at is powerful and enduring, and that it is, therefore, the duty of the rulers to see to it that Ma'at is done in the world by upholding the rights of the oppressed against their oppressors. More striking than that in this story, however, is the picture of a humble peasant who dares to make a complaint against a member of the nobility. Not only does he make the complaint, but his reliance on and trust in the power of Ma'at is so great that he has the courage to keep on repeating his complaint in the face of apparent failure and frustration in having the justice of his grievance recognized. The unknown author of this story gives herein strong evidence of a powerful social conscience which was able to recognize the rights of even the humblest commoner to justice and fairness. As the story itself makes clear, such rights are inalienable and derive from the fact that Ma'at is a reality which cannot be denied, and whose interest and protection are extended to all men. Although the plaintiff in the case is no more than a peasant, he himself feels that he has the same right to fair treatment as would any one else, one of the main moral points of the story being that such indeed is the case. In terms of Egyptian morality, therefore, it appears that even the poor and lowly were under the protection of Ma'at and the gods, and that a major tenet of proper moral activity is that fair treatment had to be extended to them. In the eyes of Ma'at, wealth and position did not give a man any favoured advantage over another, a very important precept in a society which was essentially totalitarian and governed by the royal and aristocratic classes.

We would probably be somewhat naïve if we were to accept as historical fact the idea that such an ideal as described above was indeed the actual situation in ancient Egypt, for there can be no doubt that the situation of the poor in the face of the nobility was far from being so favourable. The point remains, however, that in a story such as *The Eloquent Peasant* the ideal of absolute equality in social justice could be propounded and expanded. The Egyptian concept of morality very obviously had a high degree of potentiality. It is, furthermore, obvious that to the Egyptian mind the gods took quite seriously the rights of the poor to fair treatment, for one of the most common statements in the tomb autobiographies is the assertion on the part of the deceased that he had never oppressed the poor. If such an ideal could ever be realized in any society, then moral standards would indeed be expressive of the same power of Ma'at as is described in the Tale of the Eloquent Peasant.

The New Kingdom Text known as *The Instruction of Any* appears to have originated most likely in the Eighteenth Dynasty.[15] The text itself, due to numerous corruptions and lacunae, is relatively difficult to interpret and Gardiner has described it as "the obscurest of all Egyptian wisdom texts."[16] The most interesting fact about the text, however, is that it appears to represent the average middle class values of the New Kingdom, having nothing about it which is particularly characteristic of the aristocracy.[17] From the point of view of content, the text shows little that is of real interest and virtually nothing which is particularly novel. The thinking of Any appears to be somewhat restrained and careful, suggesting caution and discretion in one's actions, and not permitting of a great deal of individual freedom or ingenuity. The ideal life which is portrayed here appears as being marked by a typical middle class unwillingness to assert oneself and the willingness to accept a life which is simple and even relatively obscure. The reader is advised to marry young and to found a family, to build or buy a house of his own and, in readiness for death, to prepare a tomb. Reverence for one's parents is regarded as a desirable virtue, particularly the care of one's mother, as well as the duty of making the appropriate tomb offerings for them. Any's ideal man is further marked by proper reverence for the gods and due respect for his superiors and elders. Truth and honesty in both action and word is recommended, along with general restraint in one's social connections. One's friends, says Any, should be honest men, and quarrelsome types should be avoided. Strange women are also presented as individuals from whom one should stay away, for they may bring unforeseen trouble. Strangers in general should not be trusted, and a man must guard his tongue against repeating too much of what has been said to him. The major vices to be avoided appear to be excessive curiosity, gossip, quarrels and drunkenness. With regard to one's possessions and wealth, Any recommends caution lest they be lost, although he does recognize the virtue of a certain amount of generosity. His ideal man, however, does not appear to be marked by the same willingness to share with his friends as was the ideal man of Ptahhotep's text. Honesty, diligence, humility, piety and a certain degree of generosity seem to be the main marks of Any's positive moral ideology. A man who possesses these traits appears to be one who will cause no problems for those around him and will as a result avoid trouble for himself. He is not, however, the same positive, out-going and constructive man whom one finds in the ideals of Ptahhotep. Any thus appears to have added virtually nothing to any positive ideals of morality. His main ambition was basically to avoid personal problems and personal trouble, an indication of his own understanding of the dangers which can beset a man from his environment.

In contrast to Any, the writer of *The Instruction of Amenemope*,[18] a text which dates probably from the Ramesside period, shows himself to have something more of a spiritual depth and a more positive feeling towards the values of the quiet and restrained life. At the same time, one may detect in the writer some quality of resignation and the willingness and even ability to compensate for the absence of external and material comforts by a more contemplative and inward vitality. Quietness and silence seem to be the hallmarks of Amenemope's ideal of humanity, although he shows a stronger tendency than does Any towards positive ideals and actions in the area of morality. Amenemope's goodness is somewhat more positive and out-reaching than was the more restrained virtue of Any. If one attempts to see any one important characteristic in this text, its outstanding feature appears to be the marked absence of any attitude that worldly success, wealth and prosperity are the marks of a good and desirable life. Such had been characteristic of the text of Ptahhotep and the general optimism of the Old Kingdom. It appears, however, that by the time of Amenemope the older optimism had waned sufficiently that man could no longer hope for automatic prosperity as the natural result of correct living and had, therefore, to find newer values which were more in keeping with the trends of the age. We have seen above how the personal piety of the later New Kingdom was marked by a strong sense of human sin and unworthiness, and perhaps Amenemope's lack of stress on material success may be yet another manifestation of this attitude, the consciousness of sinfulness demanding also a more spiritual and contemplative nature.

The latter characteristics of the text of Amenemope are specifically evident in his repeated advice against the desire for wealth. The good man should not be eager to gain riches; he should not covet the wealth of the nobles or whatever goods and food the poor man may happen to possess. A man should rather be satisfied with what he has, for it is better to be happy with little than to possess wealth along with cares and worries. Amenemope probably realized the fact that covetousness leads to greed, and greed in turn leads to efforts to acquire, often by dishonest means, what is not one's own. Hence, he warns his readers not to rob men of lowly position and not to harm the elderly. So also one must refrain from moving the boundary stones in the fields for the purpose of acquiring land which is not one's own. Amenemope abhors all cheating, dishonesty, injuring of other people, and lying. Hence, he warns against giving false testimony in the courts, advising his readers to behave justly in court and not to deprive the lowly in favour of the wealthy and great, the latter advice echoing the ideals of *The Eloquent Peasant*. The ideal man will respect all men; he will not mock the blind man or the dwarf; he will not attempt to hinder the lame; he will not speak in an evil manner about other people. The reader is warned to stay away from one who is of a bad temper, not to provoke his enemy against himself, and not to fight back when attacked. Instead of being quarrelsome, it is better to give in to one's foes. (The idea of 'turning the other cheek was by no means peculiar to Christianity.) The ideal man will also recognize his own position and will respect those who are above him, both in age and in station. He will not attempt to exceed his position by making friends with those who are greater than himself. Above all, Amenemope sees silence as the ideal of the good man, for the silent man who keeps to himself is the one who will prosper. Aggression, even aggression which was positive, was no longer praised by the time of Amenemope, and active striving to promote oneself was not seen as a positive and desirable characteristic. Amenemope himself appears to have realized that more depends upon the goodness and graciousness of the gods than upon the natural abilities of man. Hence, true morality for him consisted of honesty, humility, respect and moderation.

By the time of the composition of the Book of the Dead during the New Kingdom, and well before the time of Amenemope, a moral and upright life had become a prerequisite for man's entering into eternal life in the next world. The Negative Confession contained in Chapter CXXV of that text is very strong in its affirmations that the deceased has avoided moral wrong, and takes great care to enumerate before the judges of the dead the various evil actions from which he has refrained. The full content of the text is too complex to be considered at any real length, but a brief perusal of its major points will help in defining the general Egyptian ideal of moral purity.

The deceased is shown in the Book of the Dead protesting to his judges that he has not done wrong (*bin*), nor has he done evil (*isft*) to man or beast. He has not been disrespectful to the gods, he has not stolen from the temples, and he has not stolen the offerings left for the dead. He has not cursed the gods, nor has he been insolent or haughty. He has caused no misery, harm or pain; he has been neither deceitful nor an eavesdropper. He has neither stolen nor cheated, nor has he coveted. He has not harmed the fields or the irrigation, he has not stolen cattle, and he has done no murder. He has committed neither fornication nor adultery, and he has not defiled himself by masturbation. He has not spoken evilly against any man; he has not been angry. He has not stirred up strife, nor has he ever stolen the bread of children. In nothing has he done those things which he ought not to have done, and he has thus never disregarded Ma'at. Hence, he is able to say to the judges of the dead, "I am pure" (*iw.i w ͑ b.kwi*). Instead of evil, the deceased has done good: he has fed the hungry, has given water to the thirsty, and has clothed the naked. Thus, he has been a positive blessing to those who were in need. In virtue of all these things the deceased may be judged as justified and so permitted to enter the realms of the blessed.

Such ideals of morality as may be seen in the Book of the Dead may be taken as normative of the morality which was held as the ideal by the average individual in ancient Egypt. Such a man would have done no harm to others and would have even brought to others whatever help and aid may have been required in each individual situation. Whether or not such was in actuality the case, or whether such affirmations one one's own goodness must be taken as pious exaggeration, it is impossible to say. The important point, however, is that from the principle of Ma'at there did eventually evolve a high degree of moral consciousness, an ideal which eventually became inseparably connected with the great gods of Egypt. It is important that the ideal of such a morality was in existence, even if it was not always fully and totally observed.

To examine the concept of morality in the Amarna system is not a difficult task, for the Amarna texts have almost no mention whatsoever of moral action. The tomb autobiographies have nothing equivalent to the Negative Confession and no statements about the goodness of the earthly life of the deceased. The tomb of Tutu does have one brief statement of moral innocence when he says, "I did not accept the reward of falsehood to repress the just man for the sake of the wrongdoer,"[19] but such a statement cannot be compared with the earlier detailed protestations of moral innocence. The Amarna nobles did, of course, append to their names the common epithet 'justified of voice' (m$^{3^c}$ ḫrw), but this was supported by no statements elaborating its significance or justifying why the deceased had the right to be so designated. One wonders if perhaps in the Amarna texts this expression was used as the equivalent of no more than the modern 'deceased', as Gardiner has suggested that it was at times used?[20] There are, however, a number of indications in the Amarna texts that the concept of justification was dependent upon the association of each individual with the fact of having done Ma'at. Ay, the father-in-law of Akhenaten, for example, states that Akhenaten had placed Ma'at in his body,[21] and that as a result he (Ay) hates lies and falsehood (grg). He states also that his mouth or speech possesses Ma'at.[22] In these, as in other instances, however, it appears that the meaning of Ma'at is more of an abstract concept of truth, rather than one of a principle of order and moral uprightness. More precisely, to live by Ma'at in terms of the Amarna system appears to have meant little more than to have accepted the official teaching (sb^{3}yt) of Akhenaten who was himself described as the 'ruler of Ma'at' (ḥḳ^3 m$^3^c$t). It thus appears that in the official Amarna theology as well as in actual practice Ma'at, although it did hold its importance as an abstract principle, had very little connection with principles of moral action. Indeed, it appears to have been entirely divorced from such. At the same time, however, this does not appear to have been a totally unusual phenomenon within the Egyptian religious experience. The official mytho-theologies did not really provide an integral place for a moral theology, morality being connected with them more as an outgrowth, as natural as that outgrowth may have been. Thus, the Amarna system, insofar as it too attempted to be a synthesis of doctrine and dogma, was under no obligation to evolve any type of systematic moral code. One may, of course, assume that Amarna morality may have consisted of an acceptance of the traditional moral values which had developed over the centuries, and that no need was felt to express one's moral uprightness in the tomb autobiographies, it being simply assumed that to follow to Akhenaten was already sufficient proof of a man's sound and wise character. Such is only speculation and no definitive statement can be made concerning the matter. Hence, it must suffice to say that the Amarna texts give little evidence of any real interest in morality or personal righteousness. At least they do not attempt to provide any elaboration of the contents of a moral system.

We have seen that in ancient Egypt moral considerations were indeed an important aspect of life. Arising out of the social and political organization as a means of regulating society, unwritten codes of action were accepted as normal standards of behaviour, and the observance of such codes was soon connected with the religious values of society. These became particularly important when it was a question of judging the worthiness of an individual to enter eternity. The leading of an upright and righteous life was seen as a sign of the principle of Ma'at within the individual. In fact we might say that moral behaviour was the practical means whereby the individual could, and was thus expected to, observe Ma'at. Finally since the gods themselves were the ones who were largely responsible for the maintenance of Ma'at in the cosmos, it was they too who came to take an interest in the moral life of the individual. In such a manner, morality evolved into an integral part of religion, both official and personal.

This does not mean, however, that the Egyptians developed any sense of moral theology. The gods themselves did not either sanction or impose any specific moral codes. What they sanctioned and upheld was the general principle of Ma'at. Nor were there ever developed any rational theological or philosophical principles which could elucidate and clarify the right and wrong which was inherent within specific actions. Such matters were left solely to the human conscience and to the talents of the writers of the wisdom literature who attempted to codify them, although these had no theological significance or moral authority. Those actions which were inherently right or wrong were known and understood solely through human experience over the centuries. The common consensus on these, it would appear, was accepted by the gods as the moral standards which they would demand and by which they would finally judge each individual. Such, however, is without doubt the source of moral values in every society and in every religion. Moral theology is, in effect, an attempt to sanctify those rules and norms which create order and decency in human society and whose value and worth have been tried and proven by centuries of experience. If the moral systems elaborated by ancient Egyptians were to be placed in any theological category, we would have to maintain that they represented a type of morality which had been revealed through the human intellect and through an understanding and interpretation of the experience of human life throughout the centuries of Egypt's history. Such a 'moral theology', deriving essentially from man himself, was probably far stronger and more natural than an ethical code which had been forcefully imposed by an outside force.

There was, however, in Egyptian thought a strong mytho-theological basis for moral action. That basis was the central place which the figure of Ma'at held in creation mythology and in cosmology. Because of this role of Ma'at in the wider order, its role of demanding a certain type of action on the part of each individual was no more than an extension of its cosmic function. Moreover, because each individual was an integral part of the cosmic and political order, taking from it the basis of his own existence, moral and upright action on his part was the practical and pragmatic way in which he could express his unity with the wider universal order of being and existence. It would be difficult to find a more valid theological reason for moral behaviour than this.

Notes

[1] A.R. David, *The Ancient Egyptians: Religious Beliefs and Practices*, 143.
[2] Translation in M. Lichtheim, *Ancient Egyptian Literature*, II, 105-107.
[3] Translation in M. Lichtheim, *Ancient Egyptian Literature*, II, 107-109.
[4] Translation in M. Lichtheim, *Ancient Egyptian Literature*, II, 109-110.

[5] Translation in M. Lichtheim, *Ancient Egyptian Literature*, I, 61-80.
[6] *Peasant*, B1, 320-321: ḏd mꜣꜥt ir mꜣꜥt
   ḏr ntt wr.s ꜥ.s wsẖ.s.
[7] Parmenides, *Fragments*, 8,13.
[8] H. Frankfort, *Ancient Egyptian Religion*, 77.
[9] J.H. Breasted, *Development of Religion and Thought in Ancient Egypt*, 174.
[10] *PT* 265c: di.n Wnis mꜣꜥt im.f m st isft.
[11] *PT* 929a: mꜣꜥ ḫrw Ppi pn
   mꜣꜥ ḫrw kꜣ n Ppi.
[12] *PT* 1238a: Ppi pw sꜣ Ḫnmw n ḏwt irt.n Ppi.
[13] *PT* 1775a-b: pt ḥtp.t tꜣm ꜣw ib
   sḏm.n.sn ddi Ppi mꜣꜥt m st isft.
[14] H. Frankfort, *op. cit.*, 73f.
[15] M. Lichtheim, *op. cit.*, II, 135.
[16] *JEA* XLV (1959): 12.
[17] M. Lichtheim, *loc. cit.*
[18] Translation in M. Lichtheim, *op. cit.*, II, 146-163.
[19] M. Sandman, *Texts from the time of Akhenaten*, p.77.1-2: bw šsp.i fkꜣ n grg r
   dr mꜣꜥty n ꜥḏꜣ.
[20] A.H. Gardiner, *Egyptian Grammar*, §55.
[21] M. Sandman, *op. cit.*, p.91.18: di.f mꜣꜥt m ḥt.i.
[22] *ibid.*, 93.2: r.i ḥr mꜣꜥt.

XI. The Egyptian Theological Synthesis

In drawing conclusions about Egyptian religion and the theological values of its mythic system, one must be careful not to make statements which are so far-reaching and so over-generalized as to create an unrealistic picture. We must not assume that some kind of homogeneity existed in which every individual had a similar comprehension and a similar understanding of the significance of the mythic system. The ordinary individual certainly was certainly far from being totally conscious of the symbolic values expressed in the mythic patterns and in the cults, and we can probably safely assume that many were not even totally familiar with the general structure and contents of the mythic patterns. The Egyptians were no more a nation of theologians than is any modern society, and one can be certain that there must have been among them a substantial number of individuals for whom religious myth and its implications held little interest or importance. Such is the situation in any culture, and there is no reason to think that the ancient Egyptians were any different. Let us also recognize the fact that many must have taken the mythic symbols at their face value and interpreted them in a purely fundamentalist fashion. In the minds of many, therefore, the individual gods would have been understood as strictly individual and anthropomorphic deities, concerned with specific aspects and interests of life. Much popular religion, therefore, must have been relatively simple in its structure and outlook, containing no deep theological insights such as may be interpreted from the official mytho-theology. The obvious existence of many rituals which were nothing more than superstitious and magic practices appear to be sufficient evidence of the latter. It is only reasonable that one would expect such levels of religious belief and experience in ancient Egypt, for they exist in virtually every culture and civilization. In brief, we must avoid being too idealistic in our general assessment of the Egyptian religious mind.

The above assertion, nevertheless, does not change the fact that the Egyptian system of mytho-theology did contain within itself the possibility of producing a more abstract and intellectual ideal which was there for the comprehension of those who had the ability to perceive its inherent implications. Such, we may say, was the highest achievement of Egypt's religious and mythic abilities. Such was the ideal which could have, and often must have, been perceived by individuals of a more astute and more acute spiritual ability. It is this which we may regard as the real heart of Egyptian religion, and hence we are justified in an attempt to define closely the Egyptian theological synthesis.

As a starting point, we may quite correctly define Egyptian religion as an all-embracing and all-encompassing system and method of perception and articulation. It was an attempt to unify all human experience of the universe, of existence and of being. It was an attempt to create a single entity out of the plurality of nature, life existence. In such a sense, Egyptian religion was both an integrating force and an integrating experience, a definition which can be applied to any valid religious concept and experience. As such, Egyptian religion was central to all life; it was the very foundation stone of existence, and not just a peripheral matter. Religion had the potential to function as the actual core and driving force of human life and existence, for in reality it was nothing more or less than the totality of that life and existence. Religion was in effect the articulation of existential being, even though the Egyptian mind itself would never have expressed it in such abstract terminology.

That Egyptian religion was able to function as has been here described was the natural result and outcome of its basic nature. As we have seen, it was marked by no doctrine or dogma, and hence the religious spirit could not have seen its needs realized by a mere intellectual assent to certain propositions. It was insufficient for the Egyptian simply to state, "I believe," and to leave it at that. Religion was rather a matter of experience, or perhaps we might better say that it was a means of experiencing the universe as an ordered cosmos. This experience was expressed through myth and mythic symbols, and created a spiritual apprehension of the realities of the universe. It is, however, important to stress again that true myth is not fundamentalism. Mythic statements are not literal expressions of the content of religion. They are rather symbols of that content, the content itself remaining intellectually undefined and being in fact the totality of the experience. To equate Egyptian myth, therefore, with the myth of the classical Greek tradition, for example, would produce a false approach to the study of Egyptian religion and a false assessment of the latter. Egyptian myth must be interpreted theologically and in terms of the Egyptian experience. It cannot be properly understood through alterior means or through the aspects and characteristics of alterior cultures and civilizations. It must be permitted to stand by itself in its own category.

Only in this way can its true nature, meaning and signification be comprehended, and only thus can it be seen as more than a collection of primitive and childish fables and traditions.

Egyptian mythology in its most authentic form remained undeveloped in the sense of saga or extended fictional creations. The very fortunate result of this was that it prevented myth from crystallizing into a hard and fast dogmatic system. Myth was able to remain symbolic, and was thus able to express both the hidden and the revealed, the two very opposite poles of reality as the Egyptians saw it. Even the gods themselves were both revealed and hidden; their essence could not be known by man, except by the dead, those who themselves had become united with the divine essence. What was thus revealed by the mythic system could not become a standard of orthodoxy. Orthodoxy by its very nature must be based on the principle of the intellectual acceptance of an official dogma or doctrine. In Egyptian religion, however, experience took the place of dogma, and experience, by its very nature, must be alive and flexible. Dogmatic statements cannot contain or limit the content of experience, for experience occurs within the specific moment and cannot be predetermined by standards which have been already set. From the experience of the cultic myth it is possible to advance to an intellectual and rational interpretation of the mythic symbols, although such is not necessary for a true appreciation of the symbols and their values. Interestingly enough, the symbol probably retains a greater value when it is left uninterpreted by the rational faculty. Although an intellectualization of the symbols was not possible for the ancient Egyptian mind, it is possible for the modern mind which wishes to comprehend the nature of the Egyptian mythic experience. In fact, for the modern rational mind such a process is even necessary, for it is no more than a translation of the mythic terminology into the abstract rational terms with which modern man is more familiar.

At the basis of the whole Egyptian mytho-theological synthesis there were two essential first principles. The primary of these, and the one which gave rise to the whole mytho-theological system, was the emphasis which the Egyptian placed on life as a real and almost tangible force. Life was a power which appeared to the Egyptian to have a separate existence of its own, one which could be hypostasized in the creator deity Atum. Life was for the Egyptian far more than a mere manifestation of physical activity; it was almost an actual substance which could be given and received. It is for this reason that the gods are so often portrayed in the royal tombs holding in their hands the symbol used to designated life, ☥, and offering it to the dead king. Life was something more than just a quality of living things; it was rather an indestructible entity in which the individual participated. Its indestructibility is shown by the tendency of the Coffin Texts constantly to deny the fact that the deceased has died. In the Egyptian way of thinking, the deceased had not in fact died; he had 'departed living'. It was this insistence on the reality of the life force which balanced for the Egyptians the stark reality of death. The latter was admitted, but it was also negated by the positive force and power of life. It was without doubt the mystic character of this life force which presented the first impetus for the rise of religious mythic expression in early Egypt.

The second principle in the foundation of Egyptian religious thought was the recognition of the reality of cosmic order, the order which was personified in the concept and goddess Ma'at, although this personification was most likely the result of earlier experience and apprehension of such cosmic order. The recognition of Ma'at must also have arisen by a very natural means as a result of the observation of the order already inherent in the physical universe. The positing of the principle of Ma'at, an abstract concept expressed by the specific symbol and goddess, was the statement of the existence of a universal order of which all things were integral parts. The very term 'Ma'at' should not be translated as 'righteousness', 'truth' or 'order' in any superficial sense. Ma'at was much more than any or all of these. It was truth in the sense of the basic fact of ordered existential reality; it was righteousness in the sense that what had come from the creator deity had to be right and just; it was the perfect and unchanging order of the cosmos. This cosmos was at once both the revealer and the revealed. It revealed Ma'at, and it was itself at the same time the physical embodiment of Ma'at. The revelation of Ma'at was, therefore, a natural revelation. It required no intellectual effort or ability to perceive it, only the normal power of the perception of the senses.

From these two basic primary principles of Egyptian religion we may move to the next logical question, that of the existence of a deity, especially a supreme deity who was the source and creator of all things. Contrary to some opinions, it seems unlikely that one can speak of any form of monotheism in either early Egypt or at any period throughout her history. One should even perhaps, at least as concerns the early stage of history, avoid speaking in terms of a supreme deity. Nevertheless, one can quite legitimately speak of a supreme *divine power*. This power was expressed and personified in such figures as Atum, Ra, Osiris, Horus, the Aten, Amun or Ptah, according to the mythic formulations of the various shrines. In actuality the supremacy of the deity could be manifested in any of the Egyptian gods. Theologically speaking, however, with the possible exception of the Aten in Amarna theology, such personifications should be seen as no more than symbols of the ultimate divine power of life, for it was this latter which was the real essence of the divine in the ancient Egyptian synthesis. Such appears to be indicated by the actual functions of the various gods. Certainly in popular religion many of the gods were concerned with specific areas and activities of life. Such characteristics, however, appear to have been secondary to their nature. The true function of the gods was to create the universe in an on-going process, to uphold the order of Ma'at, and to manifest the divine power in the person of the ruler and in the phenomena of nature. Man was, however, to a great extent free in his actions. The gods did not bind him with any strict power of fate as would be later evident in the Greek concept of μοῖρα. Any concepts of destiny and fate in the thought of ancient Egypt appear to have been restricted to the idea of fate (šꜣy) as the allotted span of human life. Such fatalism as may be found in the Homeric world seems to have been entirely absent. The Egyptian does not appear to have seen his life as so strictly bound and controlled by the divine forces. Such would not have been in keeping with the common optimism which one perceives in Egyptian thought, especially in the thought of the Old Kingdom. The Egyptian freedom from fatalism and the Egyptian love of life seem to have been two aspects of the one positive attitude towards existence. The fact that the gods did not interfere in man's life, except when it was necessary in order to re-establish Ma'at, may also serve as a further indication of their more cosmic and symbolic power. In their official capacity as state deities the gods were not a threat to human freedom. The very opposite is true, for they were the guarantors of human stability and of the freedom of man to live his life in a truly positive and constructive manner.

This latter role of the gods belonged to their function within the official mytho-theology. Nevertheless, it did not prevent them from being seen in the context of personal piety and as personal deities who could and did take a role in the lives of individuals. In the area of intercessory prayer, for example, Egypt provides much more evidence that such was a common practice than does the text of the Hebrew Old Testament.[1] That an individual could pray to the gods for specific requests and favours indicates that in popular religion they were seen as very real personal powers. The fact that there were in existence small shrines to the gods, possibly wayside shrines[2] not unlike those still to be seen in modern Greece, indicates the place which the gods could hold in the life of the individual. We have already seen the practice of erecting votive stelae containing penitential prayers or thanksgivings for the benefits of the gods, yet another indication of the power of the gods in the lives of ordinary individuals. Such a function of the gods, however, had a relatively unimportant position in the official mytho-theological synthesis.

Life, Ma'at and the existence of the divine thus appear to have been the three main foundation stones of the Egyptian religious system. From these three abstractions, abstractions which were made more specific through personification, the next logical step was the formulation of a mytho-theology of creation. This step may be described as logical insofar as it appears to have represented the concept of the divine life and order expressing itself in the tangible and visible created world. From the viewpoint of Egyptian mytho-theology, the act of creation must have appeared as a virtually necessary event, for an abstract existence of the above principles would hardly have been conceived by the non-abstract mentality of ancient Egypt. In brief, we may state that the creation was a necessary result of the power of the divine creative life force. This life force in turn provided a rationalization for all existent entities, functioning as a type of 'Ground of Being' in which they were rooted. In the Egyptian mytho-theology, therefore, all things depended on the divine for their existence and their creation, both the original act of creation and the continuing and repeated act of creation. It is for the latter reason that the creation myth was celebrated in the cult, for that celebration assured the continuity of creative and ordering powering. The creative force itself, which by its very nature had to be divine, was given specific personification, although not definition, in such deities as Atum, Min, Sobek, Ptah, Osiris and Amun. Again it must be stressed that such a personification could only give reality to the creative force, a reality which could be apprehended by experience, although not defined or explained in intellectual terms. The symbol of a specific creator deity said no more than that divine creativity was real insofar as it was embodied in a specific god, but the personality or description of that god did not define the 'How' or 'Why' of creation. Moreover, the personification of the creator deity was not a dogmatic statement. Its value depended only on the fact that it was a symbol of reality, a symbol that the universe depended on something specific and purposeful, and that its creation was not a chance occurrence. Thus, the existence of the universe appeared as a rational phenomenon. Even if its rationality could not actually be intellectually comprehended or articulated, it could at least be experienced.

The pairing of the male and female principles in the deities of the creation mythology was neither accidental nor a simple sexual motif. This too arose out of the natural experience of life, from the observation that reproduction and the continuation of life were dependent upon the combination of these two same principles. The male/female symbolism, a symbolism already inherent within the single figure of Atum, had nothing to do with fertility cults or sexual activity. It was simply the recognition of the fullness of the creative and reproductive force, the natural and obvious means of the production and continuation of life. Thus, Atum himself, a personification of creative power, was the totality of being and of the regeneration of being. This pairing of the male and female appears also in the theology of the Nun in the Hermopolitan Ogdoad through the symbols of Nun and Naunet, Kuk and Kauket, Huh and Hauhet, and Amun and Amaunet. Herein, under the double aspect of the masculine and feminine, we find a mytho-theological symbolism of chaos, darkness, infinity and the hidden, all of which were, to the non-abstract mentality, negative features. They represented that which cannot be given any clear articulation. At the same time, the balancing of the male deities by the corresponding female deities within this system implied that even in the negative chaos of Nun there was contained the possibility and the power of generation. When the figure of Atum is considered in such a context, we may see further the full and specific potentiality for being which emerges from the non-being of Nun. Hence, in the mytho-theological system the negative force of infinity had its place. It was both everything and nothing; it contained the two poles of existence, being and non-being, the former arising out of the latter. This, however, was not exactly *creatio ex nihilo*, for even non-being appears here as an actual entity. Non-being was the Nun, the primaeval waters from which all things would emerge, itself also a symbol, and a highly suitable symbol, for as the Egyptian experience of the Nile had proven, water itself was the principle and force which contained the possibilities of tangible life.

The Heliopolitan mytho-theology of creation has already been discussed above in Chapter IV. However, for the sake of the full theological synthesis, it may again be illustrated at this point:

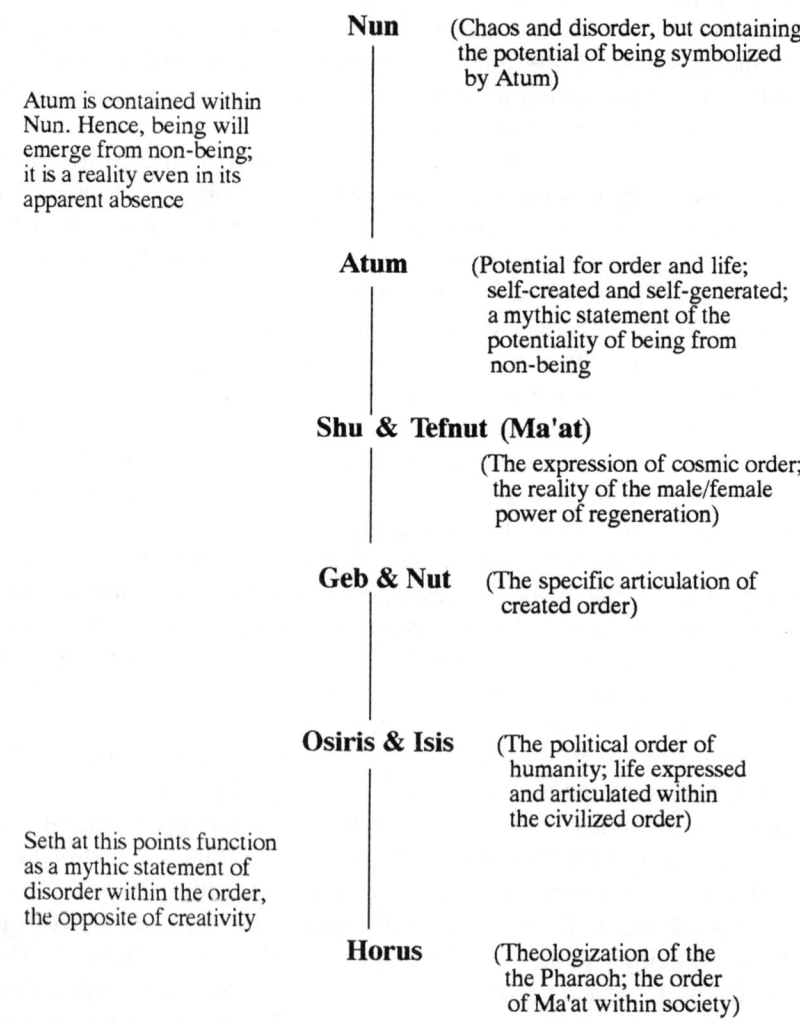

It should be noted here that the above diagram is itself intended to be seem as a representation of the Egyptian mythic symbolism, and not as a narration of mythic events which had occurred in any kind of historical or temporal sequence. If it were the latter, then it would no longer be capable of functioning as a true myth, and would constitute more of a dogmatic statement of creation. The absence of a concept of linear time, moreover, would have made a chronological and historical mythic sequence highly unlikely. Each stage of the above should be seen not as symbolic of different *events* within a saga of creation, but rather as symbolic of various *aspects* of the creative force and process. Any mythic events within the above are in essence contemporaneous. We have seen already in Chapter IV above how that in one tradition it was Atum who created the Heh gods, while in another account they had been created by Shu. At the same time, the Heh gods contained within the primaeval waters were also the source of both Atum and Shu. This apparent contradiction would have been a true contradiction only if the mythic symbolism had been regarded as a historical account or a chronological narrative. Nor is it even necessary to argue that the contradiction can be accepted on the basis that it arises from two distinct sets of symbols. The fluidity of symbolic representation is such that all symbols can be accepted and utilized, not by the intellect but through cultic experience. Since, moreover, no historical event is narrated in this pattern, the apparent contradiction becomes meaningless. The mythic symbols were arranged in a set system only in order to make them comprehensible to the non-abstract mind. The events of the creation still remained unknown and mysterious, and the actual mechanics of the creation were not actually enunciated apart from this mythic articulation. What the Heliopolitan system of mytho-theology portrayed was not the *means*, but the *meaning*, of creation. Ma'at (Tefnut) was placed in a specific position within the myth, but only because it was a concrete symbol and had, therefore, to have an actual position within the system. This, however, did not imply that Ma'at (Tefnut) had come into being at a specific time in the chronological sequence of the events of the creation. (In fact, one cannot really speak in terms of any sequence of the events of creation.) The myth contained no 'time', no temporal order of creative events. All were but symbols of the nature of created being, and in this being all aspects were contemporaneous. Hence, even though Ma'at as Tefnut was the daughter of Atum, Atum himself still lived only because of Ma'at, symbolized, as we have already seen, by his breathing of her and his eating of her. Atum and Ma'at were in effect interdependent; one could not have existed without the other, and hence to speak of a chronological order of their emergence would be pointless. In such a symbolic system, the experience of that system moves from the symbol to the reality and back again to the symbol. One cannot exist without the other. The symbol which is expressed is in actual fact the reality which still remains hidden. Hence, although the symbols themselves may be contradictory, the reality which they express still remains unaffected by the contradictions.

Through the mythic symbolism of Horus, the earthly monarch also became an integral part of both the created order and the symbolic expression of that order. He was more than just the appointed representative or regent of the divine; he was the actual embodiment of the divine in the world. He was the Good God (*nṯr nfr*), even though he remained a mortal being. What should appear as a dichotomy and a self-contradiction in such a statement was not such due to the totally symbolic nature of the statement. The Pharaoh thus became, even by his natural descent, the earthly manifestation and embodiment of Ma'at. His person could not be separated from the action of the creation, and indeed in his very succession to the throne the creation was again repeated, realized and renewed. In the person of the monarch, we may take the symbolic nature of the myth even a step further and state that the Pharaoh himself, although a specific living being, still functioned in a symbolic manner. He was the symbol of the abstract concept of kingship which had evolved from the world of the divine (Atum, Geb, Osiris, Horus) into the world of mankind, the figure of Horus, who was both the heavenly deity and incarnate in the Pharaoh, being the transition figure. Even in the death of one monarch and the succession of another, this symbolism was not broken or interrupted. Through the Horus/Osiris theology of the transformation of the dead monarch from Horus to Osiris and the transformation of the crown prince into the living Horus, the symbolic continuity still remained. The Pharaoh was in effect one being, symbolic of kingship, in the two hypostases of Horus and Osiris.

Into this latter aspect of the royal mytho-theology there entered also the symbolism of Isis and Hathor, the two goddesses on whom the royal divinity was dependent. Unlike Isis who can be characterized relatively clearly, Hathor does not so readily admit of being too closely defined. Her antiquity and early position as mother of Horus the sky god cannot be doubted, and, as is evident on the Narmer palette, she was also early connected with the earthly monarch, probably as the source of his divinity. The mythic tradition, however, makes no mention of any deity who had actually fathered the Horus whom Hathor bore,[3] even though various gods, including Osiris, Horus, Amun and Ptah, are at times said to be her husband. Hathor, despite her motherhood, also appears to have been a virgin goddess,[4] although such a logical contradiction is not necessarily a contradiction in terms of mythic symbolism. There can also be no doubt that Hathor and Isis were extremely close, similar and even at times interconnected, but this does not imply that there was ever any attempt to make an actual identification between the two goddesses.[5] Nor can an identification be made between Horus the son of Hathor and Horus the son of Isis. These latter two, although very closely linked, interconnected and sometimes even identified, were still recognizable as two separate gods.[6] An interesting suggestion has been made to the effect that the double crown sometimes associated with Hathor marked her as queen of Upper and Lower Egypt.[7] If such was the case, then it might be possible to suggest that at some stage in her history Hathor became, at least in part, a mythologization of the Great Royal Wife (*ḥmt niswt wrt*), although one must beware of attempting to interpret the mythic symbols too closely, thus creating a simplified allegorical pattern.

The birth of Horus the sky god who was incarnate in the ruling Pharaoh cannot be forced into a *logical* position in the pattern of the descent of the Pharaoh from Osiris and Isis. It can, however, be placed in a *mythical* position in this pattern through a type of parallelism as follows:

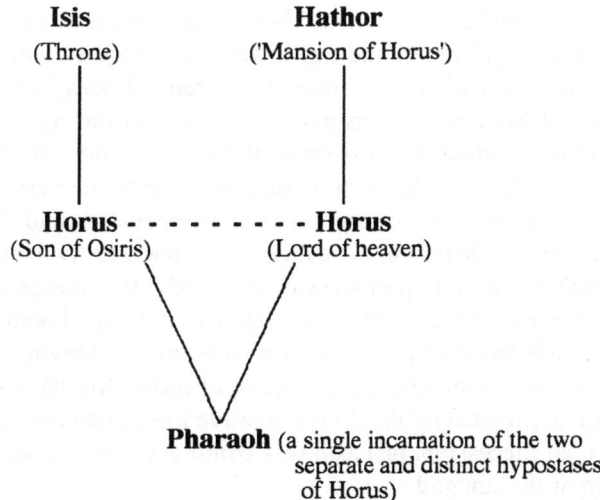

The above representation of the mythic symbolism points to three distinct and separate sources of the royal authority: Isis (the throne), Osiris (the right of inheritance) and Hathor (innate divinity). These three points of justification for the position of the monarch thus underscored the right of the monarch to rule in virtue of legal succession (Isis and Osiris) and in virtue of his own divine nature (Hathor).[8] The Horus/Osiris symbol for the monarch as representative of him as a living and as a deceased ruler had pointed to the two hypostases of the same monarch. So also the Isis/Hathor symbolism functioned to stress the two legitimate bases of royal power, legal inheritance and right of rule by divine nature. The motifs of birth from Hathor and Isis, however, were not totally parallel, for the divine nature signified by Hathor was in theory passed on to the monarch from the time of his birth, but the right of legitimate succession (*i.e.*, the transformation of the crown prince into the living and incarnate Horus) took place only at the death of the old monarch. The new reigning monarch was thus in effect 'born' of Isis, the mythologization of the throne which the new monarch assumed by right of succession, only on the death of the old monarch, *i.e.*, his transformation into Osiris, just as in the myth Horus son of Isis had been conceived and born only after the death of his father Osiris.

In terms of mythic symbolism, therefore, the incarnate Horus assumed the legal right to the throne of Osiris in virtue of being the son of that deity and of Isis, and also the son of Hathor, both goddesses being complementary aspects of royal and divine legitimacy. The succession to the throne was also the restoration of Ma'at, since, mythically, Horus had defeated Seth, the enemy of his father Osiris and had thus won the right to the throne. This aspect of the royal succession as the re-establishment of Ma'at was further expressed through the verb of succession $ḫ^ci$, the verb which was used of Atum's original appearance over the primaeval mound. Each succession of a new ruler, therefore, actualized and realized two of the basic mythic symbols of the Heliopolitan system, namely, the emergence of Atum and the emergence of Horus, both symbolic of kingship and both symbolic of Ma'at. In essence, monarchy and creation were thus two mythic expressions of one and the same principle, the principle of order (Ma'at) in the universe and in the state, founded by the divine creative force and continued and renewed in the royal succession, just as it was continued and renewed each day with the rising of the sun god.

As for the purpose of the creation, the myths themselves are silent on this point, a fact which in itself probably provides the answer to the question of why the creation took place. Very briefly stated, the creation appears to have had no purpose beyond itself, or we might better suggest that it was its own purpose and thus needed no further justification. The creation in the Heliopolitan mytho-theology appears to have been the natural result and outcome of the divine creative nature, which, in virtue of being what it was, had of necessity to express itself in creative action. Without such a creative action the creative force would have been meaningless and in fact nonexistent. The creation itself was nothing less than reality as it had emerged in Atum. It was, one might say, reality expressed in the only possible manner in which it could have been expressed, and it needed no further purposes, goals or aims to explain its existence. With an actual creation Ma'at it self could not have existed, and hence the creation existed because it was nothing less than Ma'at. To the Egyptian mind, with its absence of any tendencies towards the speculative and philosophical, the existence of a created order was sufficient to function as a kind of self-justification. No further justification or explanation for it was necessary.

The Egyptian concept of creation had two aspects, aspects which were so closely related as to form essentially one single pattern. These two aspects were the original fact of the creation at the time of Atum's emergence from the primaeval waters, and the repeated and continuous process of the creation as it was experienced with each new day and with the succession of each new ruler to the throne. In actual fact, the repetitive aspect of the creation was nothing more than an extension of the original creative act, the mythic symbolism of the former making the latter a reality when it was actualized in the cult. The basic theological significance in this total mythic symbol was the continuous and repeated process of life itself, life which was generated by the divine creative force. Thus, the whole of cosmic life was seen as a single process, and in this process the life of the individual found its meaning and its ultimate source. In effect, what this signified for the Egyptian mentality was that each individual did not live a life which was ontologically separated from the more universal reality of cosmic life. The individual life was rather an expression of the wider living reality of the universe. The positive value of this as concerned the individual was the knowledge that his own life was thereby indestructible. In such a manner, the official mytho-theology gave rise in a natural and logical manner to the hope of personal immortality. The revival of the dead individual in the next world was another expression of the creative force which sustained the universe, and hence rebirth after death could be understood as being essentially re-creation experienced by the individual. The latter possibility is evident in the pyramid structure of the royal tombs which emerged in he Old Kingdom, the pyramidal shape itself probably representing the primaeval mound which had first arisen out of the waters of Nun. Through such mythic symbolism in the royal tombs, the resurrection of the dead king after his earthly death was assured and guarantied. After the end of the Old Kingdom, when the expectation of eternal life was extended to all men, we see similar symbolism in the ritual association of the deceased with virtually any deity, but particularly with those deities who were symbolic of continuing life and rebirth. Osiris, as is well known, took the pre-eminent place among such deities, becoming the chief god of resurrection.

The figure of Sokar also entered into the mythic symbols associated with rebirth and resurrection. As a god solely of death, Sokar did not himself symbolize or effect individual resurrection. What he represented was an acknowledgement of the fact that death was a real phenomenon. It was not a mere absence of life, but a forceful power which could destroy life. At the same time, it may be recognized that Sokar contained in himself the *potential* for life, and in this way we may aptly compare him with the Heh gods of the primaeval waters. Both Sokar and the Heh gods were forces of a somewhat negative nature, but at the same time both had the potential out of which new life could arise. Hence, we may suggest that in the Egyptian thought system, Sokar, although not part of the Heliopolitan Ennead, could be connected theologically with that Ennead, for it was the reality of Sokar which made the revitalizing activity of Osiris a possibility. Sokar, as a god of death and the underworld, may to a great extent be compared with the Greek Hades, also a god of death and the underworld. At that point, however, the comparison stops, for in the mythology of Greece there was no return from Hades, *i.e.*, there was no life beyond physical death. The Egyptian synthesis on the other hand, was able to make a positive statement on death by its balance of the reality of Sokar with the opposing reality of Osiris. Moreover, the common identification of Sokar with both Ptah and Osiris may be seen further to have been an attempt to underscore the potentiality for the renewal of life which was contained in Sokar.

The role of Osiris as the main deity of resurrection appears as a logical development of the double nature of that deity. In the Heliopolitan system as it has been outlined above, Osiris appears to have been mainly a god belonging to the royal theological system. His main function in this system was centred chiefly around the double concept of the deification of the dead monarch and the legitimate succession to the throne through the transformation of the crown prince into the living Horus. This does not, however, imply that the function of Osiris within the royal theology was necessarily the original function of that deity, but the importance of this royal function cannot be underestimated. As a natural result, the final development of the mythic symbol connected Osiris more with the realm of the afterlife than with the temporal monarchy. In the course of the deification and immortalization of the dead ruler, we see the function of Osiris which was associated with his second aspect as a god of fertility and the rebirth of nature. Hence, in the final theologization of the mythic symbol, Osiris must be seen as a deity of transformation. This aspect of Osiris may again be understood as having two main functions. One of these was the idea, which we have already seen, of the transition of the earthly monarch from this world to the next. The other was a transitional function within the mechanical structure of the myth itself, that is, a means of conjoining the statement of human immortality with the wider signification of the total Heliopolitan cosmogony. The continuing aspect of life, even after physical death, thus became personified in Osiris due to his nature as a god who died and was reborn in a continual process.

Insofar as Osiris appears to have been connected at an early stage in history with the royal theology, it seems that the concept of individual immortality was more of a secondary outgrowth of that function, entering the mytho-theological system only as a later development. This may be seen in the extension of the afterlife to all men after the end of the Old Kingdom. In the latter case, the breakdown of royal authority had created a religious phenomenon which then had to be grafted into the official mytho-theology. Osiris had been the ideal figure through which to effect this connection, for his aspect as a deity of natural life allowed him to lend himself readily to such a function. Human immortality thus became an important aspect of the official mytho-theology of Egypt and, despite the secondary nature of its development, it was now inseparable from that mytho-theology. One suspects that, because of the nature of Osiris, the extension of immortality to all men might well have eventually taken place even without the impetus it was given by the breakdown of the Old Kingdom. If we conjoin the function of effecting human immortality with the role of Osiris in the royal political system of Heliopolis, we may see his full place within the mythic system as follows:

Atum: Creative Principle; Cosmic Life Force

Ma'at: Cosmic Order

Geb: Ordered Created World; Structured Universe

Osiris: Political Order; **Inherent Life Force**

> Manifest in all levels of experience:
> > cosmos
> > nature
> > state
> > human life
> > immortality

Since Osiris held this position and function, it is little wonder that the Great Hymn to Osiris (Stele of Amenmose, Louvre C 286)[9] gave to him such a universal position, for in that particular text he was given even the title of King of the Gods, not with the intention of supplanting Amun-Ra of Thebes, but solely as an indication of the universal power which he held over every aspect of life. Osiris in such a manner appears to have been (in conjunction with Horus) the final manifestation of that which was contained in the mythic symbol of Atum, the totality of the power of life. From the viewpoint of theological interpretation, Osiris and Atum do not appear as two distinct entities or concepts, but rather as two hypostatic expressions of the same reality. The creative and regenerative force as it was expressed in the figure of Atum may appear as having been somewhat shapeless and undefined, even transcendent to some extent. In the figure of Osiris, however, this same force was seen in a more specific and concrete expression, active and manifest in the particular phenomena of life, more immanent in his actual effects than was Atum. In brief, Osiris was what was symbolized by Atum, but expressed in practical reality. Osiris thus prevented Egyptian mytho-theology from becoming too abstract and too far removed from the normal experience of men. He brought a practical effect of religious experience to all individuals by assuring their eternal survival, and this immortality of man became further assured by its place in the wider mythic system.

In the Egyptian theological synthesis, human immortality eventually grew naturally out of the mythic system and was given a firm theological basis within that system. Man was understood as being part of the universal structure of cosmic life and being, and he had, therefore, out of necessity to survive into eternity. The death and resurrection of each individual became a return to the wider cosmic cycle of life, for which reason the dead could legitimately be seen as deified. In terms of the practical cultic myth, this transformation of the deceased was described by the symbol of personal resurrection through identification with Osiris as well as with others gods. This symbol of personal and individual survival was extremely important insofar as it provided a graphic and comprehensible expression of the reality of the afterlife. More important, however, was the more abstract concept that the life of the individual would return to the cosmic life of the whole universe, back to that source from which it had originated. Each individual, therefore, was able to find his place in the mytho-theological system, and through it he was given the assurance that death did not signify his utter and complete annihilation. Because of the mythic symbol of Osiris, man was assured that human life could not perish eternally.

What has been recapitulated thus far represents the basic structure of the Egyptian theological synthesis as it was expressed in official mytho-theology. It will be noted that many of the deities of ancient Egypt have been given no place or mention in the system here outlined. The reason for this is that the present theological interpretation of Egyptian religion is based mainly on the Heliopolitan mythic system, the system which appears to have been the most developed and all-encompassing of the Egyptian mythic systems. We have seen, however, that other systems were in existence among the Egyptians, and many of the other gods found their places within those systems. To attempt to conjoin the other deities with a system in which they had no mythic place or function would be to create an Egyptian pantheon and mythic system which never existed. Hence, those other gods must be left in the places and positions which were appropriately their own. This is in effect no more than to admit the already obvious fact that the Egyptian mentality was capable of permitting the existence of more than one mythic system and of not seeing in this any kind of logical contradiction. We have already seen that such a practice was an important mark of the Egyptian ideal of freedom of religion in the area of religious thought and mythic expression. The Heliopolitan system, however, which appears to have been the most complete, is also indicative of the general nature of Egyptian theology. Variations expressed in the others systems would not add anything further to our total comprehension of the Egyptian religious mind. We are concerned in this study with the theological principles of Egyptian religious thought, not with the subtleties of variation which those principles may have found in the different expressions created by the Egyptian mythopoeic mind. Thus, the achievement of Heliopolis may be taken as indicative of the Egyptian religious genius, and may provide us with a comprehension of the Egyptian cosmic outlook which served as the spiritual basis of the state for approximately three millenia.

The phenomena of universalism and monotheism have been discussed at some length in the main body of this work. Hence, very little needs to be said on these points now. A few brief remarks will be sufficient to set them in their wider context. The emergence of universalism from the concept of a creator deity may take place by a natural process once there is some impetus to start such a process. The narrower outlook of the Egyptian state during the Old Kingdom would probably not have given any such encouragement to true universalist ideas, the interest of Egypt in the outside world being too small. Definite universalist ideas, however, did manifest themselves in the New Sun Theology of the Eighteenth Dynasty and are well illustrated in the sun hymns of that period. These same universalist tendencies may be seen to an even greater extent in the texts of the Amarna movement, and are further evident in the Nineteenth Dynasty. The main cause of such tendencies was not so much development in theological thinking as it was the growth of the empire concept during the earlier part of the Eighteenth Dynasty. Due to increased political expansion and influence in the ancient Near East, Egypt was encountered with the necessity of recognizing the position of foreign nations in the international setting. This, coupled with the expansion of the Egyptian monarch into an emperor, meant that the chief deity of Egypt, Amun-Ra of Thebes, was expanded by a natural process into a universal deity. The concept of universalism, however, remained centred particularly on the figure of Amun-Ra and on the Aten during the brief time of the Amarna period. Any benefits from this new ideology (and any such benefits would have been mainly political and economic) accrued particularly to Amun-Ra, causing a further expansion of the influence of that deity. The Heliopolitan system was probably little affected by such thinking, apart from the fact that its creator god Atum had also been identified with the sun god Ra. In brief, we may speak in terms of a universalist concept of the solar deity, although it was mainly the solar deity as he was expressed in Amun-Ra who became the universal god. Indicative of this is the tendency to identify the Greek Zeus with Amun during the Ptolemaic period. Such universalism, however, did not bring about any changes in the mytho-theology of the Heliopolitan system, although it did add a wider dimension to Egyptian thought and may have partially paved the way for the eventual acceptance of a monotheistic system, although the latter lay far in the future when both Judaism and Christianity made their impact of Egypt, followed much later by Islam.

We have seen also that monotheism cannot be taken as a phenomenon of Egyptian religion, neither (contrary to some beliefs) in the Old Kingdom, nor in the New Sun Theology (where the best we can posit are henotheistic or monotheistic *tendencies*), nor in the Amarna period (where it seems safest to speak of practical henotheism). The Egyptians were definitely not monotheists, and perhaps one should not even call them polytheists, both terms being relatively meaningless in the context of the Egyptian mytho-theological system. The best one can say is that Egyptian religion was expressed by means of polytheistic symbolism. Although this polytheistic symbolism may have articulated some realization of the unity of the divine power and of the unity of the ordering principle of Ma'at, even this was far from being monotheistic. Monotheism would have been totally foreign to the Egyptian religious tradition and way of thought, and hence could never have entered into the official mytho-theology. Had it been able to do so, such would have been possible only by a total destruction of that mytho-theology and the creation of an entirely new system of mythic expression. Even in such a case, however, the Egyptian mind itself would have had to be completely restructured in its way of thinking so as to be enabled to accept such a new system. Not even Akhenaten was able to accomplish that goal. Hence, as a final conclusion we must admit that as a serious theological proposition monotheism found no place or expression within the confines of the Egyptian religious experience.

Let us recapitulate as our last point the place of morality within the Egyptian religious system. Strictly speaking, the Egyptians were not familiar with a concept of moral theology. Morals were not theological principles, but rather practical and sensible rules for the conduct of one's life. Such rules and customs had their roots in the society and in the state, but not in the religious domain. They were learned not by any form of divine revelation, but by the normal human experience of life. It was perhaps this latter fact which made Egyptian considerations of morality so totally human and humane in their approach. Nevertheless, despite its non-theological nature, morality was given at least a strong connection with the mytho-theological system by its connection with Ma'at. In a word, to live by moral standards meant to live one's life in accordance with the ordered principle of Ma'at. As a result of this, the gods, who were not by their nature moral beings, were able to function as the upholders of good and decent moral standards. Eventually, purity of life became the prerequisite for entrance into the eternal happiness and bliss of the realms of Osiris. Hence, morality, although not a theological principle or consideration, did nevertheless receive a sound theological foundation, becoming thereby an integral factor in the Egyptian assessment of the good life.

As an ultimate conclusion, we may ask what value there is in the study of Egyptian religion and theology, a system which has been dead for so many centuries. One obvious answer to this question is that since Egyptian religion was a specific phenomenon in the history of the development of human civilization, it deserves to be studied for its own sake. It gives us a further insight into the way in which the human spirit has developed over the centuries. It points to the aims, hopes and aspirations which man has conceived at a certain stage of his mental and spiritual evolution. It may thus to some extent help us to comprehend more fully our own humanity. There is no area of human achievement which does not deserve our consideration and which has not in some way made its contribution to the eventual total development of the human race. Egyptian religion, like many of the other religions and philosophical expressions in both the ancient and modern worlds, did make a number of highly positive statements concerning man and the universe in which he lives. Even though such statements were made several millenia ago, nevertheless they still have a right to be heard and to be considered within the context of man's continuing dialogue with the universe in which he lives.

We may, moreover, recognize in the Egyptian mythic statements certain theological principles and insights. Although such insights may have been been articulated by means of symbols which are foreign to the modern world, they have nevertheless been stated and were able to prove their validity by the fact that they endured for more than three thousand years, being superseded only when Christianity was able to replace them with a system based on a humane and universal belief of a loving and personal God. At the same time, however, true theology should be able to transcend the boundaries of religion and culture. It should not be sectarian in its outlook and values. It should not be confined to any specific set of symbols. True and valid theology is able to go far beyond the individual symbols and the specific culture. It can provide a means of insight which is not hampered by the strict and hard rules of religious orthodoxy, doctrine or dogma. Theology has nothing to do with individual beliefs and prejudices. Any theology which is too closely bound to the specifics of religious symbolism is nothing more than pseudo-theology. As we have seen, the Egyptian mythic symbols were not exclusive; they did not claim to represent the one and only way. They were symbols which could permit the freedom of both multiplicity and plurality. At the same time they were able to express those things which the Egyptians saw as eternal truths. The mythic symbols of Egypt provided an insight into the nature of the structure and being of the total world of human experience, and if that insight were to be measured by the norms of modern theological, philosophical and even scientific thought, what would the results of such an inquiry show? Would the Egyptian theological system have anything positive to say to the modern man? This is a question which each individual must answer for himself.

Notes

[1] D. Sweeney, "Intercessory Prayer in Ancient Egypt and the Bible," *Pharaonic Egypt, the Bible and Christianity*, 221.
[2] *ibid.*, 215. See also Davies in *Mélanges Maspero*, I, Orient Ancien (Cairo, 1935-1938), 214-250.
[3] C.J. Bleeker, *Hathor and Thoth: Two Key Figures of the Ancient Egyptian Religion* (Leiden, 1973), 38.
[4] *ibid.*, 28.
[5] *ibid.*, 70.
[6] *ibid.*, 25.
[7] *ibid.*, 58.
[8] See H. Frankfort, *Kingship and the Gods*, 44.
[9] Translation in M. Lichtheim, *op. cit.*, II, 81ff.

Select Bibliography

Albright, W.F. *From the Stone Age to Christianity*. 2nd ed. Garden City, New York: Doubleday, 1957.

Aldred, C. *Akhenaten*. London: Thames & Hudson, 1968.

----------. *Akhenaten and Nefertiti*. New York: The Brooklyn Museum in association with the Viking Press, 1973.

----------. *Egyptian Art*. London: Thames & Hudson, 1980.

Allen, T.G. "Some Egyptian Sun Hymns." *JNES* VII (1949): 349-356.

Anthes, R. "Die Maat des Echnatons von Amarna." *Supplement to the Journal of the American Oriental Society* XIV (1952): 1-36.

----------. "Egyptian Theology in the Third Millenium B.C." *JNES* XVIII (1959): 168-212.

----------. "... in seinem Namen und im Sonnenlicht." *ZÄS* XC (1963): 1-6.

Assmann, J. *Ägyptische Hymnen und Gebete*. Zürich-München, 1975.

----------. "Aton." in W. Helck, E. Otto, W. Westendorf, *Lexikon der Ägyptologie* I, Wiesbaden, 1973: 526ff.

----------. "Der König als Sonnenpriester." *Abhandlungen des Deutschen Archäologischen Instituts Kairo* VII (1970).

----------. "Die 'Häresie' des Echnaton. Aspekte der Amarna Religion." *Saeculum* XXIII (1972): 109-126.

----------. "Die 'Loyalistische Lehre' Echnatons." *Studien zur Altägyptischen Kultur*, 1980: 1-32.

----------. *Liturgische Lieder an den Sonnengott. Untersuchungen zur ägyptischen Hymnik* I, *MÄS* XIX (1969).

----------. *Re und Amun*. Freiburg: Universitäts Verlag, 1983.

----------. "Zwei Sonnenhymnen der späten XVIII Dynastie in Thebanischen Gräben der Saitenzeit." *MDAIK* XXVII, 1 (1971): 1-34.

Auffret, P. *Hymnes d'Egypte et d'Israel*. Fribourg: Editions Universitaires, 1981.

Badawy, A.M. "The Symbolism of the Temples at 'Amarna'." *ZÄS* LXXXVII (1962): 79-95.

Baikie, J. *The Amarna Age*. London: Adam & Charles Black, 1926.

Baines, J. "'Greatest God' or Category of God?" *GM* LXVII (1983):13-28.

Barton, G.A. "Tammuz and Osiris." *JAOS* XXXV (1915): 213-223.

Barucq, A. *L'expression de la louange divine et de la prière dans la Bible et en Egypte.* Cairo, 1962.

Bille-De Mot, E., *The Age of Akhenaten.* Translated by J. Lindsay. New York & Toronto: McGraw Hill, 1966.

Blackman, A.M. "A Study of the Liturgy Celebrated in the Temple of the Aton at El-Amarna." *Recueil d'Etudes Egyptologiques Dédiées à la Mémoire de Jean-François Champollion.* Paris: Payot, 1922: 505-527.

Bleeker, C.J. *De Beteekenis van de Egyptische Godin Ma-a-t.* Leiden, 1929.

----------. *Egyptian Festivals.* Leiden: E.J. Brill, 1967.

----------. *Hathor and Thoth: Two Key Figures of the Ancient Egyptian Religion.* Leiden: E.J. Brill, 1973.

----------. "The Religion of Ancient Egypt." *Historia Religionum* I. Edited by C.J. Bleeker & G. Widengren. Leiden: E.J. Brill, 1969: 40-114.

Bonnel, R.G., and V.A. Tobin. "Christ and Osiris: A Comparative Study." *Pharaonic Egypt, the Bible and Christianity.* Edited by S.I. Groll. Jerusalem: The Magnes Press, 1985: 1-29.

Bonnet, H., *Reallexikon der ägyptischen Religionsgeschichte.* Berlin: W. De Gruyter, 1952.

Breasted, J.H. *The Dawn of Conscience.* New York: Charles Scribner's Sons, 1933.

----------. *Development of Religion and Thought in Ancient Egypt.* 1912. Reprint. New York: Harper & Row, 1959.

Budge, E.A.W. *The Book of the Dead: The Papyrus of Ani.* 1895. Reprint. New York: Dover Publications, 1967.

----------. *From Fetish to God in Ancient Egypt.* London, 1934.

----------. *Osiris and the Egyptian Resurrection.* London & New York, 1911.

----------. *Tutankhamun: Amenism, Atenism and Egyptian Monotheism.* London: Martin Hopkinson, 1923.

Cerny, J. *Ancient Egyptian Religion.* London: Hutchinson's University Library, 1952.

Chassinat, E. *Le Mystère d'Osiris au mois de Khoiak.* 2 vols. Cairo: Institut Français d'Archéologie Orientale, 1966.

Clark, R.T.R. *Myth and Symbol in Ancient Egypt*. London: Thames & Hudson, 1959.
Collier, J. *The Heretic Pharaoh*. New York: John Day, 1972.
Daumas, F. *La civilisation de l'Egypte pharaonique*. Paris: Arthaud, 1965.
David, A.R. *The Ancient Egyptians: Religious Beliefs and Practices*. London: Routledge & Kegan Paul, 1982.
Davies, N. de G. "Akhenaten at Thebes." *JEA* IX (1923): 132-152.
----------. *The Rock Tombs of El-Amarna*. 6 vols. London: Egypt Exploration Society, 1903-1908.
Drioton, E., "Le monothéisme de l'ancienne Egypte." *Cahiers d'Histoire Egyptienne*, 1949.
Drioton, E., and J. Vandier. *L'Egypte*. 6th edition. Paris: Presses Universitaires de France, 1984.
Edwards, I.E.S. *The Pyramids of Egypt*. Harmondsworth, 1961.
Emery, W.R. *Archaic Egypt*. Harmondsworth, 1961.
Erman, A. *Die Religion der Ägypter*. Berlin: W. de Gruyter, 1934.
Erman, J.P.A. *A Handbook of Egyptian Religion*. London, 1907.
Fairman, H.W. *The City of Akhetaten*. London, 1951.
Faulkner, R.O. *The Ancient Egyptian Pyramid Texts*. London: The Clarendon Press, 1969.
----------. *The Ancient Egyptian Coffin Texts*. 3 vols. Warminster: Aris & Phillips, 1973-1978.
Fecht, G. "Amarna Probleme." *ZÄS* LXXXV (1960): 83-118.
Frankfort, H. *Ancient Egyptian Religion*. New York: Columbia University Press, 1948.
----------. *Kingship and the Gods*. Chicago: University of Chicago Press, 1948.
----------.*The Problem of Similarity in Ancient Near Eastern Religions*. Oxford: The Clarendon Press, 1951.
Frankfort, H., H.A. Frankfort, J.A. Wilson, and T. Jacobsen. *Before Philosophy*. Pelican Books, 1949. (Originally published as *The Intellectual Adventure of Ancient Man*. Chicago, 1946.)
Friedman, F. "*ḥḏ* in the Amarna Period."*JARCE* XXIII (1986): 99-106.
Gardiner, A.H. *Egypt of the Pharaohs*. Oxford: The Clarendon Press, 1961.
Giles, F.G. *Ikhnaton: Legend and History*. London: Hutchinson, 1970.
Griffiths, J.G. *The Conflict of Horus and Seth*. Liverpool: Liverpool University Press, 1960.

----------. *The Origins of Osiris and his Cult*. Leiden: E.J. Brill, 1980.

Gunn, B. "The Religion of the Poor in Ancient Egypt." *JEA* III (1916): 81-94.

Hayes, W.C. *The Sceptre of Egypt*. 2 vols. New York: The Metropolitan Museum of Art, 1953-1959.

Helck, W., E. Otto, and W. Westendorf. *Lexikon der Ägyptologie*. Wiesbaden: Otto Harrassovitz, 1972-1983.

Hornung, E. *Conceptions of God in Ancient Egypt: The One and the Many*. Translated by J. Baines. London: Routledge and Kegan Paul, 1983.

----------. "Monotheismus in pharaonischen Ägypten." *Monotheismus im Alten Israel und seiner Beiträge*. Edited by O. Keel. Biblische Beiträge 14 (1980): 83-97.

Ions, V. *Egyptian Mythology*. new ed. London: Paul Hamlyn, 1968.

Jequier, G. *Considérations sur les religions égyptiennes*. Neuchâtel: La Baconière, 1946.

Kees, H. *Der Götterglaube im alten Ägypten*. Berlin: Akademie Verlag, 1956.

Kramer, S.N. *Mythologies of the Ancient World*. New York Doubleday, 1961.

Le Corsu, F. *Isis, Mythes et Mystères*. Paris: Société d'Edition "Les Belles Lettres," 1977.

Leca, A.P. *The Cult of the Immortal*. Translated by L. Asmal London: Granada Publishing, 1982.

Leclant, J. ed. *Le monde égyptien: Les Pharaons*. 3 vols. Paris: 1978-1980.

Lichtheim, M. *Ancient Egyptian Literature*. 3 vols. Berkeley: University of California Press, 1973-1980.

Mercer, S.A.B. *The Religion of Ancient Egypt*. London, 1949.

----------. "The Religion of Ikhnaton." *JSOR* X (1926): 14-33.

----------. "Was Ikhnaton a Monotheist?" *JSOR* III (1919): 70-80.

Montet, P. *L'Egypte et la Bible*. Neuchâtel: Delachaux et Niestle, 1959.

Morenz, S. *La religion égyptienne*. Translated by L. Jospin. Paris: Payot, 1962.

Moret, A. *Du caractère religieux de la royauté pharaonique*. Paris, 1902.

----------. *La mise à mort du Dieu en Egypte*. Paris: Paul Geuthner, 1927.

Murray, M.A. "Burial Customs and Beliefs in the Hereafter in Predynastic Egypt." *JEA* XLII (1956): 86-96.

----------. *The Splendour that was Egypt*. London: Sidgwick & Jackson, 1949.

Nagel, G. "Les Mystères d'Osiris dans l'Ancienne Egypte." *Eranos-Jahrbuch* XI (1944): 144-166.
Osing, J. "Isis und Osiris." *MDAIK* XXX (1974): 91-113.
Oswalt, J.N. *The Concept of Amun-Re as Reflected in the Hymns and Prayers of the Ramesside Period.* Ph.D. Dissertation. Brandeis University, 1968.
Otto, E. *Egyptian Art and the Cults of Osiris and Amon.* London, 1968.
--------. "Monotheistische Tendenzen in der ägyptischen Religion." *Die Welt des Orients* 2/2 (1955): 99-110.
Pfeiffer, C.F. *Tell El Amarna and the Bible.* Grand Rapids, 1963.
Piankoff, A. "Les grands compositions religieuses du Nouvel Empire et la Réforme d'Amarna." *BIFAO* LXII (1964): 207-218.
----------. "The Theology of the New Kingdom in Ancient Egypt." *Antiquity and Survival* I (1956): 488-500.
Pirenne, J. *Histoire de la civilisation de l'Egypte ancienne.* 3 vols. Paris: Neuchâtel, 1961.
----------. *La religion et la morale dans l'Egypte antique.* Paris: Albin Michel, 1965.
Posener, G. *De la divinité du Pharaon.* Paris: Cahiers de la Société Asiatique, 1960.
----------. "Sur le monothéisme dans l'ancienne Egypte." *Mélanges bibliques et orientaux en l'honneur de m. Henri Cazelles.* Edited by A. Caquot and M. Delcor. Neukirchen-Vluyn, 1981: 347-351.
Posener, G., S. Sauneron, and J. Yoyotte. *Dictionnaire de la civilisation égyptienne.* 2nd edition. Paris, 1970.
Pritchard, J.B. ed. *Ancient Near Eastern Texts Relating to the Old Testament.* 2nd edition. Princeton: Princeton University Press, 1955.
Redford, D.B. "The Sun-Disc in Akhenaten's Program: Its Worship and Antecedents." *JARCE* XIII (1976): 47-61.
----------. *Akhenaten: The Heretic King.* Princeton: Princeton University Press, 1984.
----------. *The Akhenaten Temple Project. Vol.2: Rwd-Mnw and Inscriptions.* Toronto: University of Toronto Press, 1988.
Reymond, E.A.E. *The Mythical Origin of the Egyptian Temple.* Manchester: Manchester University Press, and New York: Barnes & Noble. 1969.
Samson, J. *Amarna, City of Akhenaten and Nefertiti.* 2nd edition. Warminster: Aris & Phillips, 1978.

Schäfer, H. *Amarna in Religion und Kunst.* Berlin, 1931.
Sethe, K. "Amun und die Acht Urgötter von Hermopolis." *Abhandlungen der preussischen Akademie der Wissenschaften* V (1929), 1-25.
Shirun-Grumach, I. "Remarks on the Goddess Maat." *Pharaonic Egypt, the Bible and Christianity.* edited by S.I. Groll. Jerusalem: The Magnes Press, 1985, 173-201.
Silverberg, R. *Akhnaton, The Rebel Pharaoh.* Philadelphia & New York, 1964.
Smith, R.W., and D.B. Redford. *The Akhenaten Temple Project. Vol. I: Initial Discoveries.* Warminster: Aris & Phillips, 1976.
Smith, W.S. The Art and Architecture of Ancient Egypt. revised by W.K. Simpson. Penguin Books, 1981.
Smith, M. "The Common Theology of the Ancient Near East." *Journal of Biblical Literature* LXXI (1952): 135ff.
Spencer, A.J. *Death in Ancient Egypt.* Penguin Books, 1982.
Stewart, H.M. "Some Pre-Amarna Sun-Hymns." *JEA* XLVI (1960): 83- 90.
----------. "Traditional Egyptian Sun-Hymns of the New Kingdom." *BIA* VI (1966): 29-64.
Sweeney, D. "Intercessory Prayer in Ancient Egypt and the Bible." *Pharaonic Egypt, the Bible and Christianity*, 212-230.
Tawfik, S. "Aton Studies I: Aton Before the Reign of Akhenaten." *MDAIK* XXIX (1973): 77-86.
----------. "Aton Studies IV: Was Aton - the God of Akhenaten - Only a Manifestation of the God Re?" *MDAIK* XXXII (1976): 217-226.
Tobin, V.A. "Amarna and Biblical Religion." *Pharaonic Egypt, the Bible and Christianity*, 231-277.
----------. "Ma'at and ΔIKH: Some Comparative Considerations of Egyptian and Greek Thought." *JARCE* XXIV (1987): 113-121.
----------. "Mytho-Theology in Ancient Egypt." *JARCE* XXV (1988).
Trigger, B.G., B.J. Kemp, D. O'Connor, and A.B. Lloyd. *Ancient Egypt: A Social History.* Cambridge: Cambridge University Press, 1983.
Vandier, J. *La Religion Egyptienne.* Paris: Presses Universitaires de France, 1944.
Varille, A., "L'Hymne au Soleil des architectes d'Amenophis III, Souti et Hor." *BIFAO* XLI (1942): 25-30.
Vaux, R. de, "The Cults of Adonis and Osiris." *The Bible and the Ancient Near East.* Translated by D. McHugh. London: Darton, Longman & Todd, 1972, 210-237.

Vernus, P. "Le dieu personell dans l'"Egypte pharaonique." *Centre interdisciplinaire d'Etude de l'évolution des idées, des sciences et des techniques, Colloques de la Société Ernest Renan.* Orsay, 1977, 143-157.

Wainwright, G.A. *The Sky Religion in Ancient Egypt.* Cambridge: Cambridge University Press, 1938.

Wallert, I. *Die Palmen im Alten Ägypten. MÄS* I. Munich, 1962.

Wente, E. "Mysticism in Pharaonic Egypt?" *JNES* XLI (1982): 161-179.

White, L.A. "Ikhnaton: The Great Man versus the Culture Process." *JAOS* LXVIII (1948): 91-114.

Wilson, J. *The Culture of Ancient Egypt.* Chicago: University of Chicago Press, 1951.

Zabkar, L.V. *A Study of the Ba Concept in Ancient Egyptian Texts.* Chicago, 1968.

----------. "The Theocracy of Amarna and the Doctrine of the Ba." *JNES* XIII (1954): 87ff.

Zandee, J. *Death as an Enemy According to Ancient Egyptian Conceptions.* Leiden: E.J. Brill, 1960.

Anthony J. Blasi

MORAL CONFLICT AND CHRISTIAN RELIGION

American University Studies: Series VII (Theology and Religion). Vol. 35
ISBN 0-8204-0497-7   190 pages   hardback US $ 33.50*

*Recommended price – alterations reserved

This work takes up the problem of moral conflict, wherein a person must choose between two or more evils. The problem lies behind such issues as the defensive war, therapeutic abortion, and contraception. It becomes a religious question because, as the author argues, religion elicits the same kind of openness to values as is needed for addressing moral dilemmas. After culling insights out of the history of Christian ethics, Blasi presents phenomenologies of both moral decision making and religion, and uses the results to address the variety of moral dilemmas.

«This is an original and enlightening study of a timely and important subject.» (Leslie Dewart, St. Michael's College, University of Toronto)

«Conflict situations will always exist. And therefore so will the need for thoughtful precision in dealing with them. Blasi's book is a significant contribution to that precision.» (Richard A. McCormick, S. J., University of Notre Dame)

«. . . the work represents a very original and inspiring contribution to moral inquiry . . .» (Béla Somfai, Regis College).

PETER LANG PUBLISHING, INC.
62 West 45th Street
USA – New York, NY 10036

Twesigye, Emmanuel Kalenzi

COMMON GROUND
Christianity, African Religion and Philosophy

American University Studies: Series VII (Theology and Religion). Vol. 25
ISBN 0-8204-0408-X   227 pp.   hardback US $ 31.00/sFr. 46.50

Recommended prices – alterations reserved

Common Ground: Christianity, African Religion and Philosophy is a result of many years of research and reflection on the problem of human existence or «the human problematic» as dealt with in the philosophical-theological traditions of both Africa and the Christian West. With the help of Karl Rahner's philosophical-theological framework, the author finds that both traditions are concerned with the same universal problems facing the human being arising out of finitude, sin and guilt. Subsequently, the author shows how in each tradition, the preoccupation of both philosophy and religion is that of soterilogy and salvation. It is also shown how both traditions are concerned with how to live a Good Life, and that the Good Life is correlative with the free human obedience to God as the Holy Creator and perfect fulfillment of all obedient human beings, everywhere.

Contents: The material of this book is theological and philosophical in nature. It deals with both Africa and the Christian West in their similar quest for a meaningful life or an authentic human existence in the One Redemptive God. The material is very academic and the language is technical at the level of scholars and advanced College students.

PETER LANG PUBLISHING, INC.
62 West 45th Street
USA – New York, NY 10036

James J. McCartney

UNBORN PERSONS
Pope John Paul II and the Abortion Debate

American University Studies: Series VII (Theology and Religion). Vol. 21
ISBN 0-8204-0349-0   176 pages   hardback US $ 28.95*

*Recommended price – alterations reserved

Karol Wojtyla (Pope John Paul II) was a professor of anthropology and ethics at the Catholic University of Lublin, Poland long before he was elected Pope. During this time, his interests centered around the concept of personhood and its many implications in the epistemological, metaphysical and ethical spheres. In this book, after considering the many philosophical and theological influences that helped to form his tought, his notion of personhood is discussed with reference to the status of unborn persons, that is of embryological and fetal life. His approach to personhood is then contrasted and compared with other contemporary notions in an effort to understand more clearly the status of life before birth.
Contents: Theological and Philosophical Influences on Wojtyla's Notion of «Person» – A Dialogue between Wojtyla and Others on Whether or Not the Living Human Embryo is a Person.
«*To relate Wojtyla's (Pope John Paul II's) more general philosophical and theological thought to his notion of personhood (its beginning, constitutive elements, etc.) is a valuable piece of research. It is what James J. McCartney has done in this careful and well-crafted study.*»
(Reverend Richard A. McCormick, S. J.)

PETER LANG PUBLISHING, INC.
62 West 45th Street
USA – New York, NY 10036